AF571799

Variations on America

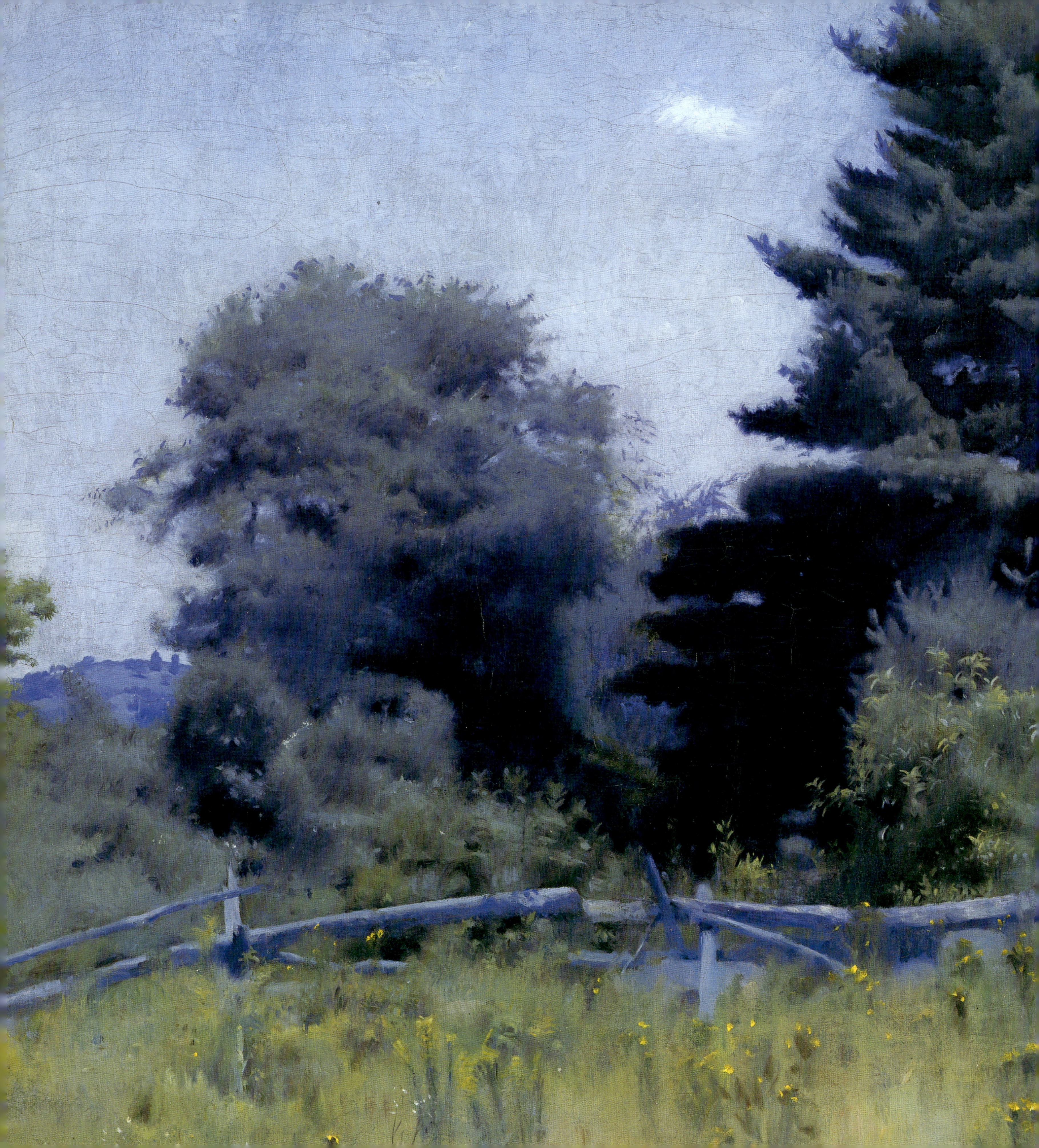

Smithsonian American Art Museum, Washington, DC,
in association with D Giles Limited, London

George Gurney

Eleanor Jones Harvey

Virginia M. Mecklenburg

Joann Moser

George Speer

Elaine Yau

Masterworks from
American Art Forum Collections

Variations on America

Variations on America

Masterworks from
American Art Forum Collections

Published in conjunction with the exhibition of the same name, on view at the Smithsonian American Art Museum, Washington, DC, April 13–July 29, 2007.

Chief of Publications: Theresa J. Slowik
Editor: Susan L. Efird
Designer: Karen Siatras

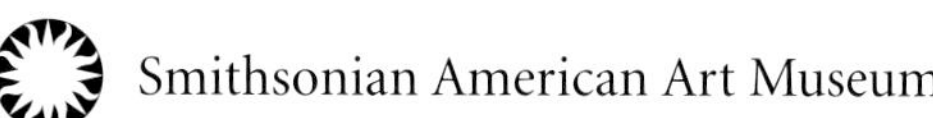

The Smithsonian American Art Museum is home to one of the largest collections of American art in the world. Its holdings—more than 41,000 works—tell the story of America through the visual arts and represent the most inclusive collection of American art in any museum today. It is the nation's first federal art collection, predating the 1846 founding of the Smithsonian Institution. The museum celebrates the exceptional creativity of the nation's artists whose insights into history, society, and the individual reveal the essence of the American experience.

For more information or a catalogue of publications, write:
Office of Publications, Smithsonian American Art Museum, MRC 970, PO Box 37012, Washington, DC 20013-7012.

Visit the museum's Web site at AmericanArt.si.edu.

Cover: George Bellows (1882–1925), *Noon* (detail), 1908, oil on canvas, 22 × 28 in., Private Collection, Washington, DC.

Frontispiece: Dennis Miller Bunker (1861–1890), *Pines beyond the Fence* (detail), 1886, oil on canvas, 28 3/4 × 21 1/4 in., Private Collection.

Frontispiece to Foreword: Andrew Wyeth (b. 1917), *Open and Closed* (detail), 1964, watercolor, 21 × 30 in. Collection of Hacker and Kitty Caldwell. © Andrew Wyeth.

Back cover: John Marin (1870–1953), *Taos Canyon, New Mexico*, 1929, watercolor on paper, 16 1/2 × 22 in. John and Dolores Beck Collection. © 2006 Estate of John Marin/Artists Rights Society (ARS), New York.

Library of Congress
Cataloging-in-Publication Data

Variations on America:
Masterworks from American Art Forum Collections, Smithsonian American Art Museum / George Gurney ... [et al.].
p. cm.
Published in conjunction with the exhibition of the same name, on view at the Smithsonian American Art Museum, Washington, DC, April 13–July 29, 2007.

Includes bibliographical references.

ISBN-13: 978-1-904832-42-3
ISBN-10: 1-904832-42-3

1. Art, American—19th century—Exhibitions. 2. Art, American—20th century—Exhibitions. 3. Art—Private collections—United States—Exhibitions. 4. American Art Forum—Exhibitions. I. Gurney, George. II. Smithsonian American Art Museum.

N6510.V38 2007
709.73'074753—dc22

2006034653

First published in 2007 by GILES, an imprint of D Giles Limited, in association with the Smithsonian American Art Museum.

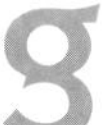

D Giles Limited
Kite Studios, Priory Mews
2B Bassein Park Road
London, W12 2RY
United Kingdom
www.gilesltd.com

Contents

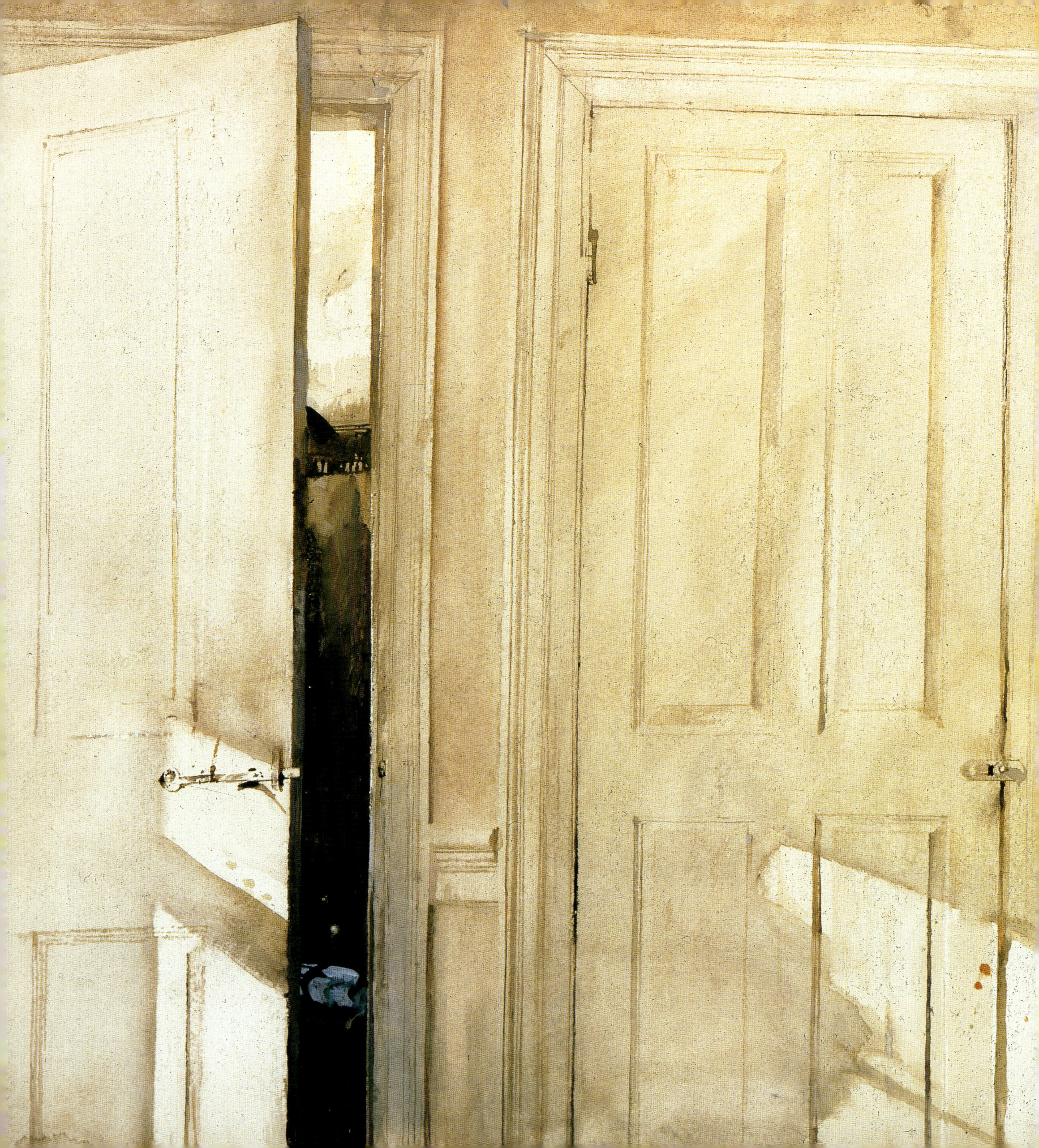

Foreword

Collectors usually begin in a private, solitary way, finding first one, then a second and third artwork that they simply cannot live without. The occasional tentative acquisition becomes a passion as confidence builds and taste matures. Along the journey, collectors come to understand that the works they love are a kind of intimate portrait of themselves, a reflection of their deepest interests and experiences. Then, it becomes urgent to find others to talk with, to compare notes and preferences, to consider a narrower or broader focus. By trading insights and questions with sympathetic friends who share the collecting impulse, and seeing the homes and collections of others, each collector discovers a special joy and finds a more profound understanding of his own artworks.

The American Art Forum, a small group of collectors from across the nation, offers an unparalleled way to share this collecting passion. The Forum was begun twenty years ago by Charles C. Eldredge while he was director of the Smithsonian American Art Museum. By founding this group, he put the museum in touch with many of the finest collectors of American art, providing us many benefits and pleasures.

The Forum plays a role in introducing far-flung collectors to each other and to the rich variety of public museums across the country. Biannual trips offer several days of camaraderie, each an occasion for trading opinions and stories, new "catches" and near-misses, record-setting prices and great bargains, exhibition experiences, and what's at auction and in the galleries. The Forum is an informal conference for the exchange of news and ideas, held in the far-ranging and ever-fascinating regions of a vast country. Barbara Cox, special assistant for Patron Programs, has managed these trips with loving attention to every detail over many years, with help from the museum's curators and others.

The chance to discover America's regions and communities has been one of the most gratifying aspects of the Forum. Art takes on a deeper meaning when the particular landscape, light, or tradition that inspired it is known firsthand. The Forum has visited all the biggest cities, including New York, Chicago, Boston, Philadelphia, Miami, Atlanta, Houston, Dallas, Los Angeles, San Francisco, and of course Washington, DC—each a story of endeavor and success. It has explored public and private collections from all points of the compass, including Chattanooga, Santa Fe, Saint Louis, Kansas City, Denver, Seattle, Phoenix, Portland (ME), San Antonio, Winston-Salem, Tuscaloosa, the Hudson River Valley, and others—each offering unusual and exciting experiences. A trip to tiny New Bremen, Ohio, provided insight into small-town life in the heartland, while an overseas visit to Paris balanced the equation with several days in a world culture capital. Both New Bremen and Paris—and all the trips in between—included superb collections of American art and a new appreciation of our artists' extraordinary reach.

We've learned from local hosts about what is unique to each place—its history, "favorite son" artists, cultural highlights, and most of all, the people whose dedication and effort have created that place as a destination. The indelible memories of so many trips come from the generous private collectors who have invited us into their homes, artists who opened their studios for us, and museum colleagues who offered behind-the-scenes tours of galleries and storerooms. The trips are extended tutorials by the finest experts who have lived each day with the art they love, collapsing years of learning into an exhilarating moment of connection with new friends.

Perhaps a similar avid friendship springs naturally among new acquaintances in other areas of art, but those committed to American art have an unusual bond that is linked to a common identification with the country's development and spirit. As each collector explains why favorite works are so affecting and resonant, each story seems a microcosm of the larger collective world of experience that built this country and sustained it through the generations.

The American Art Forum's membership is small, so it stays within the narrow number accommodated in private homes. Turnover is gradual, but over twenty years it has been almost complete, with only a handful of the founding members still participating. Current and former members stay in touch, and the network of connections becomes more profound as mutual art interests blossom into deeper friendships.

Thanks to the generosity of Forum friends, the museum's chief curator, Eleanor Jones Harvey, and deputy chief curator, George Gurney, have gathered seventy-two treasured artworks for this exhibition. Senior curators Virginia M. Mecklenburg and Joann Moser also contributed to the catalogue in their areas of specialization. George Speer, former Luce Foundation Center curator, and Elaine Yau, curatorial assistant, wrote significant contributions for this book. Fine landscape masterpieces in the Hudson River tradition, light-filled impressionist canvases, dazzling Gilded Age decorative objects and paintings, gritty Ashcan records from a dynamic New York City, vivid aesthetic creations of the modern age, triumphant abstract expressionism, and moving contemporary works are shared here, for the enjoyment of all. During the twenty years of the Forum's existence, art of the West has achieved a major place among art historians and collectors, and this is also reflected in the exhibition. The collectors have lent their best art in the same spirit of warm collaboration that unites all in this field.

The Smithsonian American Art Museum is happy to be the place where so many visitors will discover these wonderful selections. Just maybe, some of these visitors will be inspired to buy that special work they've been considering, and begin the journey for themselves.

Elizabeth Broun
The Margaret and Terry Stent Director
Smithsonian American Art Museum

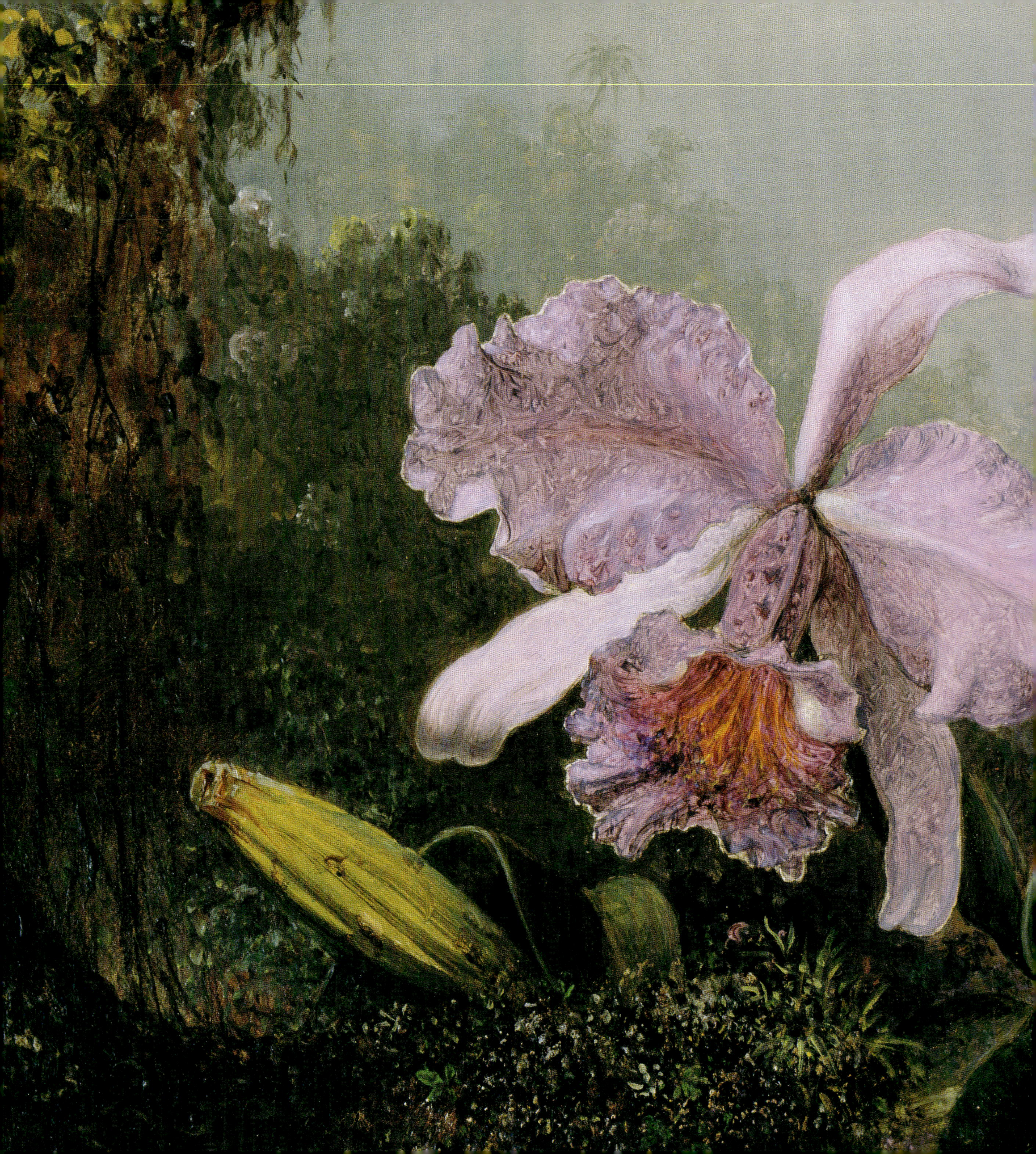

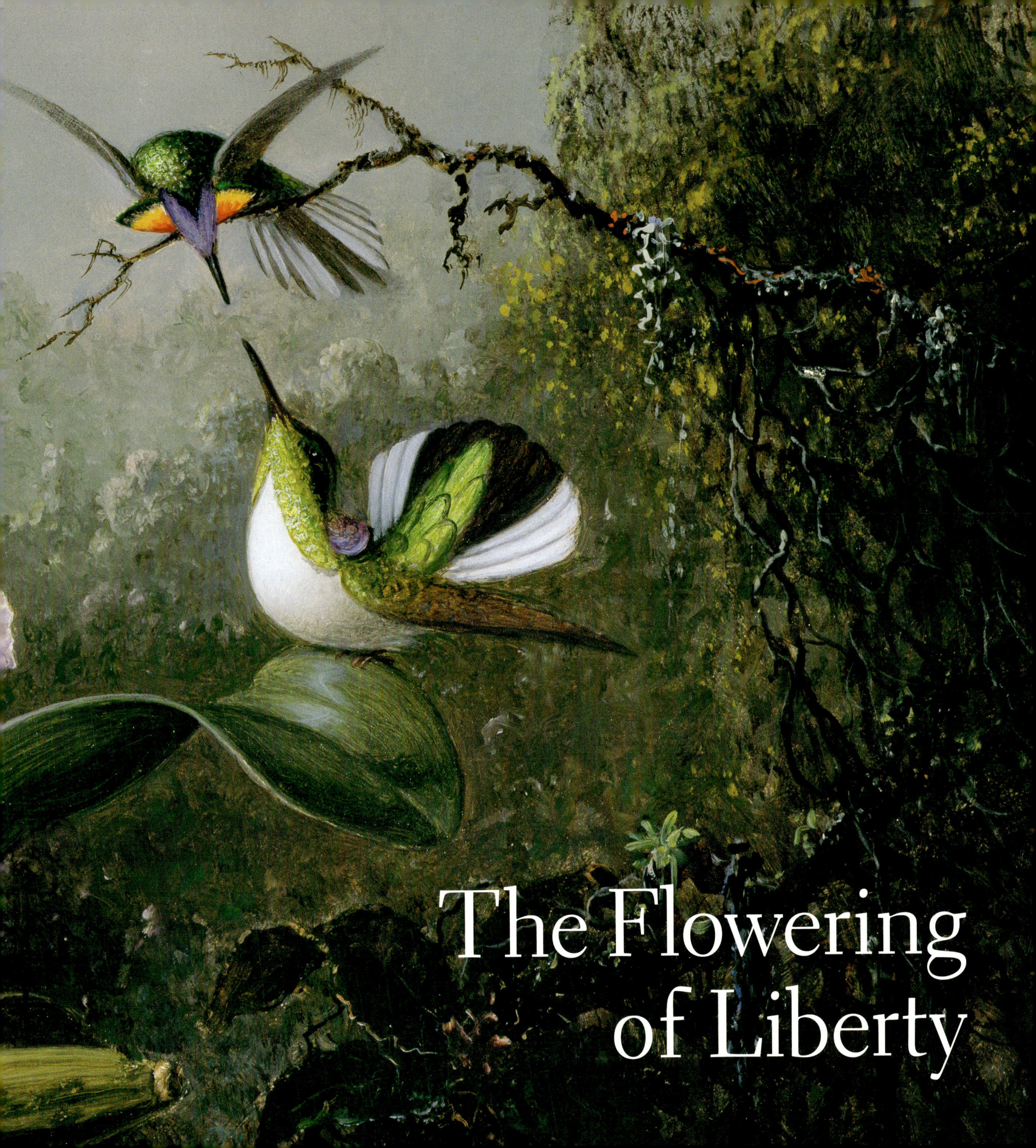

The Flowering of Liberty

Sarah Miriam Peale 1800–1885

On January 10, 1841, Priscilla Stump Griffith noted in her diary the first signs of her daughter's illness: "Found my darling [Mary] very sick with high fever and vomiting." On January 28, two days after Mary's death, she recorded the visit of "Miss Peale" at her request, who made a plaster cast of the deceased child's face to memorialize her in this posthumous portrait.[1] Sarah Miriam Peale was one of the leading portrait painters in Baltimore during the mid-nineteenth century. She was the youngest child of miniaturist James Peale, cousin of the noted painter Rembrandt Peale, and niece of well-known portraitist Charles Willson Peale. The Griffiths, who lived in Havre de Grace, Maryland, northwest of Baltimore, may have commissioned her to execute the portrait because of her reputation for painting the city's fashionable elite.[2]

This portrait most likely hung in the Griffith family's parlor for public viewing and contemplation, a vital part of the mourning process.[3] Central to the painting, which integrates symbols of childhood, death, and new life, is the serenity radiating from the life-size child. Delicate wisps of hair frame clear eyes that look toward the viewer, and a slight smile warms her face. Though the chair behind her has tumbled over and books lie scattered, they do not disturb the gentility with which she grasps the scissors or crosses her ankles. She is no bumbling toddler, but an angelic form floating above the shadows of her well-appointed surroundings.

Peale's portrait offers comfort to the grieving parents through this visual reincarnation of their lost child. Despite Mary's youth, the artist shows her absorbed in preparation for her future as a wife and mother, when she would have served as guardian of and advocate for the domestic arts and the education of youth. As she snips the paper with blunted scissors, which allude to the sudden sundering of life, she looks up. A primer at her feet ominously reveals the end, not the beginning of the alphabet. Though death has denied her the chance to instill republican virtues in future generations by direct tutelage and example, her gravity suggests an awareness of her symbolic importance in supporting the moral and democratic underpinnings of the new nation.[4] For a young America, death and loss were allayed by a belief in social progress and expressed in such images of robust optimism.[5] [EY]

Mary Leypold Griffith (1838–1841)

1841, oil on canvas, 35 1/2 × 30 3/4 in.
Private Collection

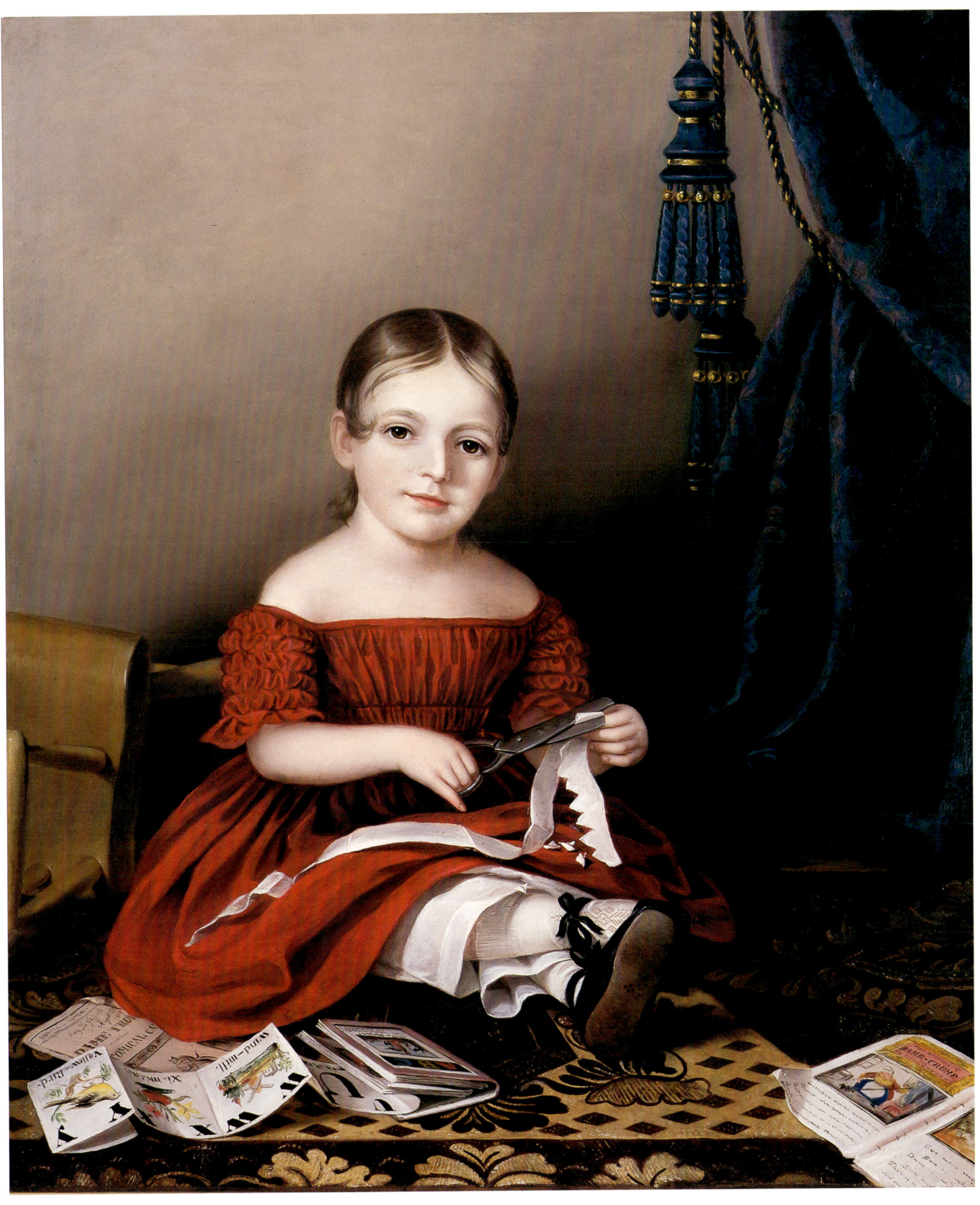
DAME-CRUMP

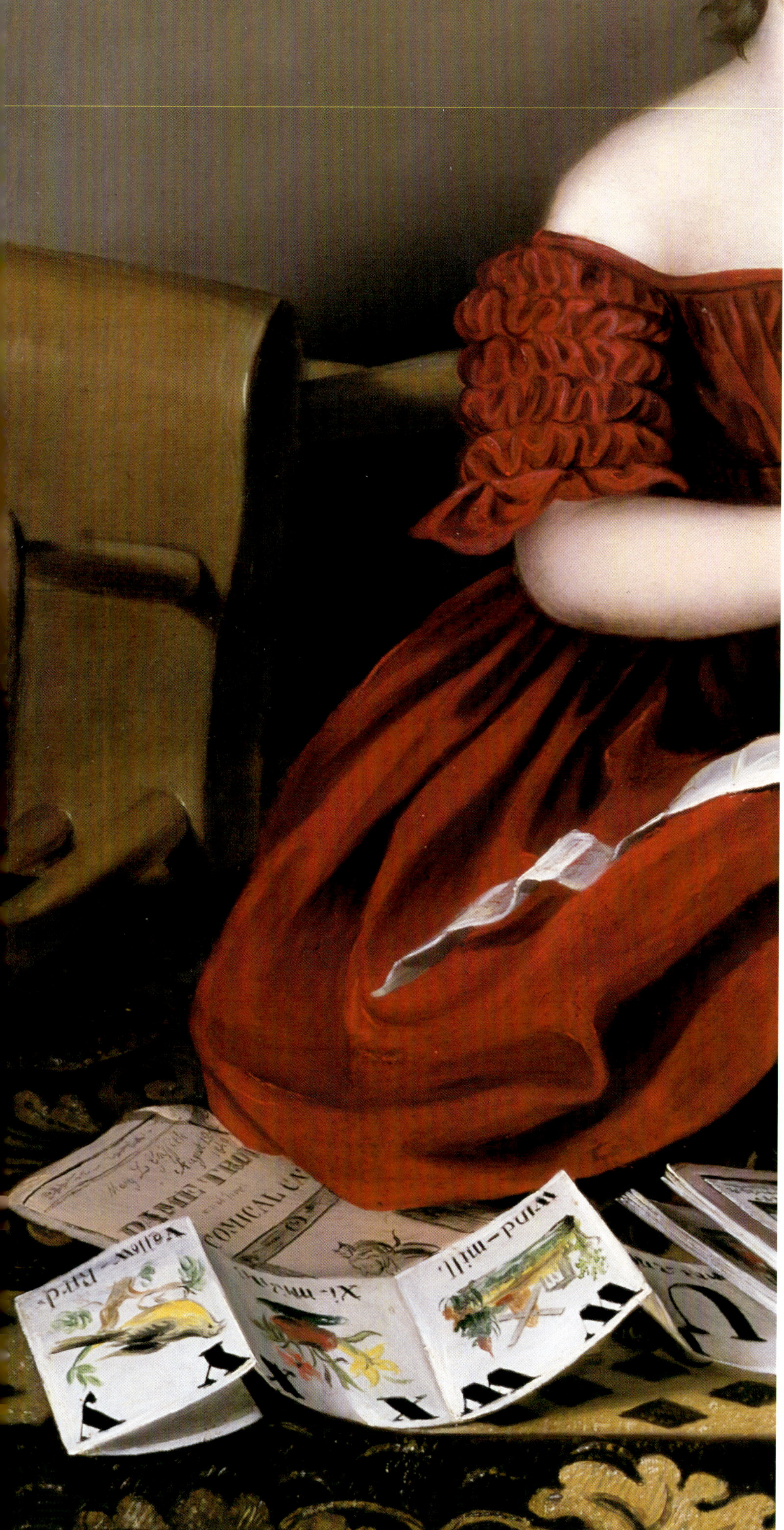

Sarah Miriam Peale

[1] January 28th, 1841, diary entry of Priscilla Stump Griffith, no. pag. A copy of the diary was provided by Stephanie Strass and Carlton Neville.

[2] Anne Sue Hirshorn describes the relationship between artist and family as "seemingly distant, or, at least, formal" and concludes that "categorized as neither friend, servant, nor tradesman, Miss Peale appeared to occupy a niche of her own." See Hirshorn's "Sarah Miriam Peale," *American Women Artists: 1819–1947: The Neville-Strass Collection* (Hagerstown, MD: Washington County Museum of Fine Arts, 2003), p. 35.

[3] Phoebe Lloyd refers to posthumous mourning portraits as "icon[s] for the bereaved." See "Posthumous Mourning Portraiture," in *A Time to Mourn: Expressions of Grief in Nineteenth-Century America*, Martha V. Pike and Janice Gray Armstrong, eds. (New York: Museums at Stony Brook, 1980), p. 74.

[4] Claire Perry, *Young America: Childhood in Nineteenth-Century Art and Culture* (New Haven, CT: Yale University Press and the Iris & B. Gerald Cantor Center for Visual Arts, Stanford University, 2006), pp. 39–43. Chapter 2, entitled "Daughters of Liberty," offers an in-depth discussion of the many representations of girls in art and popular imagery as future wives and mothers who would nurture the male citizenry and balance the "expansive energies of liberty."

[5] See Chapter 2, "The Era of Jacksonian Democracy: O Lovely Appearance of Death" in Phoebe Lloyd's *Death and American Painting: Charles Willson Peale to Albert Pinkham Ryder* (PhD diss., City University of New York, 1980), p. 84.

Detail:

Mary Leypold Griffith (1838–1841)

Henry Inman 1801–1846

after Charles Bird King

During the winter of 1825–26, Mistippee accompanied his father, Yoholo-Micco, to Washington with a delegation of thirteen Creek chiefs from Alabama to protest a dishonorable treaty signed earlier in the year in which the Creeks ceded all their lands in Georgia and agreed to move west of the Mississippi. During the negotiations, the delegates agreed to sit for their portraits at the request of Thomas McKenney, the superintendent of the Bureau of Indian Affairs of the War Department. McKenney was creating an Indian Gallery of historic portraits and commissioned Charles Bird King to paint the Creek chiefs and Mistippee in all their finery in his Washington studio. As a result of other commissions from McKenney, King became one of the first American artists to paint numerous portraits of Native Americans. His images were based on the European tradition of portraiture with a new ethnographic interest that was to become the hallmark of another major painter of Indians, George Catlin. Whereas King painted his relatively small canvas, about seventeen by fourteen inches, in his studio, Catlin's portraits of the Plains Indians are nearly double that size and were painted from life on the plains.[1]

In the early 1830s, McKenney became involved in a project with James Hall to publish the sumptuously illustrated three-volume *History of the Indian Tribes of North America* (1837–44). McKenney commissioned Henry Inman, a leading New York City portrait painter, to make copies of the War Department's Indian Gallery paintings, including King's. These served as the basis for the lithographic illustrations in the publication.[2] In 1832 Inman moved for two years to Mount Holly, New Jersey, just outside Philadelphia, where he was in partnership with lithographer Cephas G. Childs, who initially produced illustrations for McKenney and Hall's publication. McKenney had King's paintings shipped from Washington to Mount Holly, where Inman copied them and returned them to the Capitol.[3] Inman's copy of *Mistippee* is reasonably faithful to King's version, although he used a much larger canvas and simplified the forms so the portrait would be easier for the lithographer to transcribe. The lithographer in turn simplified the composition even more by leaving out the background with the exception of the rock.[4]

As painted by Inman, Mistippee stands in a forest and leans his elbow on a mossy rock. A young hunter and future brave, he holds three small arrows and a bow with the string running through his fingers. His face is painted with a delicate pattern of dots, reflecting the colors in his outfit. He is dressed in "civilized" clothes, a white shirt, brown jacket or vest, and long white coat, possibly made

Mistippee

about 1833, oil on canvas, 30 × 25 in.
Collection of Ann and Tom Cousins

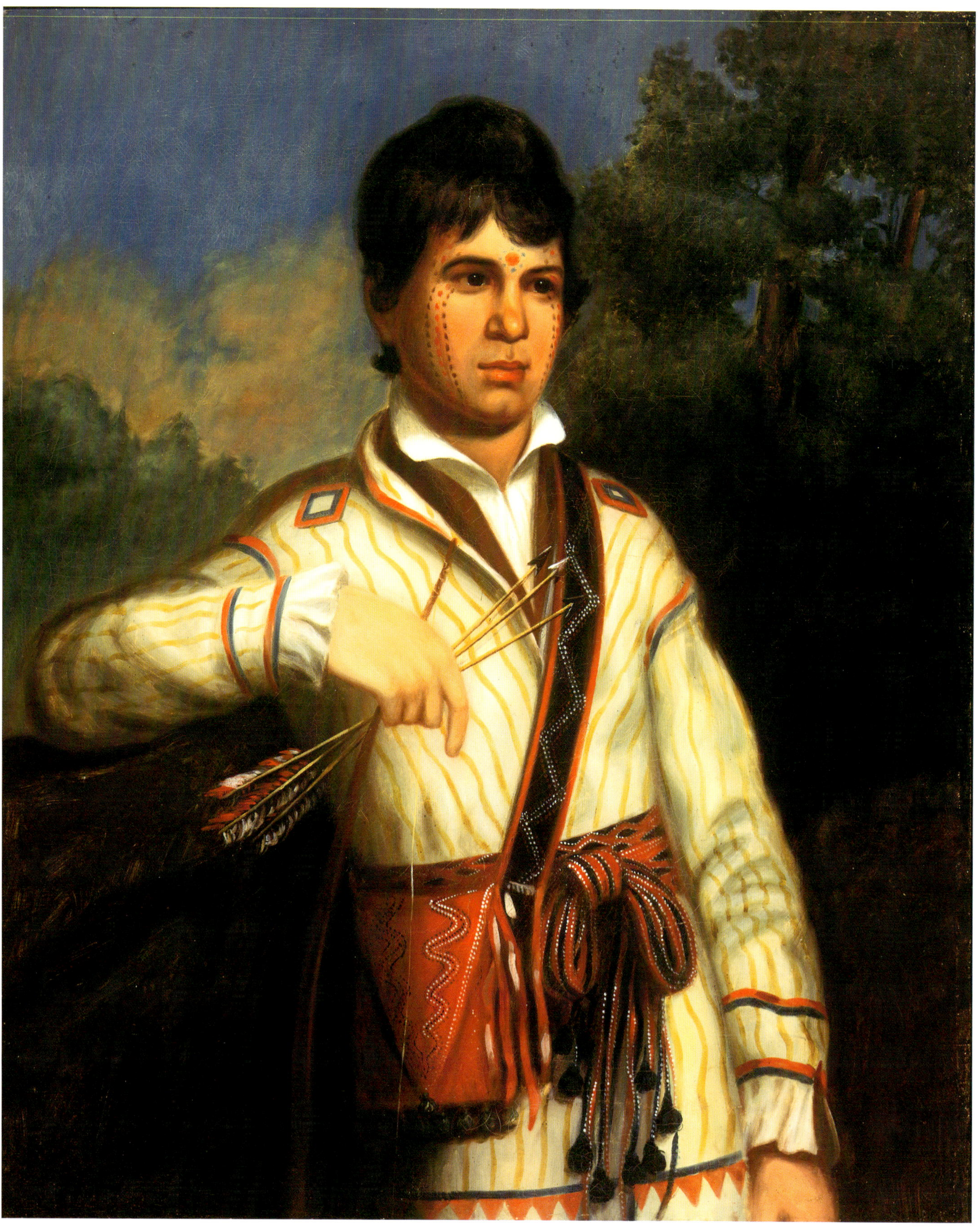

of calico, embellished with painted diamonds and stripes. The sash, pouch, tassels, and belt are made from trade cloth decorated with designs of glass pony beads that hark back to older, more traditional regional motifs made from natural materials.

Not an ordinary Indian boy, Mistippee was the son of Yoholo-Micco, a brave and eloquent Creek chief, who raised his children "after the fashion of their white neighbors." His parents bestowed on him the name Benjamin from which, as was later recorded, "soon arose the usual abbreviation of Ben and Benny.... To this familiar name, respect for his family soon prefixed the title of Mr, and, in the mouths of Indians, Mr. Ben soon became Mistiben, and finally Mistippee."[5]

In his *History of the Indian Tribes*, McKenney related that Mistippee was given "unusual advantages in regard to education," wed a comely woman, and "emigrated to the new home provided for his people, west of the Mississippi." His father was not so lucky, for he "fell victim to the fatigues attending the emigration."[6] The forced removal of the Creeks from Alabama in 1838 was required by the provisions under Andrew Jackson's Indian Removal Act of 1830. It decreed that all Indians on land east of the Mississippi be removed to land on the western side. The route that the Cherokee, Creek, and other tribes traversed is known as the Trail of Tears. [GG]

---

[1] Andrew J. Cosentino, *The Paintings of Charles Bird King (1785–1862)* (Washington, DC: Smithsonian Institution Press and the National Collection of Fine Arts, 1977), pp. 60-78. See Herman J. Viola, *The Indian Legacy of Charles Bird King* (Washington, DC: Smithsonian Institution Press, 1976), pp. 50–51.

[2] Thomas L. McKenney and James Hall, *History of the Indian Tribes of North America with Biographical Sketches and Anecdotes of the Principal Chiefs*, 3 vols., ed. Frederick Webb Hodge (1837–44; repr., Totowa, NJ: Rowman and Littlefield, 1972).

[3] William H. Gerdts, *The Art of Henry Inman* (Washington, DC: National Portrait Gallery, 1987), pp. 40–41, 94–95.

[4] A version of the King painting from which Inman made this copy was destroyed in a fire in the Smithsonian Castle on January 24, 1865. Another King version was willed by the artist to the Redwood Library in Newport, Rhode Island, which sold it at Parke-Bernet on May 21, 1970, to the Museum of Early Southern Decorative Arts in Winston-Salem, North Carolina. See Parke-Bernet Galleries, Sale Number 3056, May 21, 1970, Lot 10, p. 24. This copy by Inman commissioned by McKenney found its way into the Peabody Museum, Harvard University, until it was deaccessioned and acquired by the current owners.

[5] McKenney and Hall, *The Indian Tribes of North America*, vol. 2, p. 39.

[6] Ibid., pp. 37, 44.

17

Mistippee

about 1833, oil on canvas, 30 × 25 in.
Collection of Ann and Tom Cousins

George Henry Durrie 1820–1863

George Henry Durrie's images of New England were popularized through lithographs produced by Currier and Ives in the last six years of the artist's life. Durrie encircled the luminous middle ground of this canvas, in which all of the lively action unfolds, with rich shades of gray and brown in the trees, water, and mountains. *Winter in the Country, Distant Hills* echoes Henry Ward Beecher's contemporaneous description of winter's "bracing air" and "hills lying clear upon the sky [and] exquisite tracery of trees."[1] In an 1854 advertisement, Durrie offered his paintings to America's middle class, to "the admirers of the fine arts and all who would adorn their parlors with pictures that will stand for ages as an evidence of a cultivated and refined taste."[2] Seven years later, when Durrie painted this work, the nation was at war. The small homestead in this scene, complete and self-sufficient, seemed more like a comforting fiction built on a vision of New England that had endured for generations.

And yet, the artist's life was truly as peaceable and serene as his paintings. Some seventy years after this work was created, Mary Clarissa Durrie wrote of her father's devotion to his family and the sweet tenor voice he raised at New Haven's Trinity Church.[3] Durrie's joy in making these winter scenes mirrored his popularity with patrons. The artist created *Winter in the Country, Distant Hills* at the height of his career, when the annual lotteries of the Cosmopolitan Art Association in New York City offered Durrie's winter scenes to the exclusion of all others on the theme.[4] On his twenty-sixth birthday, Durrie had exhorted himself to "improve the time as it flies, and increase in all good works, so that when my short race is run, I may not have lived in vain."[5] Throughout his career, Durrie traveled extensively across New England in search of his subjects. He blended his love of painting with his appreciation for the region's distinctive identity, epitomized in his classic winter views. [GS]

---

[1] Quoted in Martha Hutson, *George Henry Durrie, 1820–1863: American Winter Landscapist, Renowned through Currier and Ives* (Santa Barbara, CA: Santa Barbara Museum of Art, 1978), p. 109.

[2] Colin Simkin, *George Henry Durrie, Connecticut Artist, 1820–1863* (New Haven, CT: New Haven Colony Historical Society, 1966), p. 14.

[3] Mary Clarissa Durrie, "George Henry Durrie: Artist," *Antiques* 24, No. 1 (July 1933): 13–15.

[4] Hutson, *George Henry Durrie: American Winter Landscapist*, pp. 109–10.

[5] Simkin, *George Henry Durrie, Connecticut Artist*, p. 16.

Winter in the Country, Distant Hills

1861, oil on canvas, 32 × 40 in.
Collection of Ted Slavin

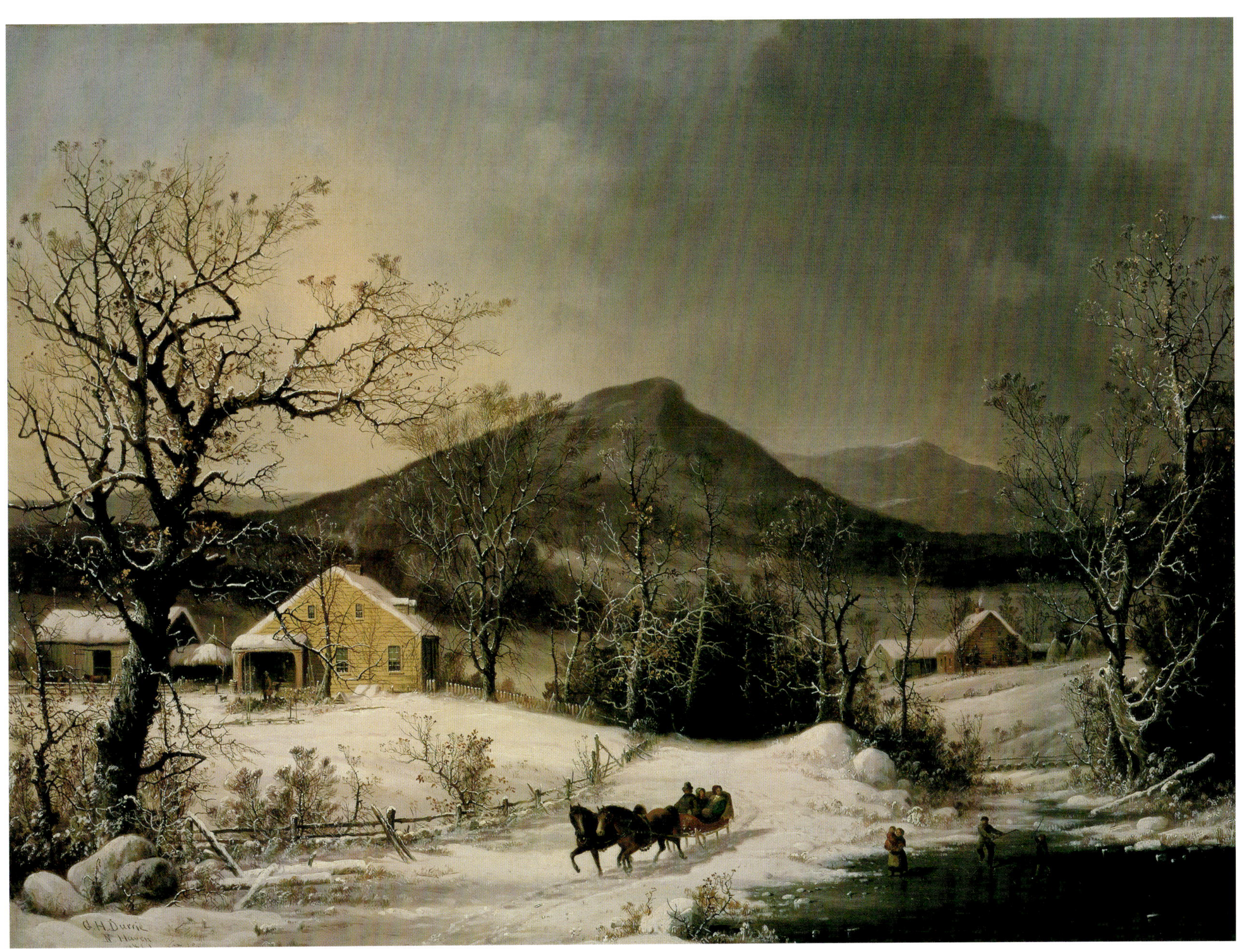
G.H.Durrie
N Haven

Fitz Henry Lane 1804–1865

Fitz Henry Lane's serene *View of Norwich* reflects the ten years of work in which the artist refined his drawing, perspective, and effects of light and atmosphere.[1] From the late 1830s to roughly 1850, his lithographs and oils of Boston, Washington, Baltimore, and other burgeoning cities on the eastern seaboard show a painter coming of age as his young country grew into an industrial power. Norwich, Connecticut, lies fourteen miles above Long Island Sound at the point where the Thames River becomes unnavigable by larger ships. The city was settled in the late seventeenth century and by Lane's day had become a trading center where manufactured goods were loaded onto vessels for shipping up and down the Atlantic coast.

View of Norwich shows steamboats and sailing sloops pulling up to the wharves and rail lines that served the settlement. The bustle of trade fostered a strong middle class, symbolized by the gentleman in white breeches and top hat strolling along the lower margin of the painting. But for all its mercantile strength, Norwich remained an ideal Jeffersonian community surrounded by forests and farms. Among the houses of worship across the harbor are the First and Second Congregational churches established in the seventeenth and eighteenth centuries.[2] Their spires echo the ships' masts, pointing to a radiant late afternoon sky that suggests a benediction on a healthful and industrious city.

Lane had supported himself much as America's early limners had done, traveling from one settlement to another and painting whatever his clients needed. *View of Norwich* demonstrates how far Lane had come, and how thoroughly he had trained himself to be a great painter. The gentle clarity of figures and shadows arrested in motion and the soft colors stitching together a seamless image of nature and industry anticipate Lane's luminous marines painted in the following decade. [GS]

---

[1] John Wilmerding, *Fitz Henry Lane* (1971; repr., Danvers, MA: Bradford & Bigelow and the Cape Ann Historical Museum, 2005), pp. 25–29. Page references are to the 1971 edition, published by Praeger.

[2] Norwich Board of Trade, *Norwich Connecticut: Its Importance as a Business and Manufacturing Centre and as a Place of Residence: A Brief Review of its Past and Present* (Norwich, CT: Press of the Bulletin Company, 1888), pp. 11–67.

View of Norwich

1849, oil on canvas, 12 1/2 × 17 in.

Collection of Mr. and Mrs. Thomas M. Evans Jr.

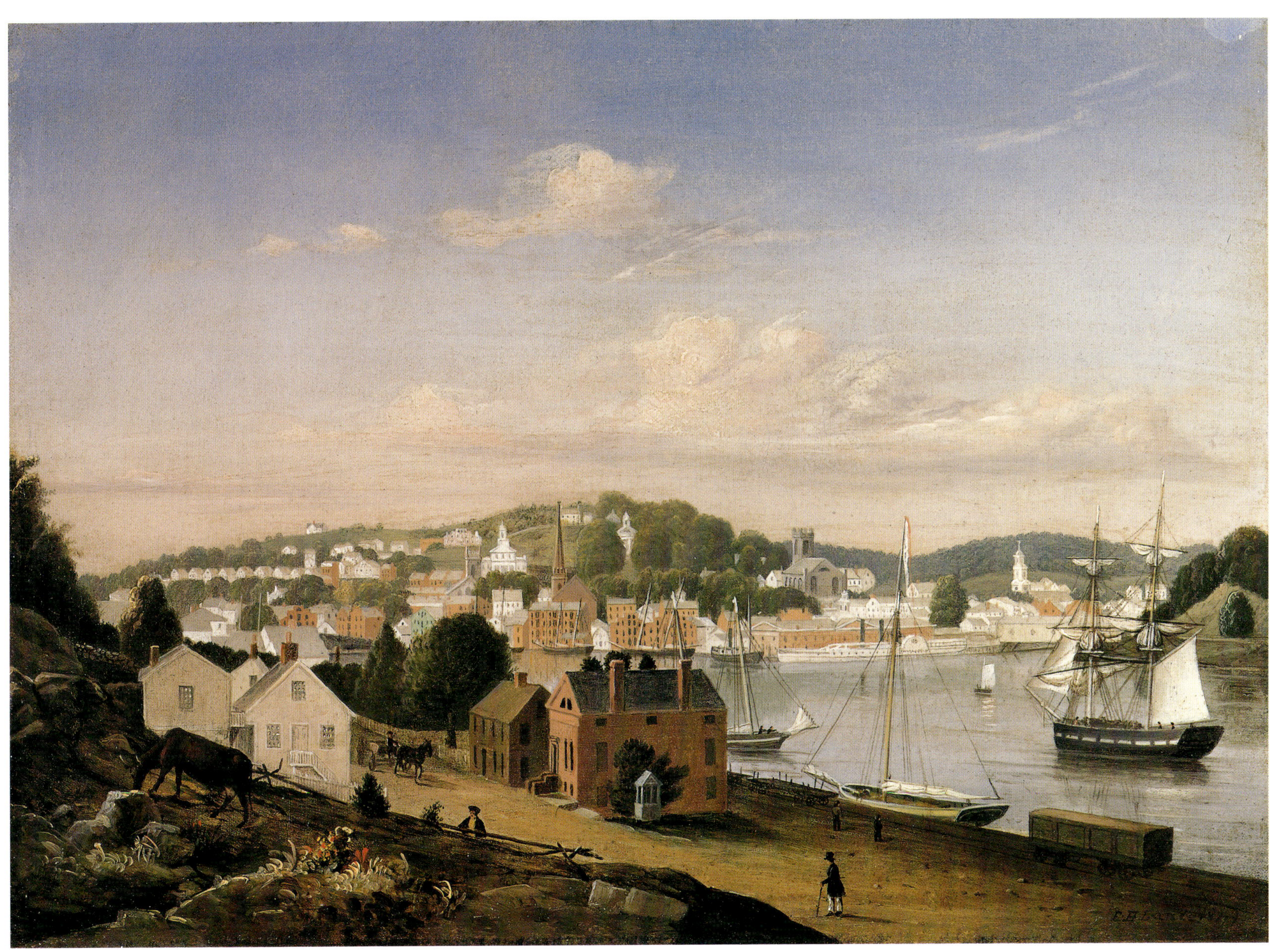

Francis A. Silva 1835–1886

Evening in Gloucester Harbor captures a moment of perfect peace in a New England locale that, in Francis Silva's day, was favored by tourists and artists alike. In 1865, military service brought the artist north from New York to Massachusetts, where he discovered the coastal landmarks made famous by artists Fitz Henry Lane, Martin Johnson Heade, and others. Poised to inherit Lane's mantle, Silva began painting the New England coastline in 1865, the year Lane died. Like Lane, Silva had worked for several years as a trade painter, creating signs and decorative side panels for coaches and fire engines.[1] And, like Lane before him, Silva taught himself how to capture the luminous colors and vibrant atmosphere of the coast, raising his journeyman painting to the level of a master.

Silva was a man of strong opinions who felt that native-born painters should work to make American art great rather than paint "the everlasting and insipid Seine" as expatriates in Paris.[2] But Silva believed that a painting must be poetic as well as skillful. He heightened the humid haze and raking light for greater effect and calibrated the brightness and scale of the sails to express the breadth of sea, sky, and horizon. *Evening in Gloucester Harbor* pictures a line of sloops moving gently southward past two lighthouses that stood between Gloucester and the Atlantic.

Gloucester Harbor is a place of industry as well as a haven suffused with spiritual grace. Silva's love of the tranquil moments associated with early morning and evening resonated with his American audience. A pair of lighthouses watching over schooners and sail boats underscores the sense of stability and calm Silva vested in this work. The artist's easy command of the details of sails and rigging, and the deft mirroring of sea and sky across the watery horizon, are hallmarks of his best work. The image of a safe harbor resting under the light of heaven struck a chord with Americans still shaken by the Civil War. Such works played an important role in the healing process of the 1870s. [GS]

---

[1] Mark D. Mitchell, *Francis A. Silva (1835–1886): In His Own Light* (New York: Berry-Hill Galleries, 2002), p. 23; John I. H. Baur, "Francis A. Silva: Beyond Luminism," *The Magazine Antiques* 118 (November 1980): 1021.

[2] Francis A. Silva, "American vs. Foreign-American Art," *The Art Union* 1, nos. 6–7 (June–July 1884): 131.

Evening in Gloucester Harbor

1871, oil on canvas, 20 × 40 in.
Collection of Paul Leach and Susan Winokur

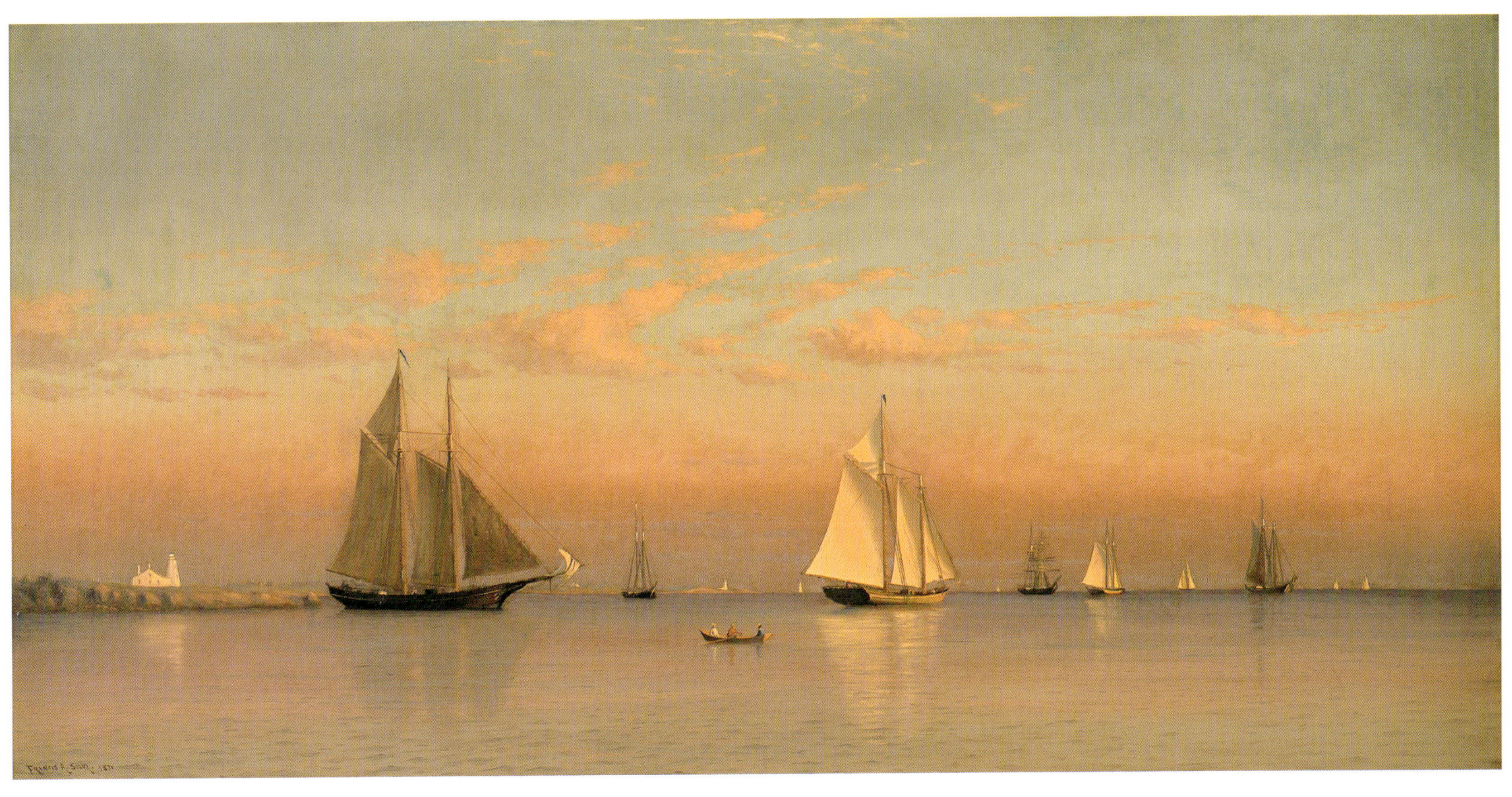

David Johnson 1827–1908

The Torne at Ramapo appeared in an exhibition of David Johnson's paintings in New York City in 1890. The catalogue noted that "it was from this peak that Washington viewed the manoeuvres of the British forces after his retreat from Long Island."[1] That comment encapsulates Johnson's approach to landscape painting, as he embued his compositions with the aura of history. Embracing topographic accuracy and specificity as one of his goals, Johnson catered to an audience familiar with the associations at each site he painted. This merging of landscape and history painting gave Johnson the ability to focus with delight on recording directly his observations in nature, while creating scenes resonant with important events from the past. Like the second-generation Hudson River painters with whom he traveled and sketched, Johnson measured his success by working "earnestly to find out how Dame Nature made things, divesting myself of all thoughts of pictures or studio effects."[2]

A small clearing north of the river and a split-rail fence in the foreground are the only clues that Johnson worked in a thoroughly settled area along the New Jersey state line. From 1872 to 1874, he painted views along the Ramapo and Genesee rivers and around Lake George. A related work, *October at Ramapo, Rockland County* (1874), employs the same soft brushwork and gentle gradations of autumn color. The minutely observed rocks and feathery clouds in *The Torne at Ramapo* are the particular hallmarks that earned Johnson a reputation as "a close student of Nature, looking upon her as his teacher and master."[3] Although he studied informally with Asher B. Durand, John Frederick Kensett, and John W. Casilear, and admired the work of Jean-Baptiste-Camille Corot, little is known of Johnson's formal training or his mature career. Instead, we are left to extrapolate the missing details from his paintings, encouraging the close observation of which the artist surely would have approved. [GS]

[1] David Johnson, *Catalogue of Paintings in Oil* (New York: Fifth Avenue Art Galleries and Ortgies and Co., 1890), p. 17.

[2] Gwendolyn Owens, *Nature Transcribed: The Landscapes and Still Lifes of David Johnson (1827–1908): An Exhibition* (Ithaca, NY: Herbert F. Johnson Museum of Art, Cornell University, 1988), p. 15.

[3] John I. H. Baur, "'...the exact brushwork of Mr. David Johnson,' An American Landscape Painter, 1827–1908," *The American Art Journal* 12, no. 4 (Autumn 1980): 34, 57–62.

The Torne at Ramapo

1873, oil on canvas, 15 1/2 × 25 1/2 in.
Collection of Mr. and Mrs. Thomas M. Evans Jr.

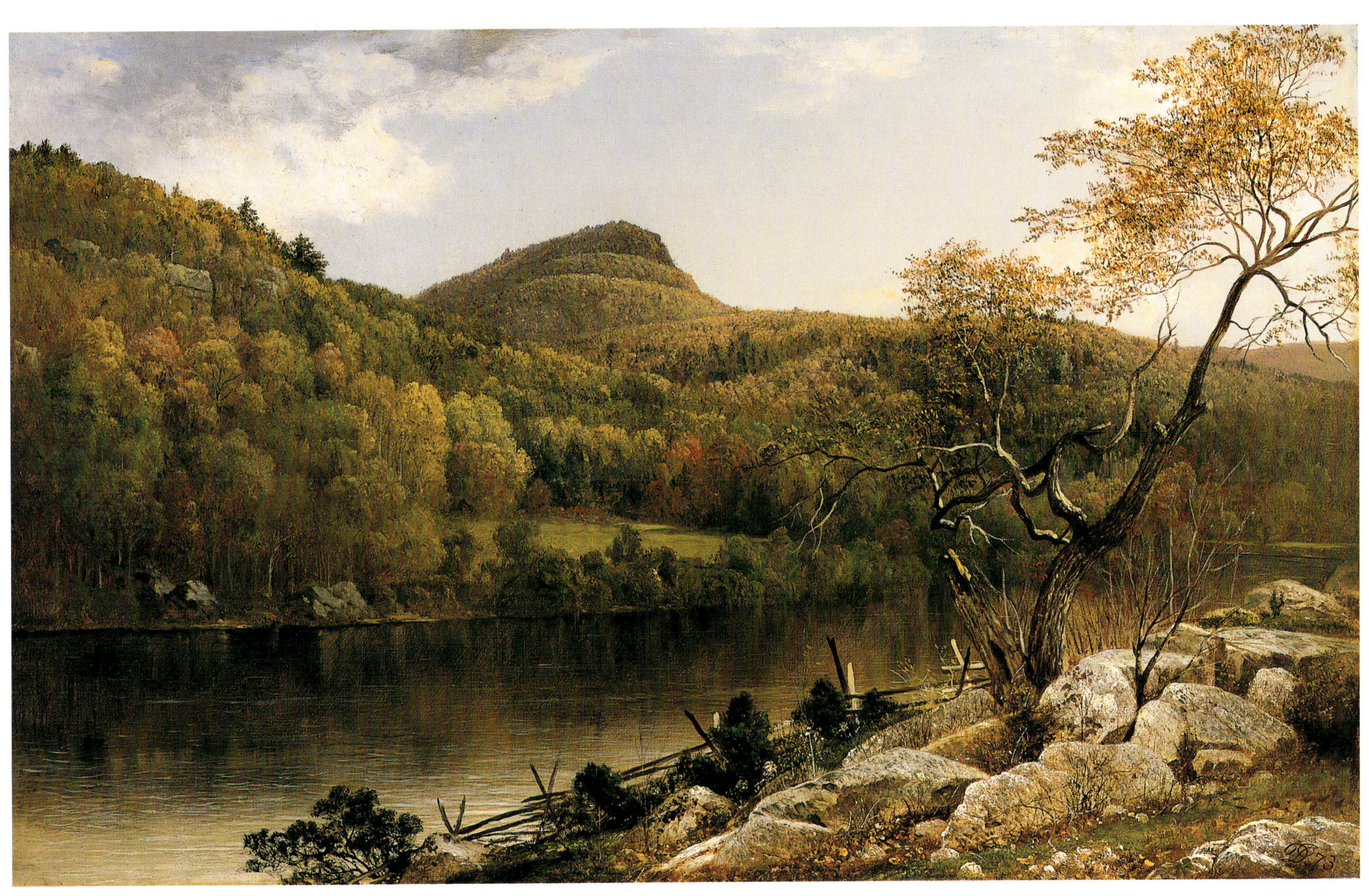

Eastman Johnson 1824–1906

Eastman Johnson grew up in Fryeburg, Maine, a small town near the border of New Hampshire, and had fond memories of the rituals involved in making maple sugar. Those rituals took on amplified significance during the Civil War, and between 1861 and 1865 Johnson spent the early spring months in the maple forests, sketching and painting the activities associated with maple sugaring, as a reprieve from his Civil War subjects.[1]

Cardplaying at Fryeburg, Maine captures the second stage of the process, called "sugaring off," when sap from the maple trees was hauled to a clearing to be boiled down and poured into trays to make maple syrup and cakes of maple sugar. Dominating the center of the composition is the large cast-iron kettle suspended from a long birch trunk over a fire that had to be kept burning day and night. Behind the kettle four indistinct figures keep each other company. Two keep watch over the boiling sap, while another pair passes the time playing cards under the cover of the shed. A fifth young man pulls up to the shack with a sled bearing a fresh barrel of sap to add to the kettle. On the far left, cakes of maple sugar cool in a snow bank.

These details eloquently capture the timeless qualities associated with maple sugaring, centered on the long hours spent checking the trees, hauling fresh buckets of sap, and tending the kettle fire. Johnson preferred to paint in his studio, and for this work and the many others he painted of the maple harvest, he took his studio to the woods: "The artist... had a house built on wheels and provided with a stove, so he was able to move his temporary studio and work in comfort, and in this way make accurate and careful studies of all details of the sugar camp."[2]

However, Johnson deliberately rusticated the process of sugaring off, invoking the traditional methods of tapping trees and boiling down the fresh sap rather than featuring the newer, more efficient equipment widely in use by then.[3] His purpose was likely to reaffirm the old New England traditions as a fundament of American society at a time when the country was racked by internal strife. The symbolism of sugaring in New England accorded with the painter's strong abolitionist views. Slave labor was required to harvest sugar cane from southern and Caribbean plantations, which would be refined into white table sugar. To abolitionists like Johnson, maple sugar was not "sprinkled with the tears and blood of slaves," but was the wholesome nourishment of "those who are happy and free."[4] Johnson's interpretation of the maple harvest in *Cardplaying at Fryeburg, Maine* evokes the cycles of nature and human history. A hard winter

Cardplaying at Fryeburg, Maine

about 1865, oil on canvas, 18 ⅞ × 29 in.
Private Collection, Washington, DC

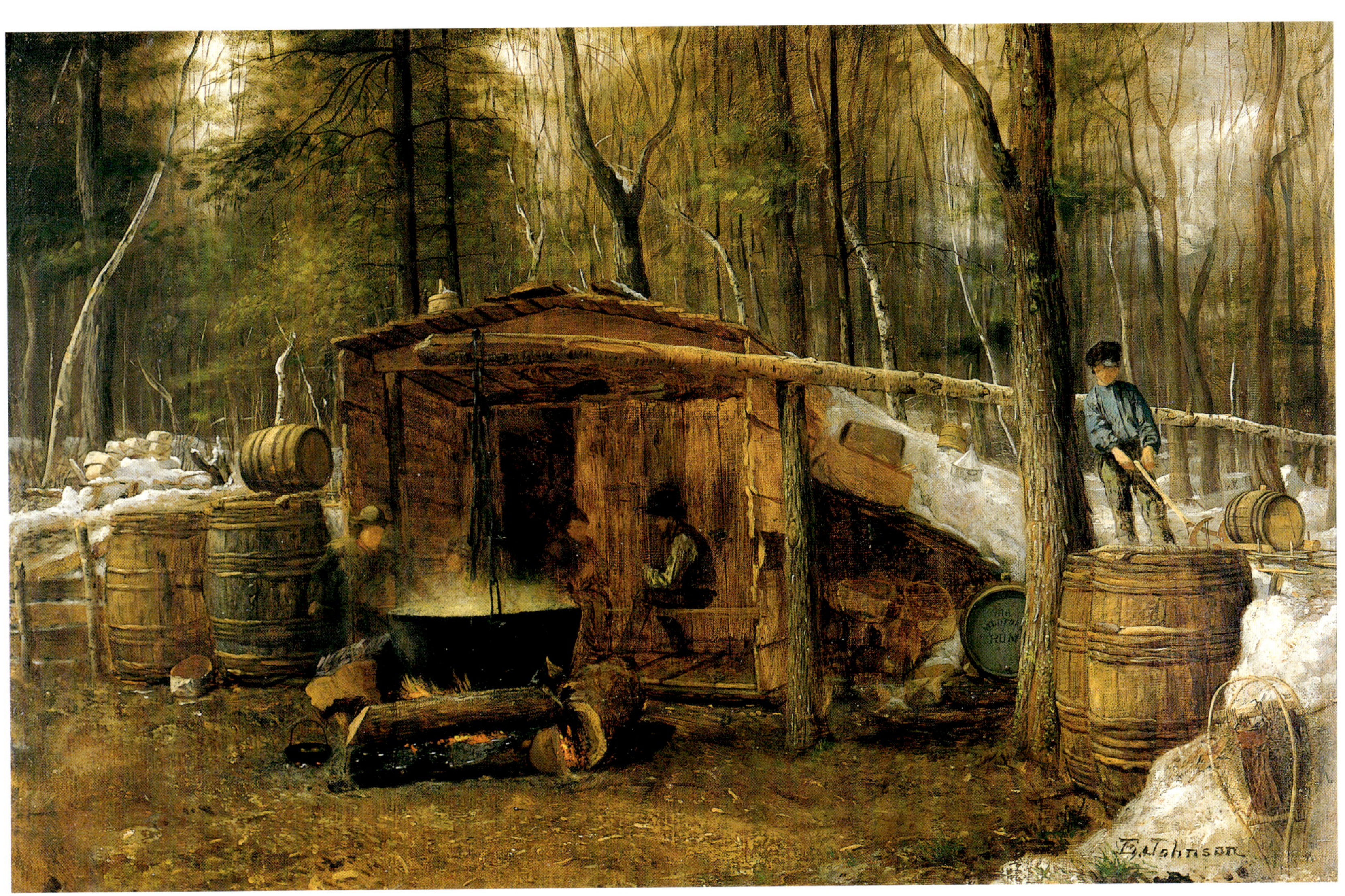
RUM
E.Johnson

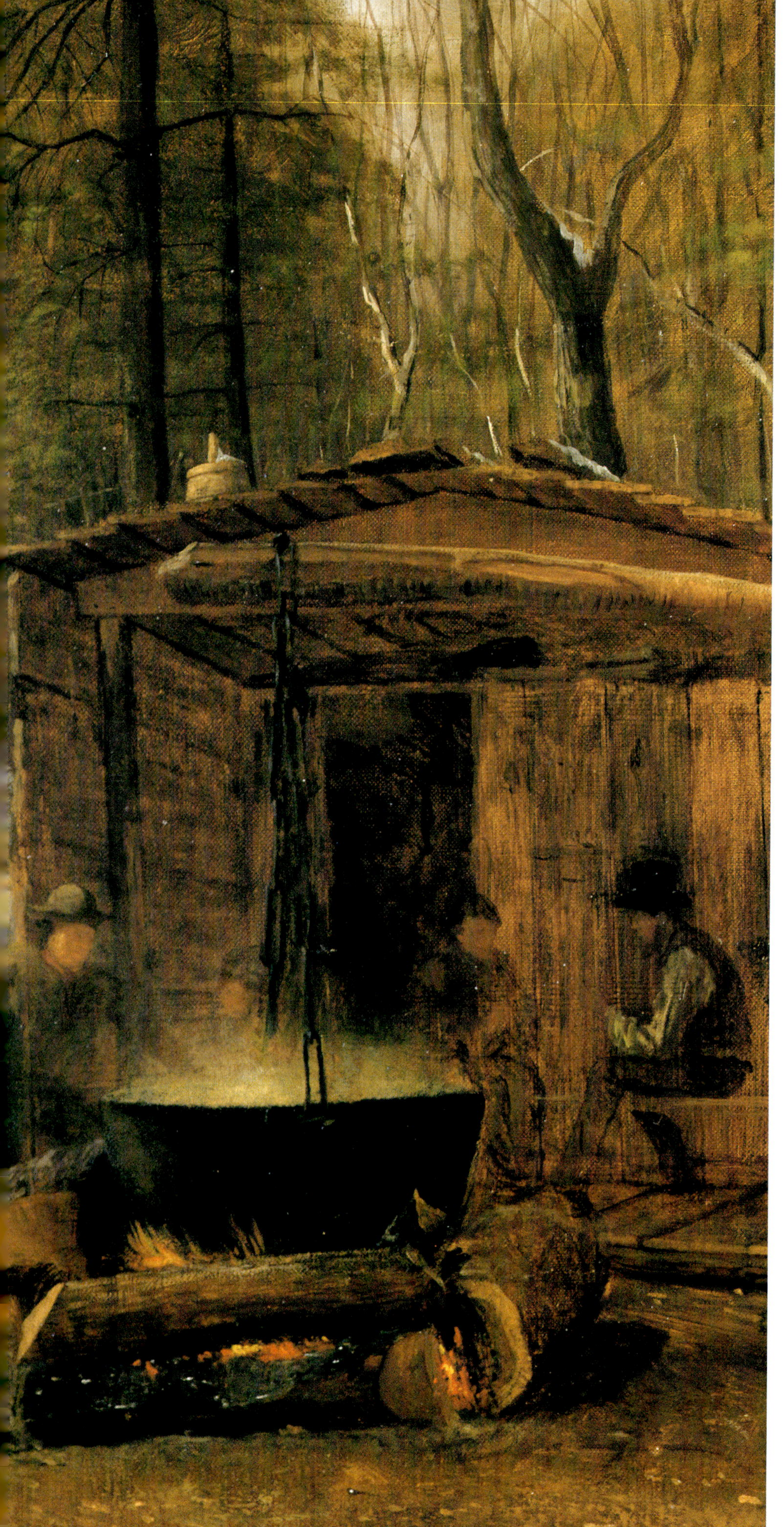

will lead to spring, industrious farmers will reap nature's bounty, and a nation will survive a fratricidal war, protected and renewed by the values of Johnson's New England community. [GS and EJH]

---

[1] "For five years in the early sixties [Johnson] spent three months each year in the maple groves at Fryeburg, Maine, and in the summer seasons of those years sought his subjects on the battlefields of the Civil War." See *The Works of the Late Eastman Johnson, N. A.* Roll N51, frame 1015, Archives of American Art, Smithsonian Institution, Washington, DC.

[2] Ibid.

[3] Brian T. Allen, *Sugaring Off: The Maple Sugar Paintings of Eastman Johnson* (Williamstown, MA: Sterling and Francine Clark Art Institute, 2004), p. 34.

[4] Ibid., pp. 38–39.

Detail:

Cardplaying at Fryeburg, Maine

Martin Johnson Heade 1819–1904

Martin Johnson Heade's luminous images of the Atlantic salt marshes testify to his love of nature and to his unorthodox professional choices. Other prominent painters had built their reputations on dramatic canvases of Niagara Falls or the Rocky Mountains, but Heade looked elsewhere, capturing the beautiful effects of weather and light from the placid fields of salt hay that had sustained generations of farmers in Massachusetts and New Jersey. The marsh in *Newburyport Meadows I* lies under a humid sky. A moving cloud shadow and a stream winding past haystacks and harvesters subtly suggest the passing of seasons. Heade's painting suspends a moment in time, preserving a way of life that was disappearing as America marched forward into the Gilded Age. His beloved marshes were drained throughout the 1860s and 1870s, until, by the time Heade painted this scene, three-quarters of the hay farms were deserted.[1]

Henry David Thoreau wrote that the coastal wetlands brought him the same pleasure as Walden Pond, where he had "my own sun and moon and stars, and a little world all to myself."[2] Heade experienced a similar emotional bond with the marshes, where he walked and hunted at all hours of the day. The painter railed against the privileges of the rich and the destruction of these last natural landscapes. Ironically, *Newburyport Meadows I* was the sort of painting that appealed to the captains of industry whose success had transformed the eastern seaboard forever. Heade's paintings of the salt meadows, like Eastman Johnson's scenes of cranberry picking, or Winslow Homer's depictions of carefree children, sought to recapture a Golden Day when America seemed more innocent. [GS]

[1] Nancy Frazier, "Mute Gospel: The Salt Marshes of Martin Johnson Heade," *Prospects* 23 (1998): 201.

[2] Quoted in Theodore E. Stebbins Jr., *The Life and Work of Martin Johnson Heade: A Critical Analysis and Catalogue Raisonné* (New Haven, CT: Yale University Press, 2000), p. 119.

Newburyport Meadows I

about 1876–82, oil on canvas, 9 × 20 in.
Collection of Paul Leach and Susan Winokur

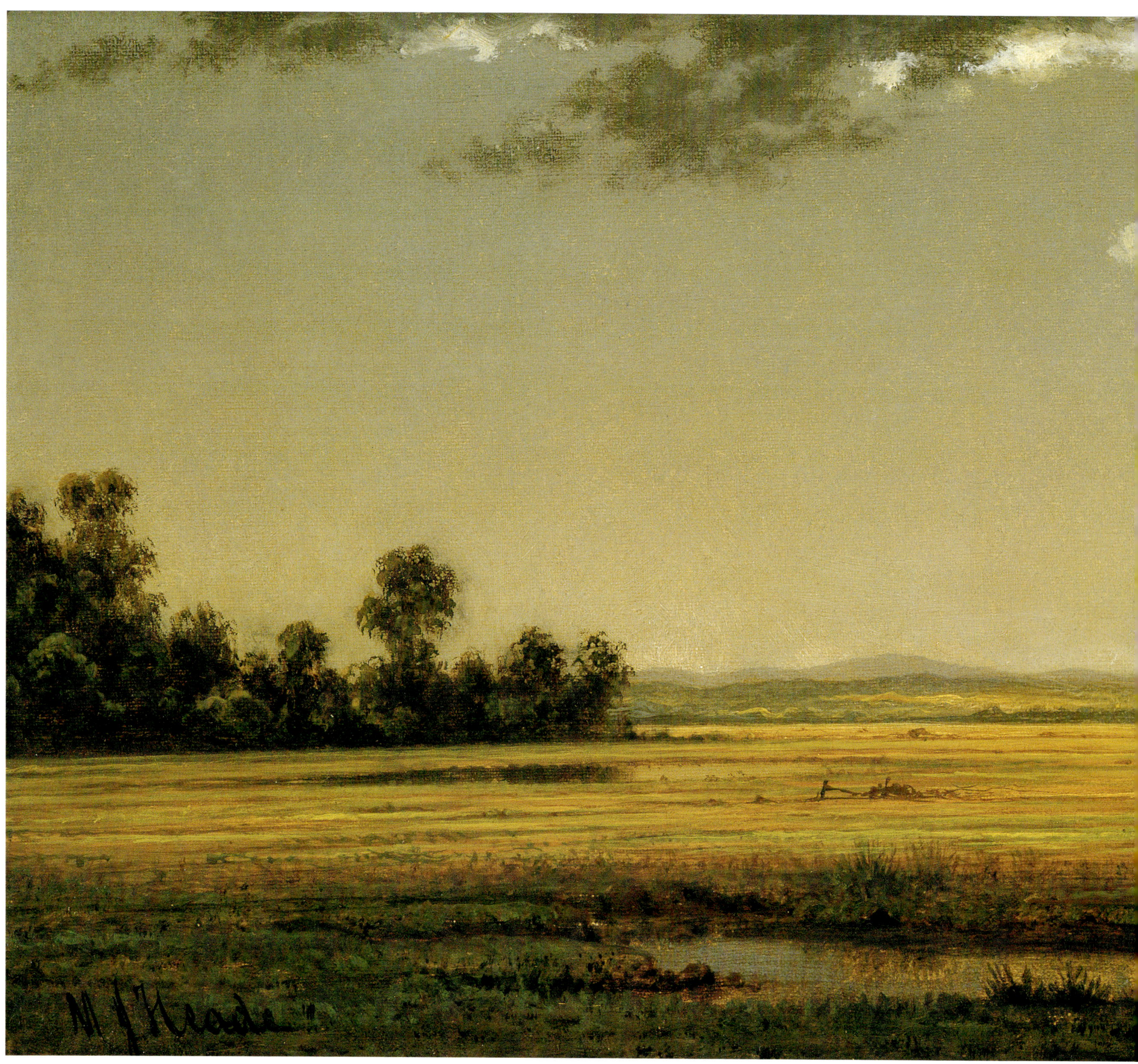

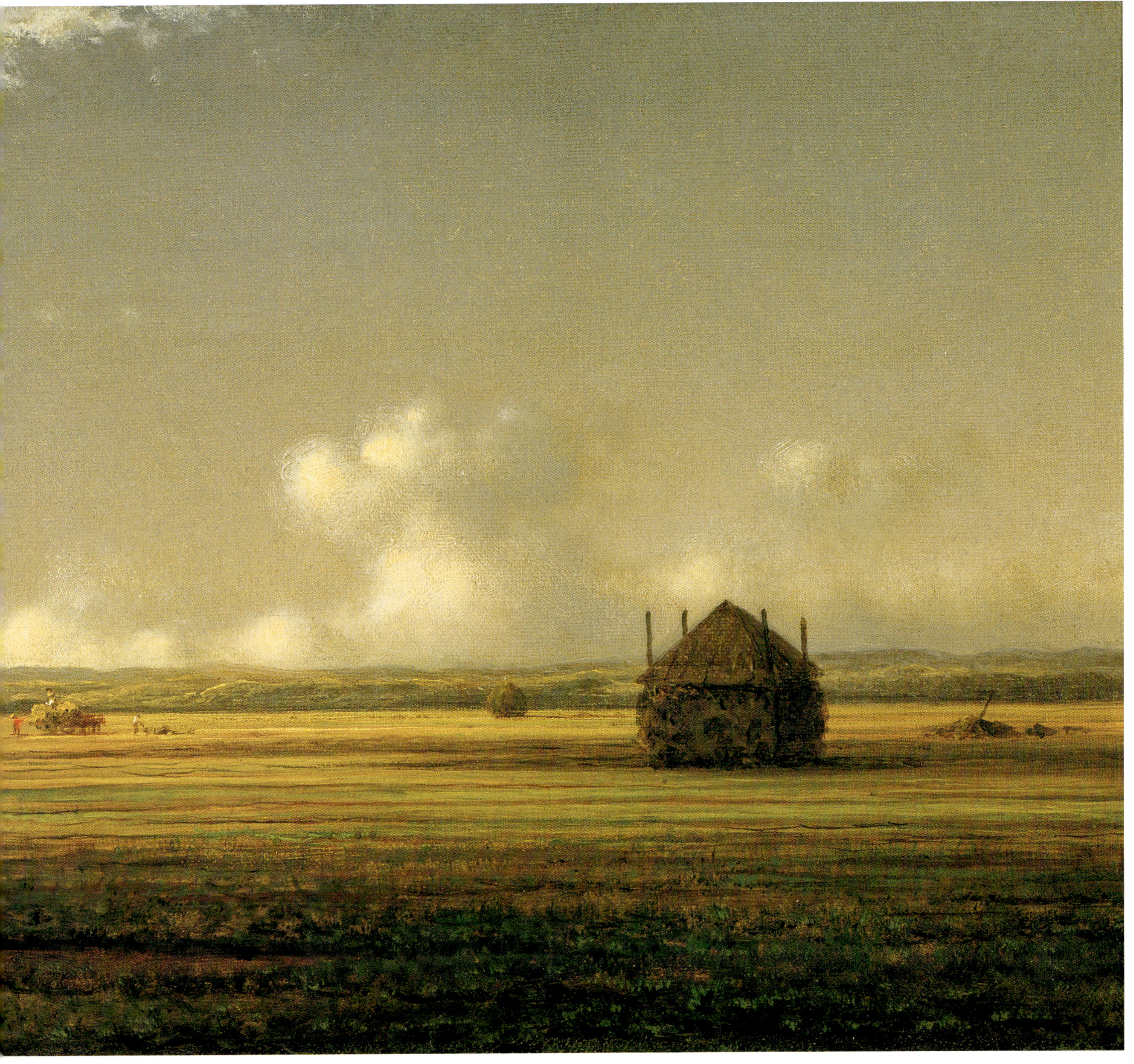

Martin Johnson Heade 1819–1904

Cattleya Orchid with Two Brazilian Hummingbirds is based on Martin Johnson Heade's notes from three trips to South America. Heade said of Brazil that "there is probably no country where a person interested in ornithology, entomology, botany, mineralogy or beautiful scenery could find so much to keep him entertained."[1] But it was only after his last equatorial trip that Heade hit upon a theme combining his passion for orchids, a confessed "monomania" for hummingbirds, and his love of landscape. Here, a male horned sungem hummingbird courts a black-eared fairy female. The birds are painted to scale, as is the *Cattleya labiata* orchid, suggesting the interrelatedness of plant and animal kingdoms. The humid landscape and heavy rain clouds beyond underscore the transient, violent energy of nature's cycles. The *Cattleya labiata* grew wild only in Brazil, but it had been cultivated for decades. It was popular in the United States as much for its horticultural beauty as for its sexually suggestive form.[2]

The small scale and wealth of details of this painting reflect a profound change in Americans' philosophical and scientific understanding of the world in the mid-nineteenth century. Heade's explorations followed in the footsteps of the naturalist Alexander von Humboldt and American painter Frederic Edwin Church. But, unlike Church, who painted enormous canvases that expressed the ordering hand of God in the sweep of nature, Heade trained his eye on the microcosm. He captured the tiny incident that described Charles Darwin's world, which was not a static manifestation of divinely ordained harmony, but an arena of sex, death, adaptation, and survival.[3] *Cattleya Orchid with Two Brazilian Hummingbirds* expresses Heade's respect for science and his profound emotional connection to the natural world. [GS]

---

[1] Quoted in Theodore E. Stebbins Jr., *Martin Johnson Heade*, with contributions by Janet L. Comey, Karen E. Quinn, and Jim Wright (Boston: Museum of Fine Arts, 1999), p. 71.

[2] Theodore E. Stebbins Jr., *The Life and Work of Martin Johnson Heade: A Critical Analysis and Catalogue Raisonné* (New Haven, CT: Yale University Press, 2000), p. 91.

[3] Ibid., pp. 75–78.

Cattleya Orchid with Two Brazilian Hummingbirds

1871, oil on panel, 13 ¾ × 18 in.
Private Collection, Washington, DC

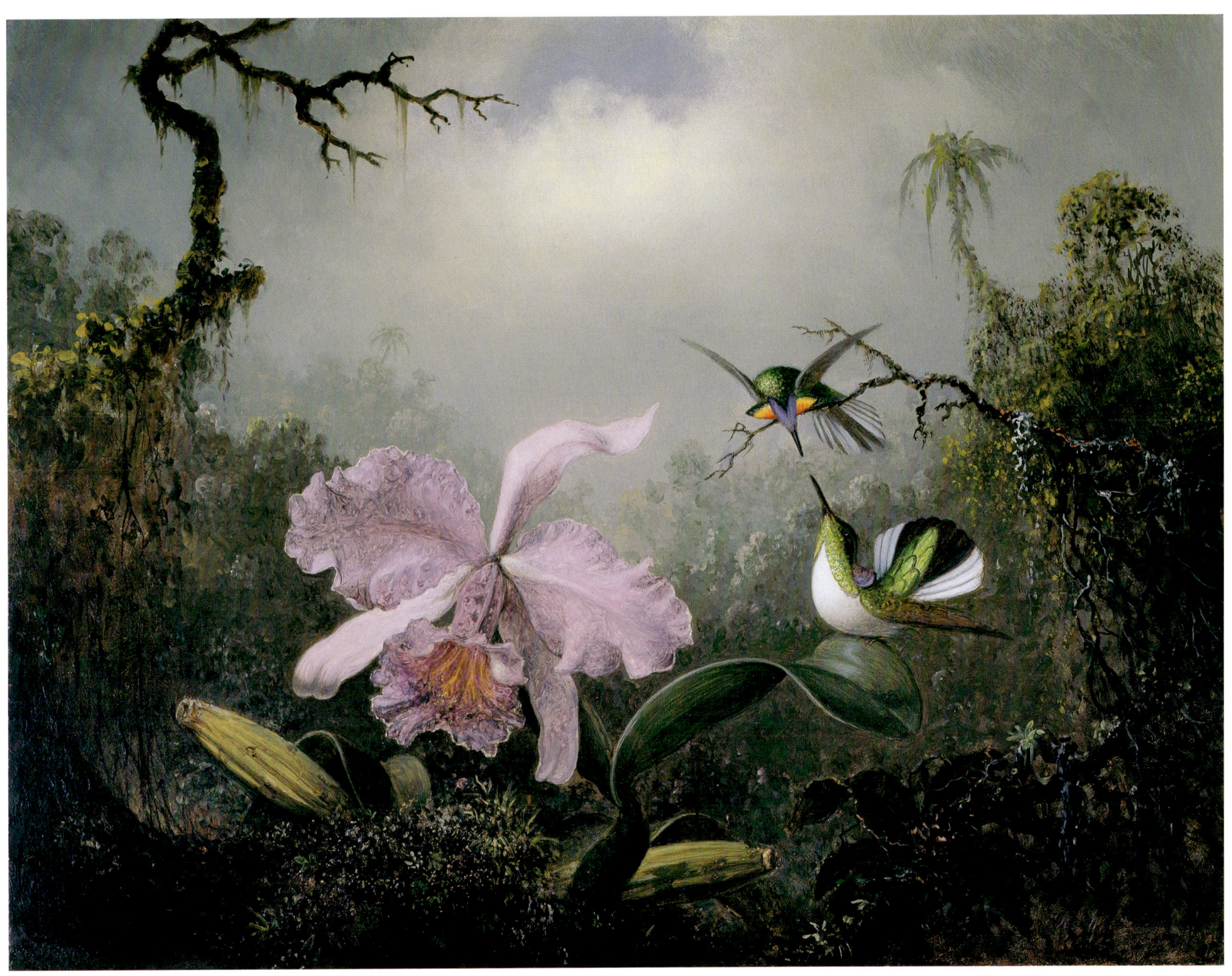

Winslow Homer 1836–1910

Winslow Homer's paintings of children at play and idle young women earned the praise of critics who saw in these images the "freshness" and "solid worth" of American life. That his canvases lacked the smooth finish of European academic paintings only made them more "redolent of the soil."[1] In *Girl in the Hammock*, a young woman lies in the half-light between the full glow of sun on the grass and the deep shade of an orchard. Across the canvas, confident dabs of pigment capture the scintillating effects of breezes and warm air, echoing the assurance that Homer achieved in his watercolors during these years. The luminous green behind the shadowed figure is so densely painted over a darker ground color that it pushes outward toward the surface of the canvas, nearly breaking the illusion of light and becoming less a field of grass than a field of brushstrokes.

Throughout the 1870s, Homer painted idyllic scenes of couples or of women alone. He created many of these on summer visits to upstate New York with the Valentine family, who were staunch supporters of his career. Late in the decade, the artist appears to have experienced a personal crisis brought about, perhaps, by a disappointing end to a friendship with a woman from the Valentines' social circle. The red-haired girl in this painting, with her distinctive white skin and strong jaw, appears in *Summer Afternoon* and *Sunlight and Shadow*, both from 1872, and most notably in *A Temperance Meeting (Noon Time)* of 1874. If she is the mystery woman in Homer's life, her retreat into the pages of a book could signal her indifference to the painter and a rejection of his attentions. Soon enough, Homer himself would withdraw into a solitary life in which his only concern was for his painting. [GS]

[1] Nicolai Cikovsky Jr. and Franklin Kelly, *Winslow Homer* (New Haven, CT: Yale University Press and the National Gallery of Art, Washington, DC, 1995), p. 95.

Girl in the Hammock

1873, oil on canvas, 13 ½ × 20 in.
Private Collection

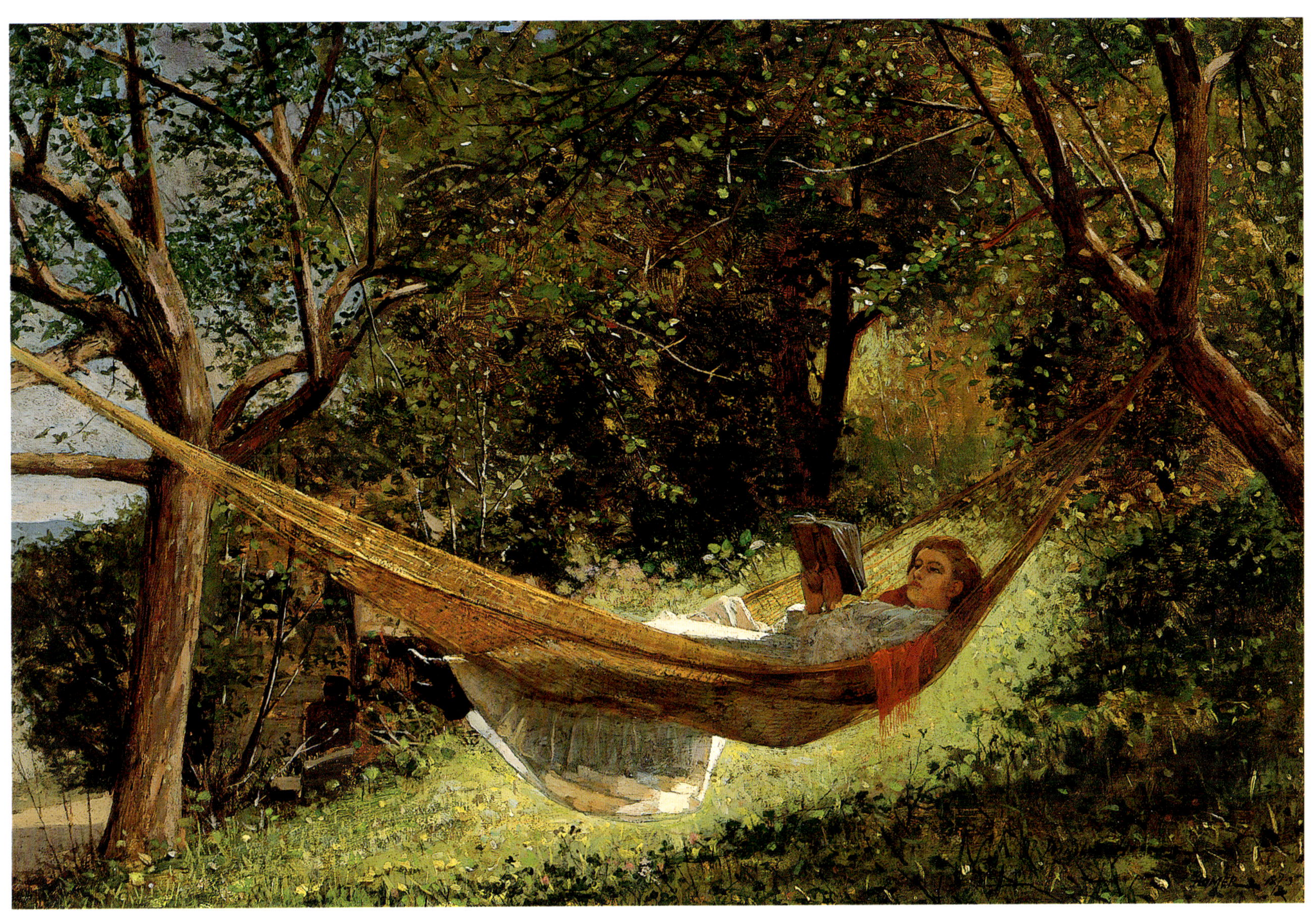

John Frederick Peto 1854–1907

A teetering match beckons the viewer into John Frederick Peto's still life of the stalwart companions of male leisure. A burned match lies at the left, along with ashes spilled from the pipe, which rests on the edge of a worn book. Rather than evoke overt nostalgia or seduce the eye with hyper-real, glossy finishes, *Beer Mug, Book, and Pipe* suggests melancholy and introspection, thus moving it beyond mere artistic showmanship.[1]

That same hovering match and its singed counterpart lead the viewer's eye along another diagonal, the stem of the pipe, to the blue bands circling the mug. The reclining bowl of the pipe and the spine of the book reinforce these strong horizontals. Though awkward in its nonforeshortened treatment, the handle of the mug and the rim of the bowl function as a pair of parentheses and create a sense of internal unity.

Peto also built a conceptually linked structure within his formal one. The pipe's stem links the bit, or mouthpiece, with the lip of the mug, setting up a sensory resonance between smoking and drinking. That the pipe and mug are both objects meant to be held further strengthens the overall effect of the pairing. The book, located between the two, suggests the act of reading or, as Peto has positioned it, with spine facing the viewer, *looking*. By tapping into such multisensory engagement, or "incarnating vision," the artist enlivened the physicality of an intimate environment.[2]

This trio of parlor objects connects Peto to other still-life painters, notably William Harnett. In 1878, Peto enrolled at the Pennsylvania Academy of the Fine Arts where he met Harnett, and the two artists decisively influenced each other's work. While Harnett left for Europe in 1880, regularly exhibited and sold his paintings, Peto withdrew to Island Heights, New Jersey, in 1889, where he worked in obscurity until the end of his life. Harnett focused on surfaces that recall old-master paintings, and Peto sought comfort and stability in the pleasures of painting familiar objects in an era that straddled post-Civil War recovery and the advent of the modern age. [EY]

---

[1] John Wilmerding, *Important Information Inside: The Art of John F. Peto and the Idea of Still-Life Painting in Nineteenth-Century America* (Washington, DC: National Gallery of Art, 1983), p. 37.

[2] For a discussion on "incarnating vision," see Alexander Nemerov, *The Body of Raphaelle Peale: Still Life and Selfhood, 1812–1824* (Berkeley, CA: University of California Press, 2001), p. 31.

Beer Mug, Book, and Pipe

1884, oil on canvas, 10 × 14 in.
Collection of Frederick D. Hill

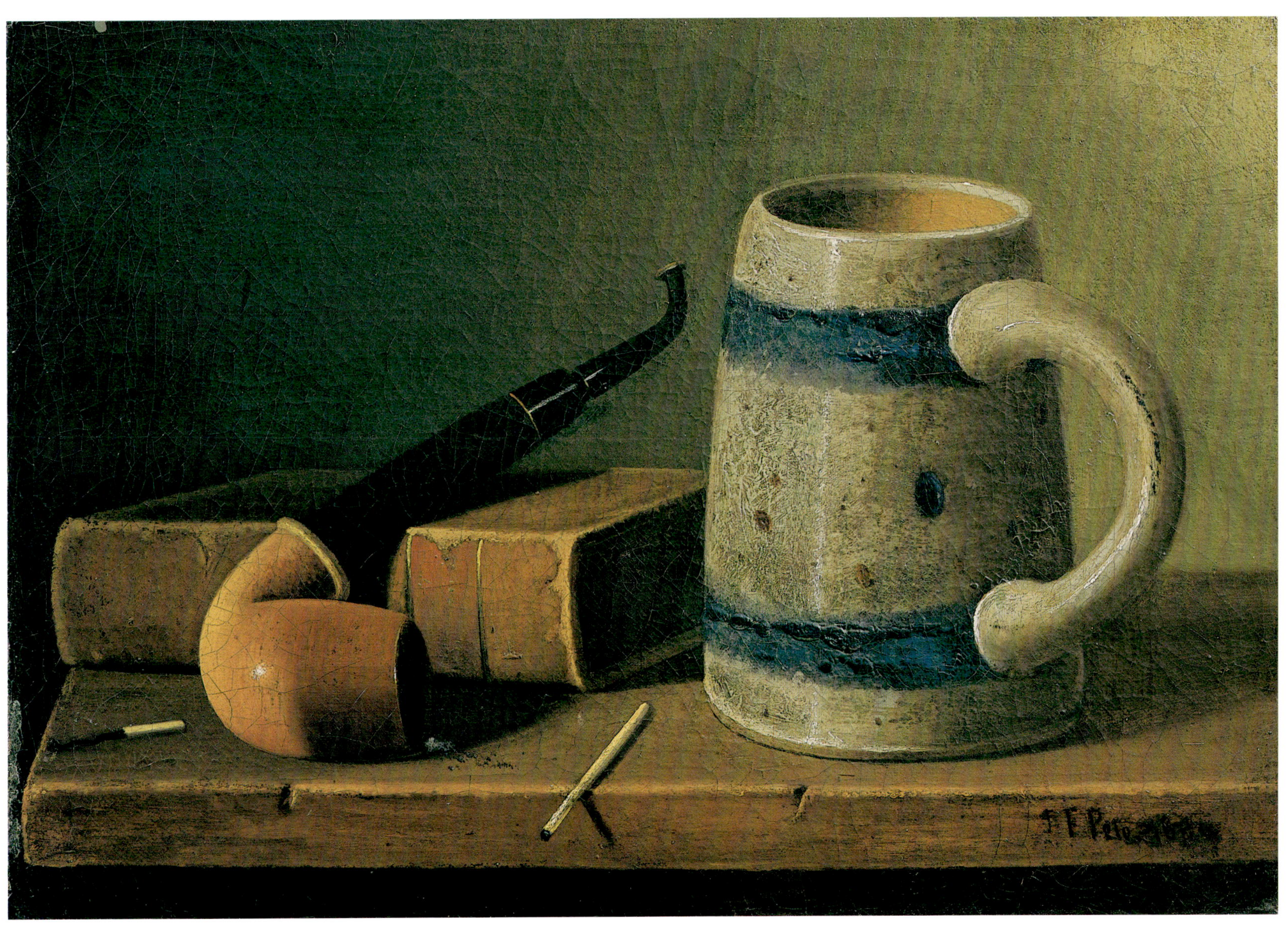

Frederic Edwin Church 1826–1900

During the two winters spanning 1870–72, Frederic Edwin Church reveled in two related projects: building his new home, Olana, on a high hill near Hudson, New York, and painting a suite of oil sketches and freely brushed small paintings of the vistas from his property. In 1867, Church had finally purchased the land at the summit of the Sienghenbergh, or "Long Hill," as the site of his new home. From that lofty vista, Church painted more than twenty winter views, ranging from exuberantly brushed sketches to more finished oil studies, all on paper or academy board.[1] Nearly all these winter scenes, and numerous small works painted the rest of the year, adopt the view looking south and southwest down to the Hudson River from Church's old studio on the property.

View from Olana in the Snow is the largest known of these works, and preserves what was clearly Church's favorite vantage point. In the right middle distance is the forested outcropping of Quarry Hill, and beyond that the hazy purple contours of the Catskills' Sleeping Giant, across the river. Church painted the fresh snowfall covering the silent and undulating hills. The traces of the meandering carriage road leading up to the house are barely discernible as sinuous strokes of contrasting white paint within the landscape. The vibrant brushwork and opalescent palette convey the artist's delight in capturing the nuances of the snow-covered landscape.

Church kept the majority of the Olana oil sketches and framed a number of them to hang throughout his new home. Mrs. Church's bedroom, in the family's private quarters on the second floor, was hung with numerous examples of her husband's work. *View from Olana in the Snow*, which eventually left Olana, most likely was displayed there. The artist's surviving daughter, Isabel "Downie" Church, inherited many of the paintings that had hung in her mother's bedroom and wrote in her diary of her great joy upon receiving them, singling out "the Olana view in winter, long, long ago, just the way it looked in my childhood."[2] Church's views from his family's new home form the most personal and private aspect of his oeuvre, cherished by family and friends as much for their intimate associations as their painterly virtuosity. [EJH]

---

[1] See Gerald Carr, *Frederic Edwin Church: Catalogue Raisonné of Works of Art at Olana State Historic Site*, 2 vols.(Cambridge: Cambridge University Press, 1994), vol I, pp. 375–80.

[2] Diary of Isabel Church Black, October 25, 1901. Olana Archives; quoted in Eleanor Jones Harvey, *The Painted Sketch: American Impressions from Nature, 1830–1880* (New York: Harry N. Abrams and the Dallas Museum of Art, 1998), p. 94.

View from Olana in the Snow

about 1871–72, oil on paper, 13 × 21 ¼ in.
Private Collection

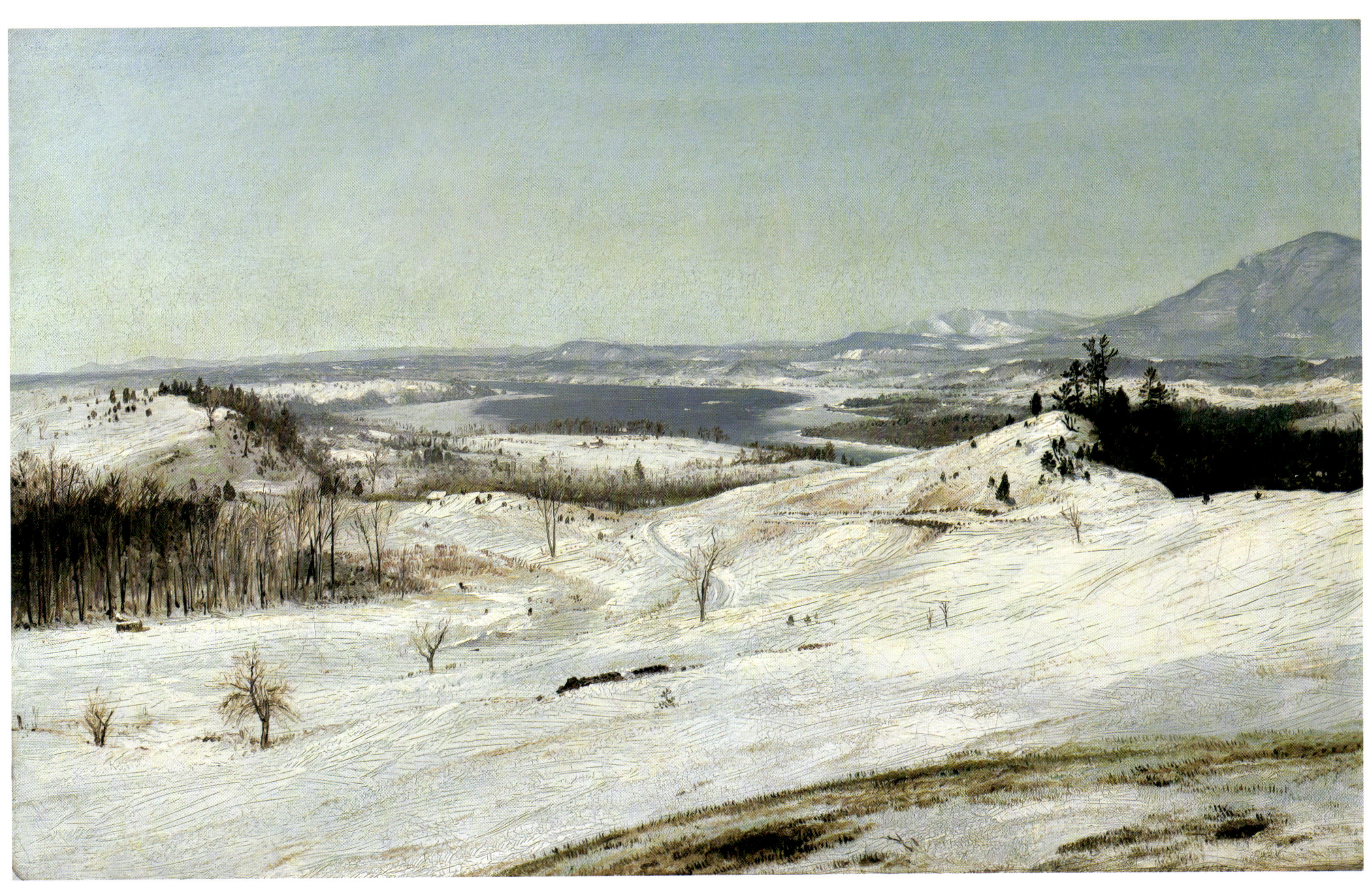

James McNeill Whistler 1834–1903

In March 1863, James McNeill Whistler moved into Number 7 Lindsey Row in Chelsea (now 101 Cheyne Walk), where his view of the Thames River and Battersea Bridge would inspire some of his most memorable painted harmonies and nocturnes. Whistler's early fascination with plein-air painting extended to painting the views through his open windows during all seasons, including winter. January and February of 1864 were particularly bitter and cold, and the Thames froze over in places.[1] Then as now, such weather in London was worthy of note. The artist's mother came to live with her son that winter. She observed that "during a very sharp frost of only a few days I think for two days ice was passing as we look out upon the Thames, he [Whistler] could not resist painting while I was shivering—at the open window—two sketches & all say they are most effective, one takes in the bridge, of course they are not finished; he could not leave his Oriental paintings."[2]

Her account has helped settle a long-running debate among scholars about whether *Harmony in Grey: Chelsea in Ice* was painted early in Whistler's career, in 1864, or closer to 1887, the year it was exhibited at the Royal Society of British Arts.[3] Stylistically the work fits comfortably in the earlier period, when Whistler, in his evolving approach to abstracting the familiar London cityscape, first experimented with bold diagonals and flat planes of color inspired by Japanese prints. Here Whistler explored ideas he would take up again a decade later with such seminal paintings as *Battersea Bridge*. In this winter scene he counterbalanced the white diagonal, zigzag profile of the ice floe with the strong, pale brown wedge formed by the open water, and the prow of the oncoming steamer. Mist shrouds the far shore, where two tall smokestacks loom like giants over the craggy contours of the city, which resembles a small mountain as much as a cluster of crowded dwellings along the riverbank.

Whistler's mood that winter mirrored the bleak palette and icy gloom of this painting. His mother's arrival signaled the end of his autonomous, bohemian lifestyle, since she had come, in her own words, "to render his home as his father's was."[4] Her presence also meant that Whistler's mistress and favorite model, Jo Hiffernan, had to find another place to live. Whistler was left to wrestle with many conflicting emotions: his liberated freedoms and passions were tempered now by old family constraints and obligations. Whistler's studio remained his private refuge. He stipulated that although his mother might run his household, she was not to

Harmony in Grey: Chelsea in Ice

1864, oil on canvas, 17 ¾ × 24 in.
Private Collection

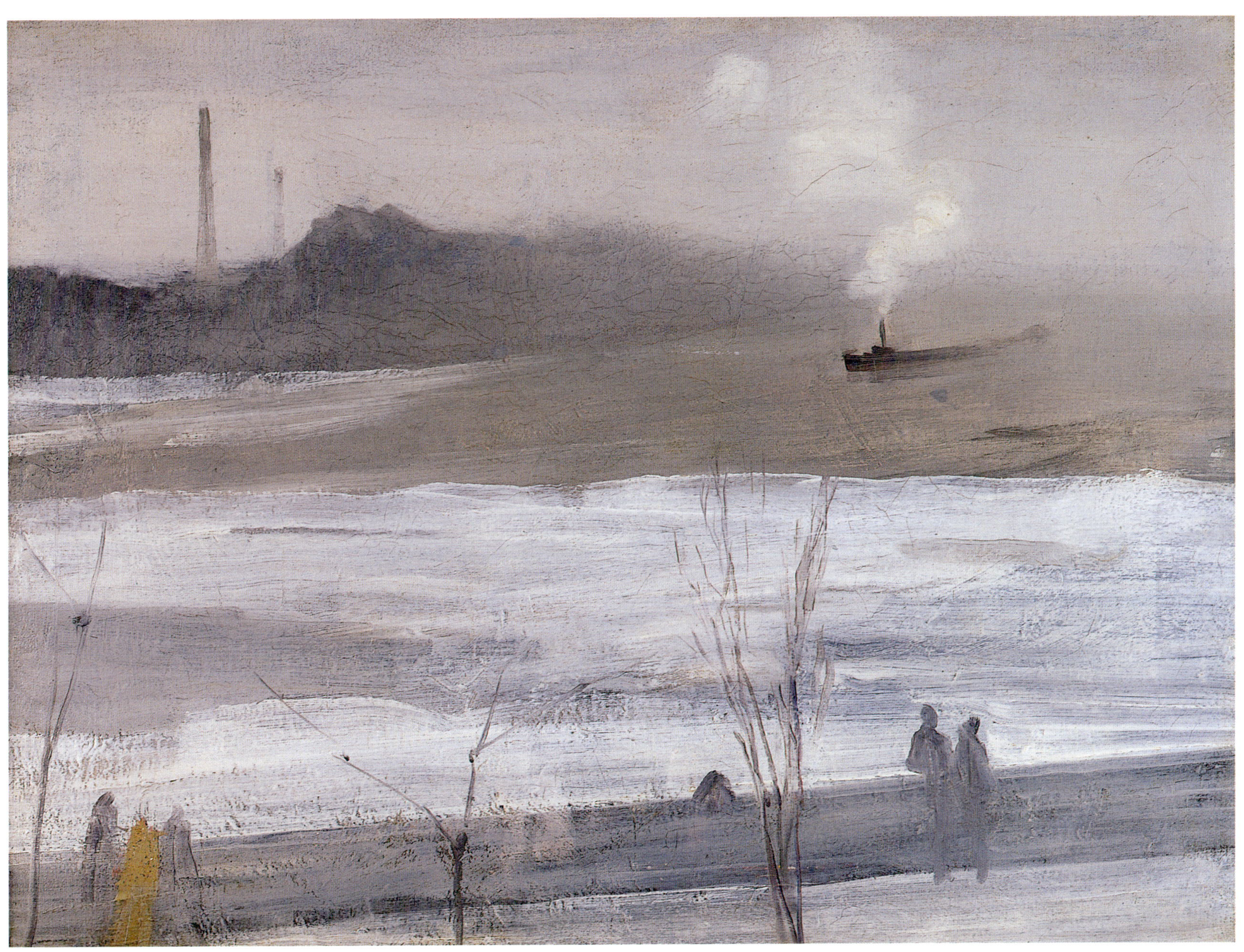

enter his studio. There, as she noted in her diary entry, her son's orientalist work—that in some ways represented that once-unfettered lifestyle—still held sway.

Chelsea in Ice is Whistler's earliest foray into abstraction, prefiguring the later nocturnes and harmonies such as *Battersea Bridge* in which the actual subject of the work plays a subservient role to his growing fascination with a "purer" form of painting. Beginning with this work, he adapted his rapid plein-air technique to larger studio paintings, borrowing the use of thin layers of paint from his own work in watercolor to lend his surfaces a more ethereal note. His delight in titles inspired by music and color found voice in an article he published in 1878, in which he declared, "As music is the poetry of sound, so is painting the poetry of sight, and the subject-matter has nothing to do with harmony of sound or of colour."[5]

Whistler's evocative title for this painting calls attention to his genius for establishing a mood by suggesting color and tone, all while anchoring the composition with a recognizable subject. Thus *Harmony in Grey: Chelsea in Ice* is simultaneously a landscape and a tonal progression. Whistler lovingly captures all forms of water: ice, mist rising off the river, and steam from the oncoming ship set against the gray winter clouds. The vaporous clouds of steam appear more solid than the spindly branches of the naked trees that screen the view from Whistler's window out to the river. The single note of yellow ochre in the otherwise muted palette is a subtle but distinct chord vibrating in the lower corner, a figure nominally in motion in this otherwise frozen world. [EJH]

---

[1] The London *Times* reported the bitter cold weather of January 8–9, 1864. On January 5–7, London registered twenty-four degrees of frost, and during that week ice in the harbor was floating downstream. See Andrew MacLaren Young, Margaret MacDonald, and Robin Spencer, *The Paintings of James McNeill Whistler* (New Haven, CT: Yale University Press and the Paul Mellon Centre for Studies in British Art, 1980), p. 30.

[2] Anna McNeill Whistler to James Gamble, February 10, 1864. Additional manuscripts, Glasgow University Library, 1962, letter w/35, cited in Andrew McLaren Young, et al., *The Paintings of James McNeill Whistler*, pp. 29–30.

[3] Ibid.

[4] Anna McNeill Whistler to James Gamble, February 10, 1864. "The Lady of the Portrait: Letters of Whistler's Mother," *The Atlantic Monthly*, vol. 136 (1925), p. 323; quoted in Elizabeth Broun, "Thoughts that Began with the Gods: The Content of Whistler's Art," *Arts Magazine* 62, no. 2 (October 1987): 40.

[5] James McNeill Whistler, "The Red Rag," *The World* (March 22, 1878), reprinted in Denys Sutton, *James McNeill Whistler: Paintings, Etchings, Pastels and Watercolours* (London: Phaidon Press, 1966), p. 58.

Sanford Robinson Gifford 1823–1880

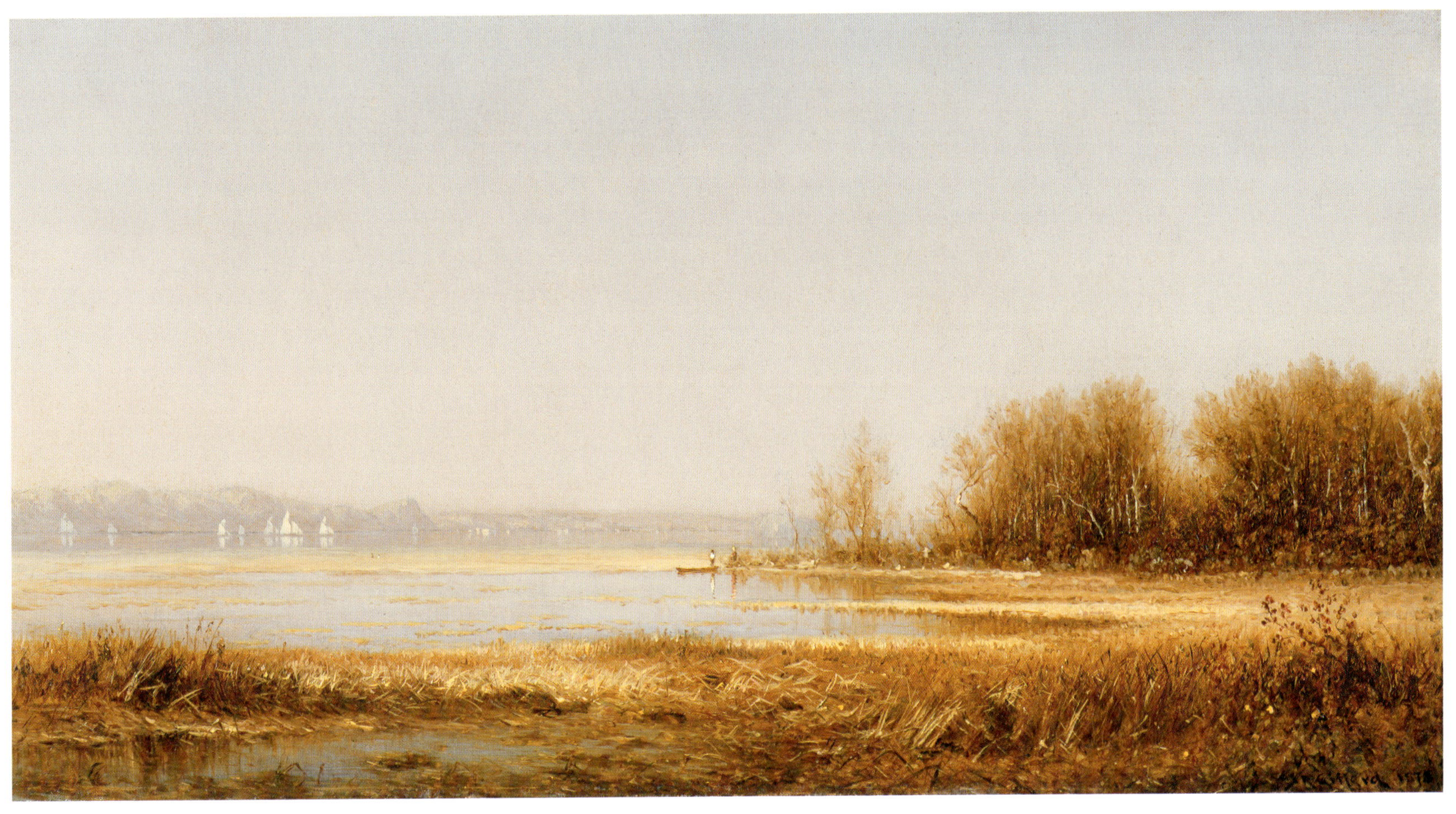

The Marshes of the Hudson

1878, oil on canvas, 16 ½ × 30 ¼ in.
Private Collection

Sanford Robinson Gifford

Sanford Robinson Gifford brought a different kind of atmosphere and a more subtle appreciation of narrative to his landscapes than that employed by the other artists associated with the Hudson River school. Perhaps owing to his collegiate training in religion and philosophy, and his circle of erudite literary friends, Gifford invested many of his paintings with an understated intensity centering on a sophisticated use of color and atmosphere.[1] Another, often overlooked, yet significant aspect of his work is the way in which his diminutive figures engage with the landscape.

In this work Gifford painted the expanse of marshland along the Hudson River, with the hills of Irvington-on-Hudson dissolving into the hazy atmosphere along the horizon. Clusters of boats provide scale and emphasize the distance from near to far shore. The grasses and stands of river birch lend the work an autumnal feel. They help anchor the foreground, but the focus of the painting is the pair of tiny figures facing each other at the juncture of land and water. Their forms and reflections provide a still point in this fluid environment, and their deliberate placement at the horizontal midpoint of the composition suggests several levels of interpretation.

Two years earlier Gifford had painted a small oil sketch bearing the same title, in which the same couple, together in a small boat, cross the open water toward the spit of dry land nearly at the center of the foreground. A woman dressed in vibrant red sits in the stern while her companion, standing in the prow, poles them along. Gifford made a significant change in the finished painting when he took the woman out of the boat and placed her on dry land facing the man in the skiff. She now awaits the man's final stroke of the pole that will either bring him closer to her or further separate them. Gifford created his large-scale painting of *The Marshes of the Hudson* the year he secretly married Mary Cecilia Canfield, a recent widow and childhood friend.[2] The relationship between these two tiny figures in the painting is one of intimacy and independence, mirroring Gifford's personal life at this pivotal point. What began in the sketch as the pair together in the boat has now become a moment of transition between separation and union, and between mutable water and solid ground.

Gifford often made oil sketches in two smaller sizes before embarking on a major painting, with each successive stage further distilling the keenly observed detail from his initial sketches into a finished scene of balance and luminosity. The sketch of *The Marshes of the Hudson* portrays the physical character of the marshes as they give way to open water; the finished painting focuses on the

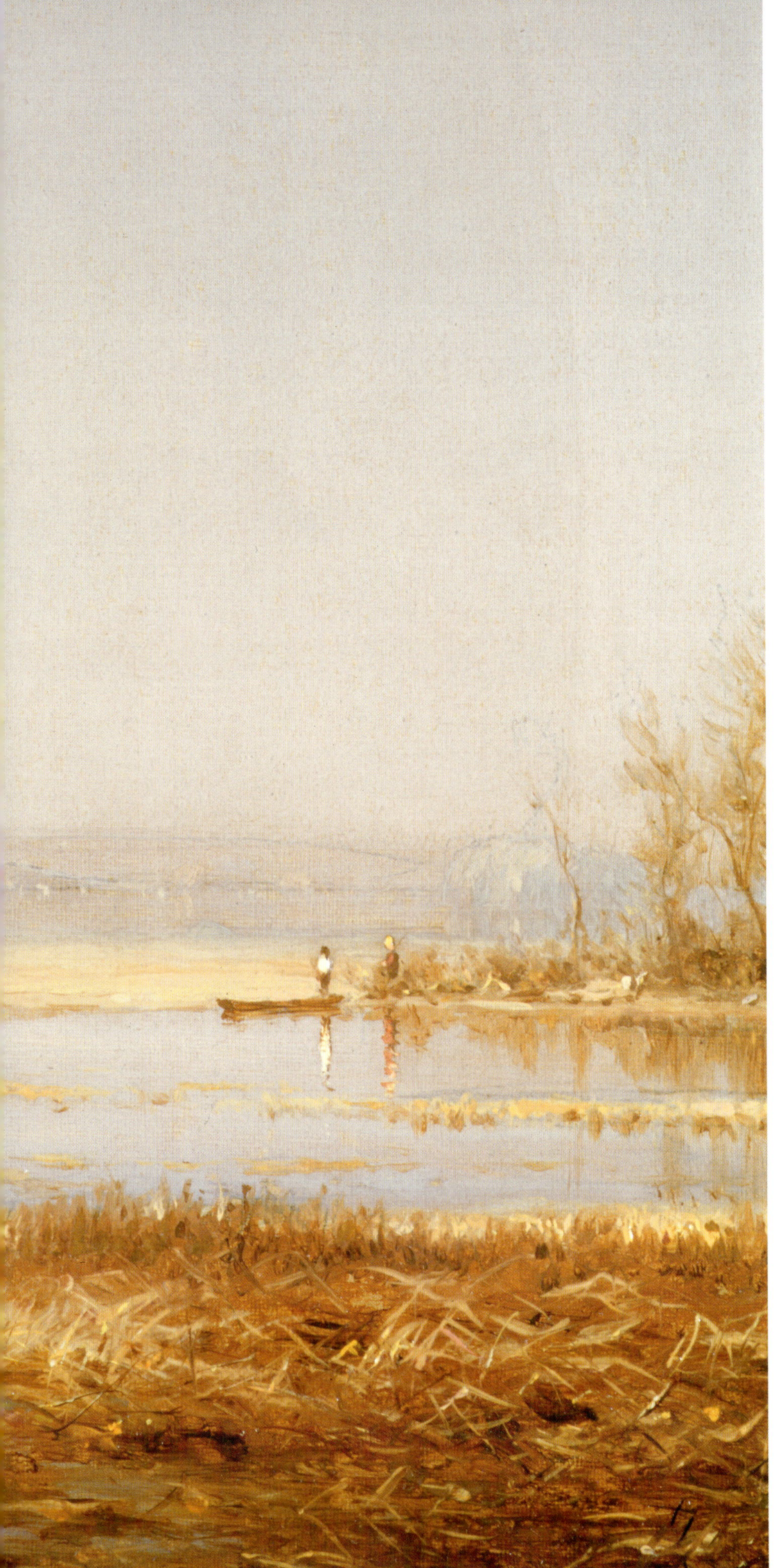

intimate intensity of Gifford's tiny figures in this liminal environment. The space between them becomes crucial to the painting's composition and illuminates how Gifford invested his finished paintings with universal and personal meaning. [EJH]

---

[1] Gifford was the only Hudson River school painter to attend college; he studied at Brown University for three semesters. Close friends included Richard and Elizabeth Stoddard, Clarence Stedman, Candace Wheeler, and the Rev. Henry Whitney Bellows. For an extensive discussion of Gifford's patrons and friends, see this author's essay "Tastes in Transition: Gifford's Patrons," in Kevin Avery and Franklin Kelly, eds. *Hudson River Visions: The Landscapes of Sanford R. Gifford* (New Haven, CT: Yale University Press and the Metropolitan Museum of Art, 2003), pp. 75–89.

[2] Ila Weiss first suggested the woman in the sketch might be Mrs. Canfield, and points to several small oil sketches from 1876–79, in which Gifford paints a couple together in nature. See Ila Weiss, *Poetic Landscape: The Art and Life of Sanford Robinson Gifford* (Newark, DE: University of Delaware Press, 1987), especially pp. 307–9.

Detail:

The Marshes of the Hudson

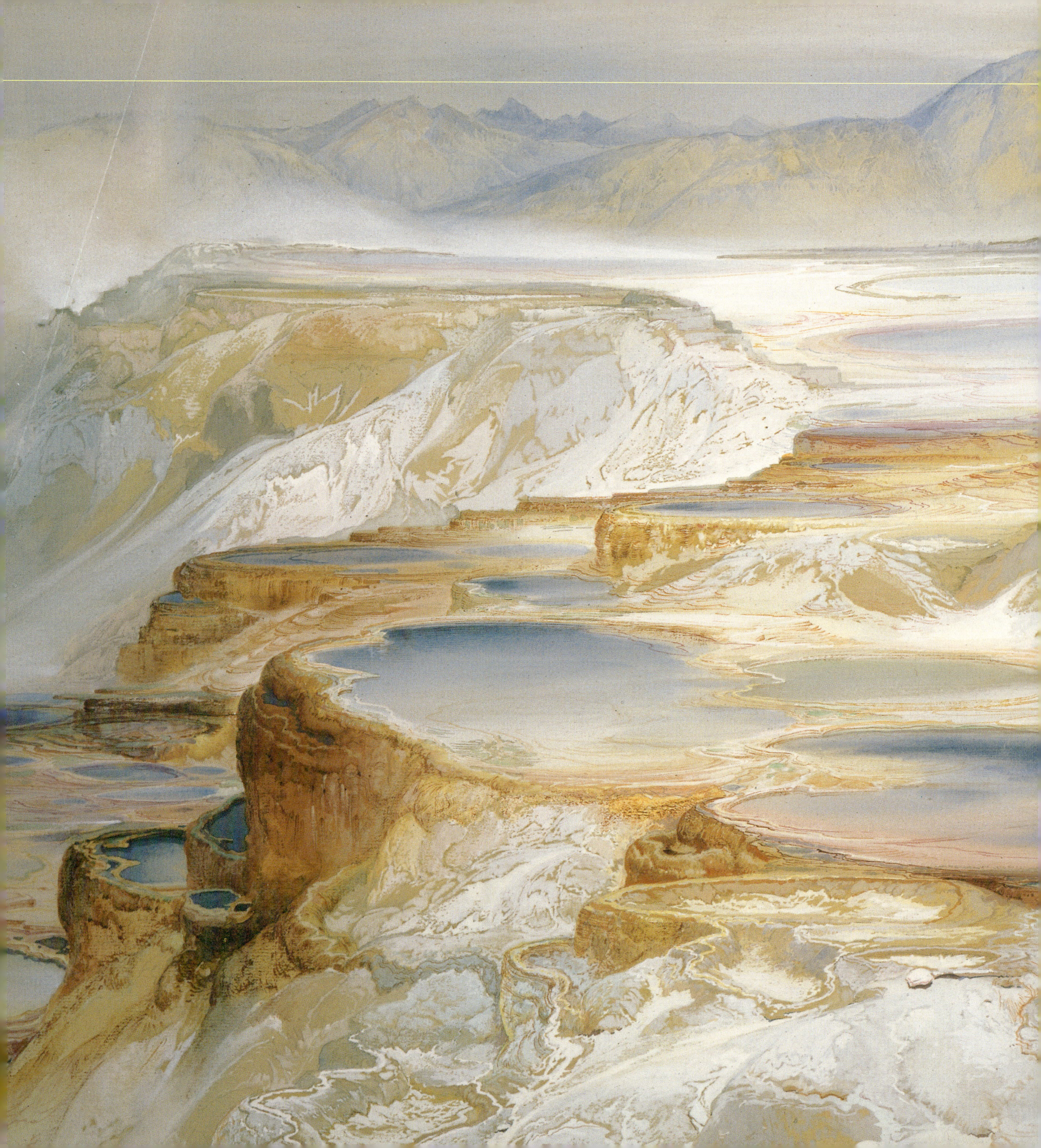

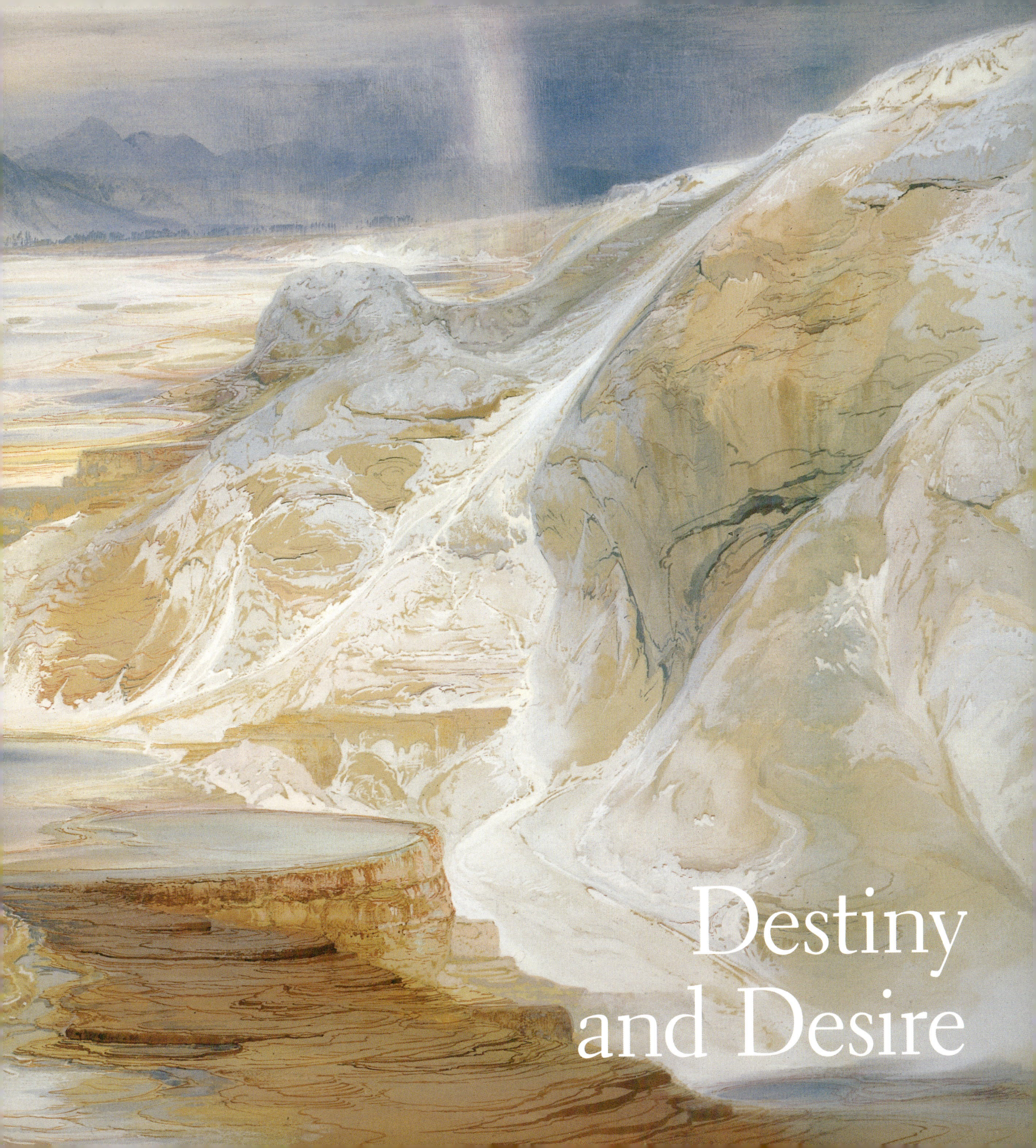

Destiny and Desire

John Singer Sargent 1856–1925

François Flameng and Paul Helleu were among the young artists John Singer Sargent came to know while he was a student in the Paris atelier of portraitist Émile Auguste Carolus-Duran. This double portrait marks a pivotal year for Sargent, who had been to Madrid to see the masterpieces of Velázquez and, late in 1880, traveled to Holland, where he studied the works of Frans Hals, the great portrait and genre painter of the Dutch Golden Age. Carolus-Duran learned from Hals and Velázquez the technique of painting *au premier coup*, with touches of color adjoining one another to suggest highlights, shadows, and volumes. Carolus-Duran's—and Sargent's—method challenged the realist tradition of painstaking glazes and illusionistic modeling taught at the École des Beaux-Arts.[1]

François Flameng and Paul Helleu reveals Sargent's mastery of these influences, which would carry him into the Venetian scenes and commissioned portraits that quickly established his reputation. The portrait also conveys the audacious spirit of Sargent's contemporaries, who, like him, were intent on making names for themselves. The portrait heads, different in scale and bearing no psychological relation to one another, acknowledge these men as individual personalities.[2] Helleu's brooding, romantic profile conveys the magnetism to which Sargent and many others in the Paris scene responded, while Flameng's uptilted chin and appraising gaze signal the ambitions of the young history painter. Sargent appears to have inscribed their names with the butt of his brush, as if to emphasize the spontaneous gesture of painting the portraits.

The tradition of exchanging portraits and student works cemented personal and professional relationships among the aspiring artists of Paris. Sargent took a particular interest in Helleu, whom he introduced to potential patrons and encouraged with small purchases and public support. Decades later, Helleu wrote to his daughter that he had wanted to photograph Sargent, "who has been for me, all my life long, more than a father."[3] [GS]

---

[1] Richard Ormond and Elaine Kilmurray, *John Singer Sargent: Complete Paintings*, vol. 1 (New Haven, CT: Yale University Press and the Paul Mellon Centre for Studies in British Art, 1998), pp. 1–6.

[2] Ibid., p. 90.

[3] Ibid., p. 93.

François Flameng and Paul Helleu

about 1880, oil on canvas, 21 × 17 in.
Collection of John Liebes

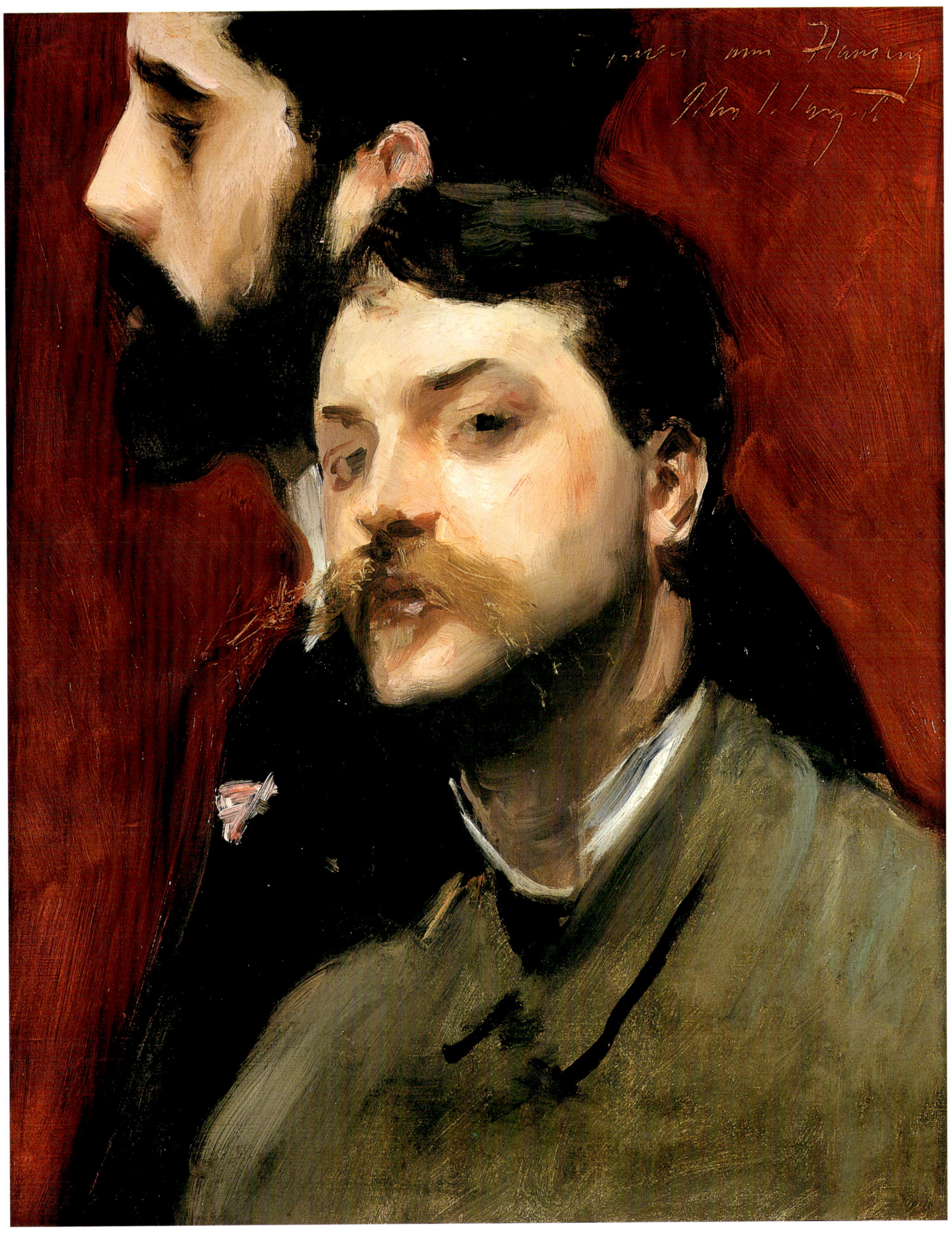

John Singer Sargent 1856–1925

From 1884 through 1886, John Singer Sargent spent his summers in the English countryside away from the professional pressures of Paris and the controversy that his painting *Madame X* had generated. Sargent's portrait of the celebrated beauty had shocked Parisians with its unconventional pose and flagrant sexuality, scandalizing the wealthy middle class upon whom he depended for commissions. The artist spent the warm months of 1885 in the village of Broadway in the Cotswolds, among a colony of expatriate American painters. *Garden Study with Lucia and Kate Millet* shows the wife and daughter of the artist Frank Millet gathering rose petals in the garden of Farnham House, across the village green from Sargent's lodgings.

Sargent had challenged himself to paint outdoors, to capture fleeting effects in nature like the French impressionists. But his "studies" were very studied, indeed, and for this work (and two related canvases, *Garden Study of the Vickers Children* of 1884 and *Carnation, Lily, Lily, Rose* of 1885–86), he planted the garden with blooms in his desired hues, dressed his models to harmonize, and timed his work to capture the tones of twilight. The Broadway paintings have high horizon lines or none, suggesting a protected world of domestic pleasures and childlike innocence.[1] The flattened pictorial space and "dab-and-spot" brushwork of the Broadway paintings struck English audiences as impressionistic.

Sargent's elaborate stagings, his symbolism, and the decorative effect of colors arranged across the canvas also aligned his work with English aesthetic movement paintings of women and children.[2] In *Garden Study with Lucia and Kate Millet,* the standard roses—bred and shaped to grow as small trees—evoke the training of children, who were brought up to be morally and socially upright. White, pink, and red flowers suggest the stages of a girl's life from innocence to motherhood, a reference underscored in the different lengths of the white dresses worn by mother and daughter. The unfinished image of five-year-old Kate corresponds to the idea of children as not yet fully formed, always in the process of "becoming."[3]

The protective embrace of the garden at Farnham House parallels the supportive environment Sargent enjoyed among his friends at Broadway.[4] Letters written by Sargent and others in his circle leave no doubt that the months in the Cotswolds were a pleasant round of picnicking, boating, and conversation. Even while he was on vacation, however, Sargent was calculating his career moves. He was "trying out" impressionism as yet another phase of his artistic development, but far from the vituperative Parisian critics. Impressionism by this

Garden Study with Lucia and Kate Millet

1885, oil on canvas, 24 × 36 in.
Private Collection, Washington, DC

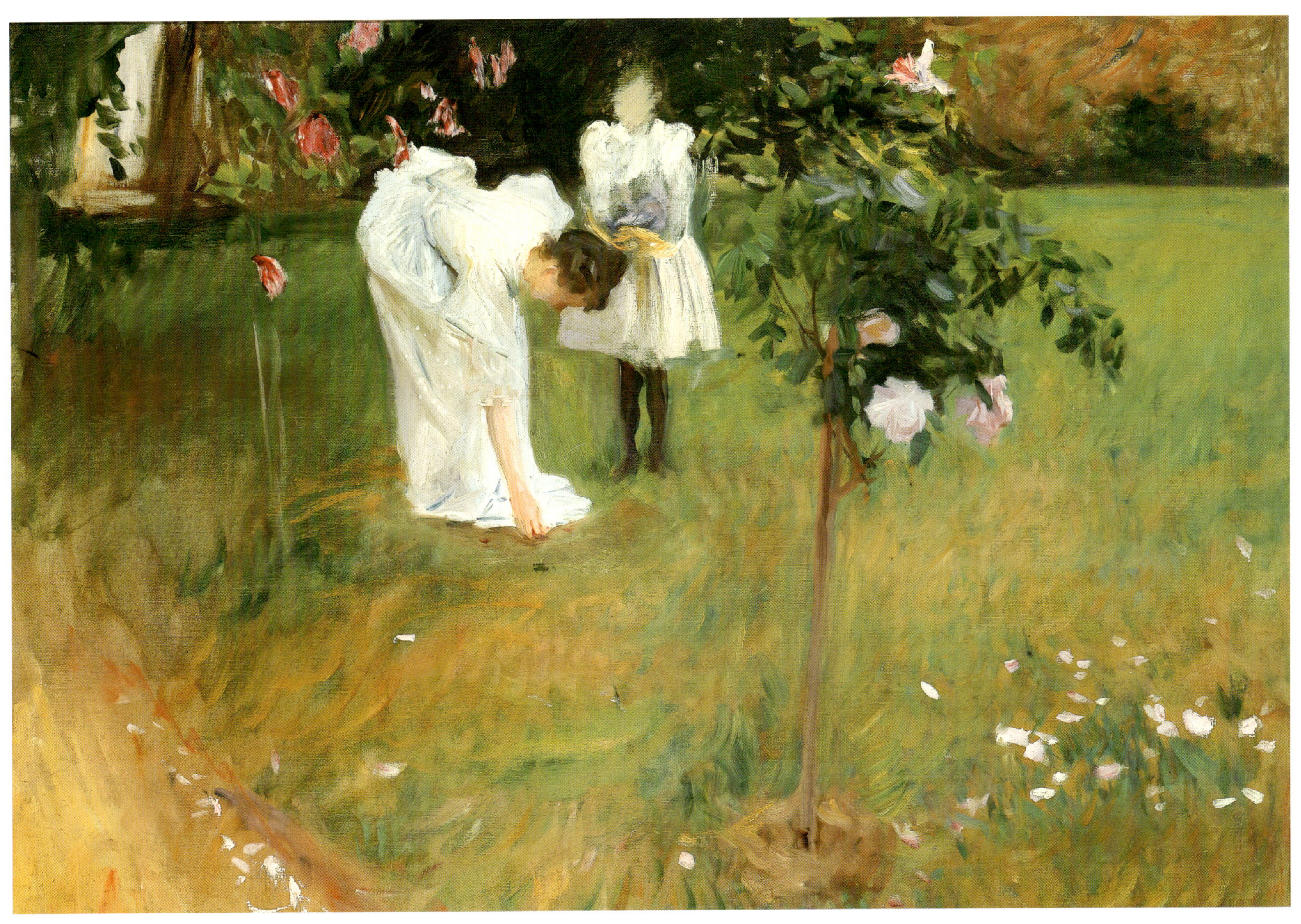

time was already accepted in France, but relatively new in England, leaving Sargent in a safer position than if he had gone up against Claude Monet and Camille Pissarro. In the garden at Broadway, Sargent assimilated what he needed from French art. *Garden Study with Lucia and Kate Millet* led immediately to *Carnation, Lily, Lily, Rose*, a finished work that won critical acclaim when it was shown at London's Royal Academy in 1887 and cemented Sargent's reputation as a modern painter. [GS]

---

[1] See Richard L. Ormond, "Carnation, Lily, Lily, Rose," in Warren Adelson et al., *Sargent at Broadway: The Impressionist Years* (New York: Universe Books and the Coe Kerr Gallery, 1986), pp. 63–75.

[2] Bonnie Barrett Stretch, "Fragments of a Lost World," *Artnews* 86, no. 1 (January 1987): 122–29; William H. Gerdts, "The Arch-Apostle of the Dab-and-Spot School: John Singer Sargent as an Impressionist," in Patricia Hills, *John Singer Sargent*, with essays by Linda Ayres et al. (New York: H. N. Abrams and the Whitney Museum of American Art, 1986), pp. 111–45.

[3] Barbara Dayer Gallati, *Great Expectations: John Singer Sargent Painting Children* (Brooklyn, NY: Bulfinch Press and the Brooklyn Museum of Art, 2004), p. 91.

[4] Ibid.

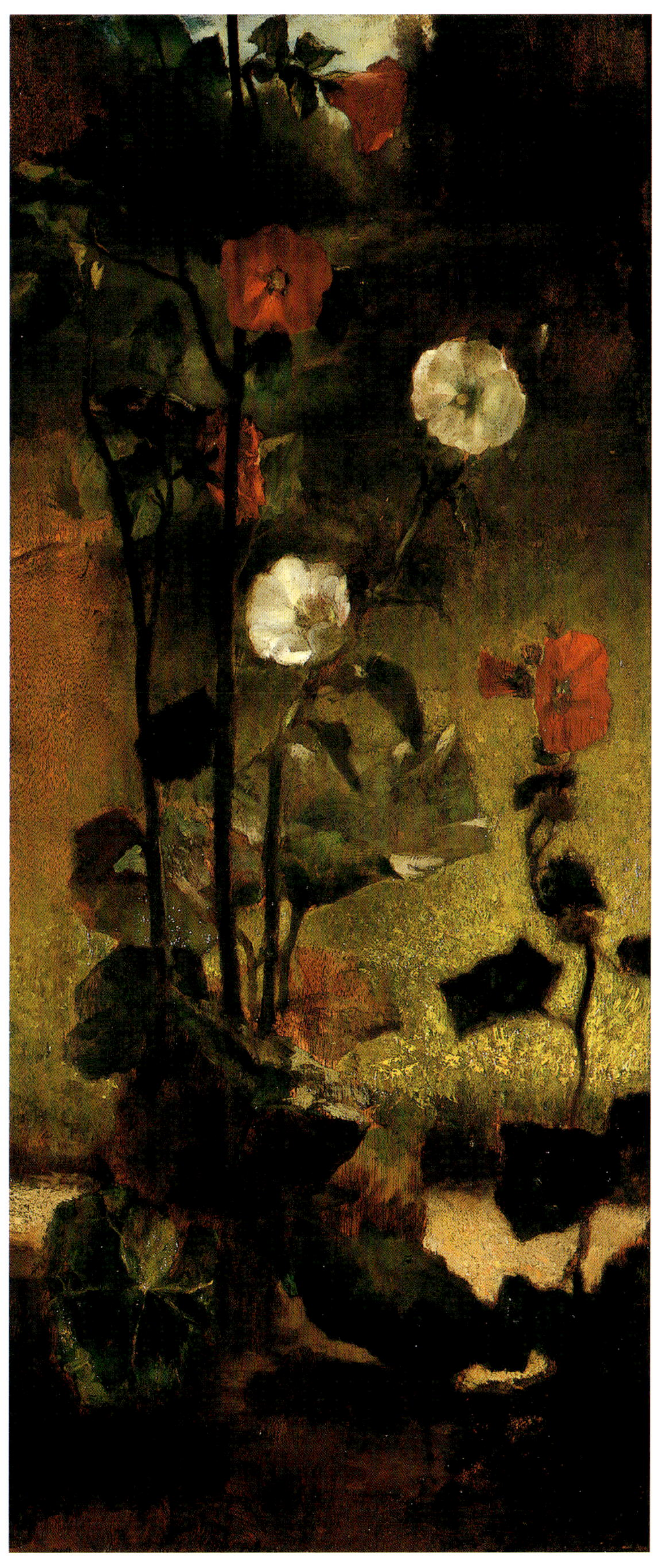

John La Farge 1835–1910

Hollyhocks signals John La Farge's transition from easel painting to the decorative works that would establish his fame in Gilded Age America. The painter learned the recipe for encaustic—a mix of oil, pigment, and wax—from an artist who had worked in England's great cathedrals. The pink and white blossoms glowing against an iridescent background suggest the works of England's Pre-Raphaelite painters, whose canvases La Farge had seen in the 1850s. In his theme, as in his use of an archaic medium, La Farge harked back to a Ruskinian ideal of a purer past, when art and beauty were woven into the fabric of everyday life and exalted the human spirit.

At the same time, *Hollyhocks* unmistakably reflects La Farge's fascination with the Japanese prints that he and a colleague were importing into the United States in 1863. The tall, elegant format recalls *kakemono*, scroll paintings displayed in traditional Japanese homes and usually accompanied by a spray of blossoms. La Farge married a grandniece of Commodore Oliver Hazard Perry, who had opened Japan to Western trade the decade before, and it was partly through this connection that he grew interested in Japanese art.[1]

But La Farge's panel is unlike Pre-Raphaelite or Japanese images in that he painted the flowers not with crisp drawing or flat planes of colors, but as if he were

Hollyhocks

1863, encaustic on panel, 34 × 15 in.
Collection of John Liebes

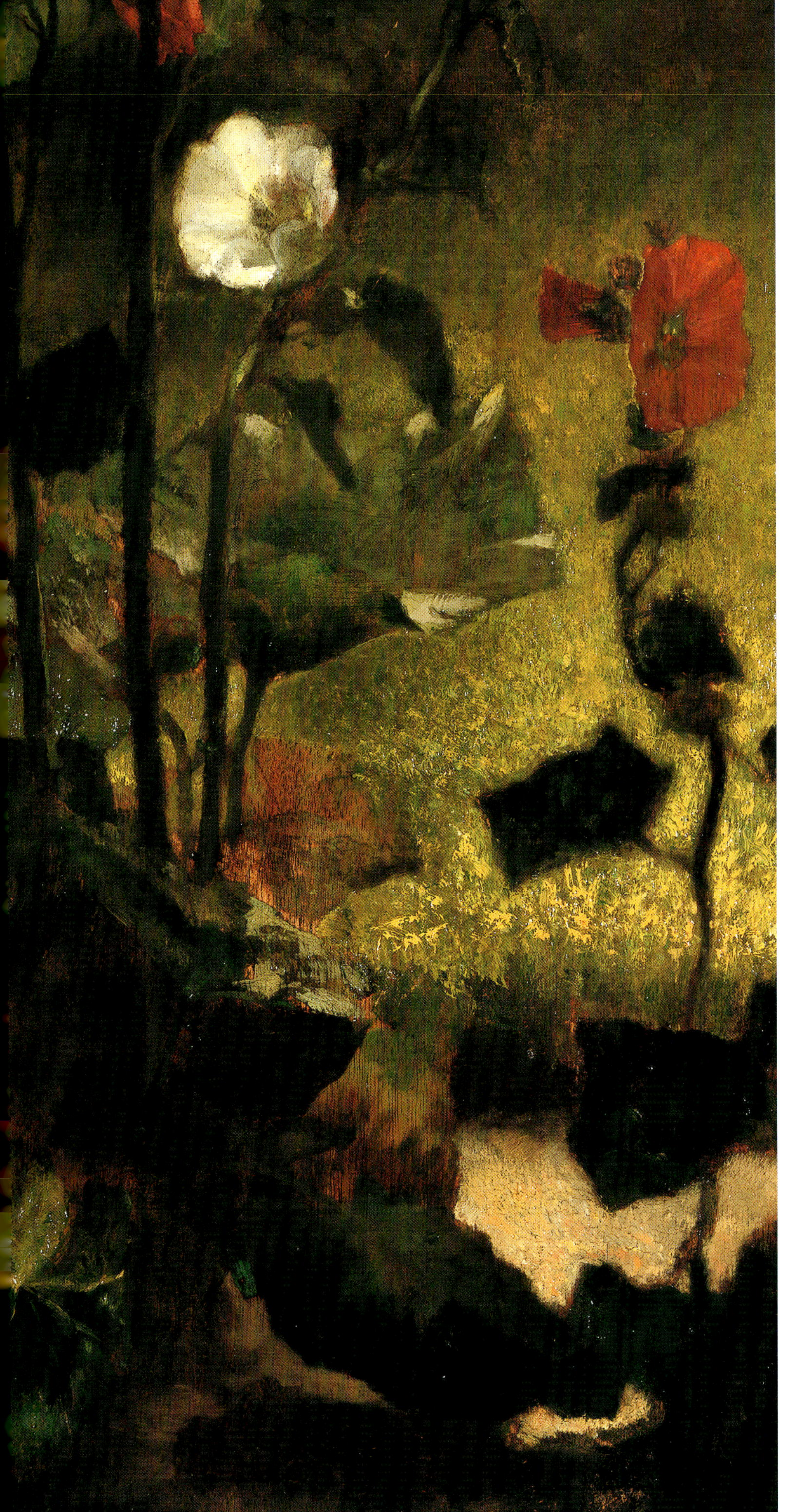

John La Farge

sensing their texture and scent, absorbing the atmosphere of the "Sacred Grove" near his home in Newport, Rhode Island, where the hollyhocks grew.[2] In 1864, the art critic James Jackson Jarves wrote that La Farge's flowers "have no botanical truth, but are burning with love and beauty."[3]

In *Hollyhocks*, La Farge's use of encaustic and his synthesis of Eastern and Western ideas of beauty look forward to the commissions he would complete in the following decades. He used the same composition, for example, in a stained-glass window for J. P. Morgan's New York townhouse in 1881. For the Morgan commission, La Farge recast the intimate experience of seeing and painting the hollyhocks in Newport into a semi-public work of art that the artist hoped would be no less transcendent for a new generation of viewers. [GS]

---

[1] James L. Yarnall, *Nature Vivante: The Still Lifes of John La Farge* (New York: Jordan-Volpe Gallery, 1995), pp. 31–32, 118.

[2] Kathleen A. Pyne, *Art and the Higher Life: Painting and Evolutionary Thought in Late Nineteenth-Century America* (Austin, TX: University of Texas Press, 1996), p. 51.

[3] Quoted in Henry T. Tuckerman, *Book of the Artists: American Artist Life: Comprising Biographical and Critical Sketches of American Artists* (1867; repr., New York: James F. Carr, 1966), p. 489.

Detail:

Hollyhocks

John La Farge 1835–1910

The art critic James Jackson Jarves wrote in 1864 that John La Farge's flower paintings spoke "the language of the heart," and that "we bear away from the sight of them, in our inmost souls, new and joyful utterances of nature."[1] La Farge created *Bowl of Flowers* and related works while living among the insular and privileged circle that summered in Newport, Rhode Island. In this painting, a white curtain masks the bright sun of the coast, reducing the light around the pansies, zinnias, roses, and poppies to a spectral gloom from which one flower and then another emerges before falling back into the shadows. A contemporary of La Farge, painter Elihu Vedder praised the "never-to-be-forgotten" blooms in La Farge's paintings, in which "the outdoor air faintly stirring the lace curtains seems to waft the odour toward you."[2]

Bowl of Flowers conveys little of the nation's turmoil in the middle of the Civil War. The cloistered room evokes the introspective lives of La Farge and his friends, among them the writer Henry James and his brother, the philosopher William James. The war shattered the certainties by which Americans had lived, leaving figures like La Farge and the James brothers to believe that ideas, "truth," even the objective reality of the things around them were all products of "seeing and being," existing only from one moment to the next.[3] La Farge was not concerned, as earlier American still-life painters had been, to record faithfully the stems and petals, the God-given attributes of carefully selected blooms. He wanted to record instead the quality of light at that particular moment and the soft, shifting colors of the flowers that would quickly fade. The nation, however, was poised on the threshhold of the Gilded Age, when modern life would offer few opportunities for such a meditative pursuit of beauty. [GS]

[1] Quoted in William H. Gerdts and Russell Burke, *American Still-Life Painting* (New York: Praeger, 1971), p. 182.

[2] Quoted in Gerdts and Burke, *American Still-Life Painting*, p. 186.

[3] Henry Adams, "The Mind of John La Farge," *John La Farge: Essays* (New York: Abbeville Press, Carnegie Museum of Art, and National Museum of American Art, Smithsonian Institution, 1987), pp. 19–30; Henry Adams, "William James, Henry James, John La Farge and the Foundations of Radical Empiricism," *American Art Journal* 17, no. 1 (Winter 1985): 63.

Bowl of Flowers

1863, oil on canvas, 9 × 16 in.
Collection of John Liebes

John La Farge

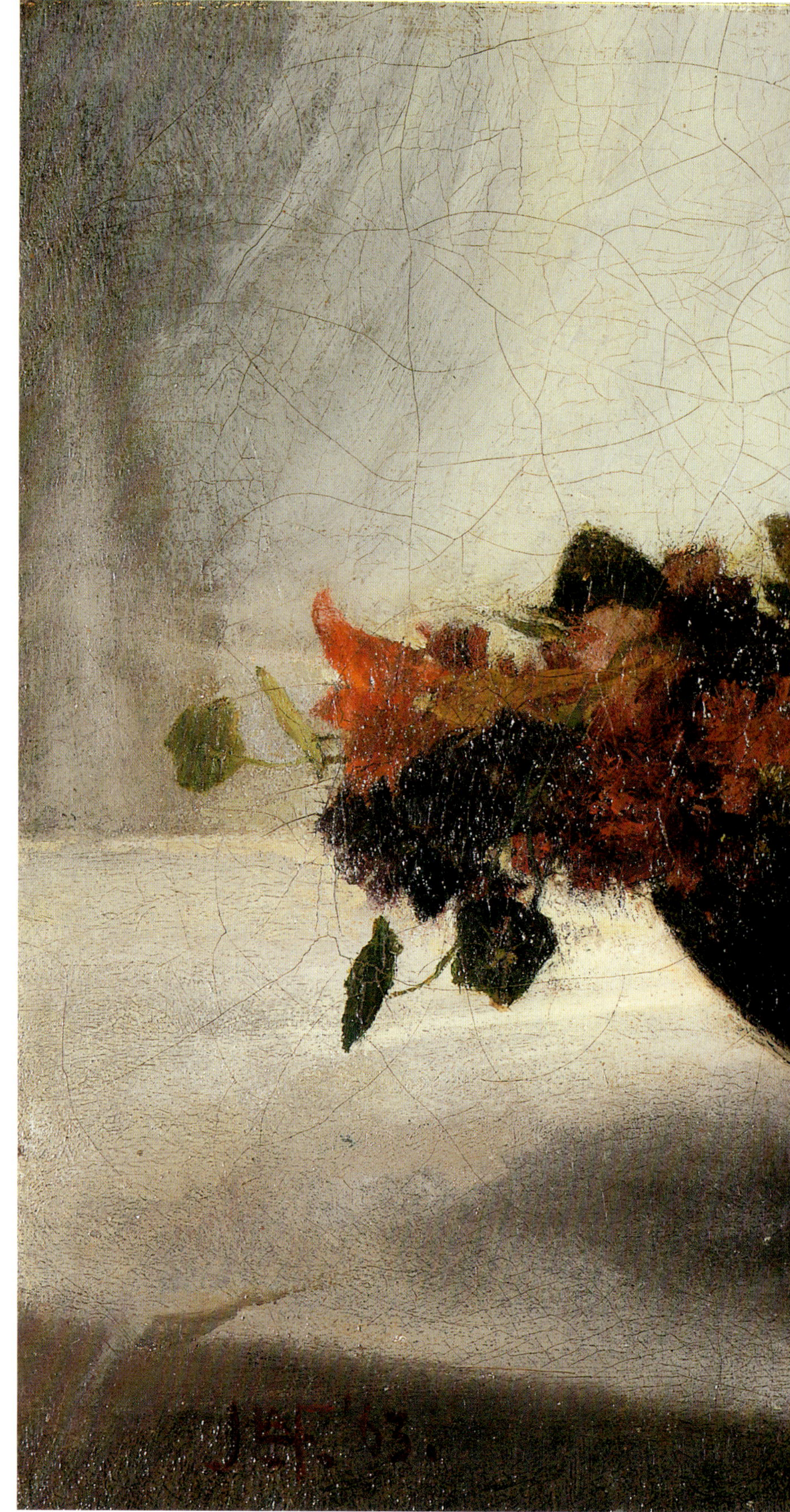

Bowl of Flowers

1863, oil on canvas, 9 × 16 in.
Collection of John Liebes

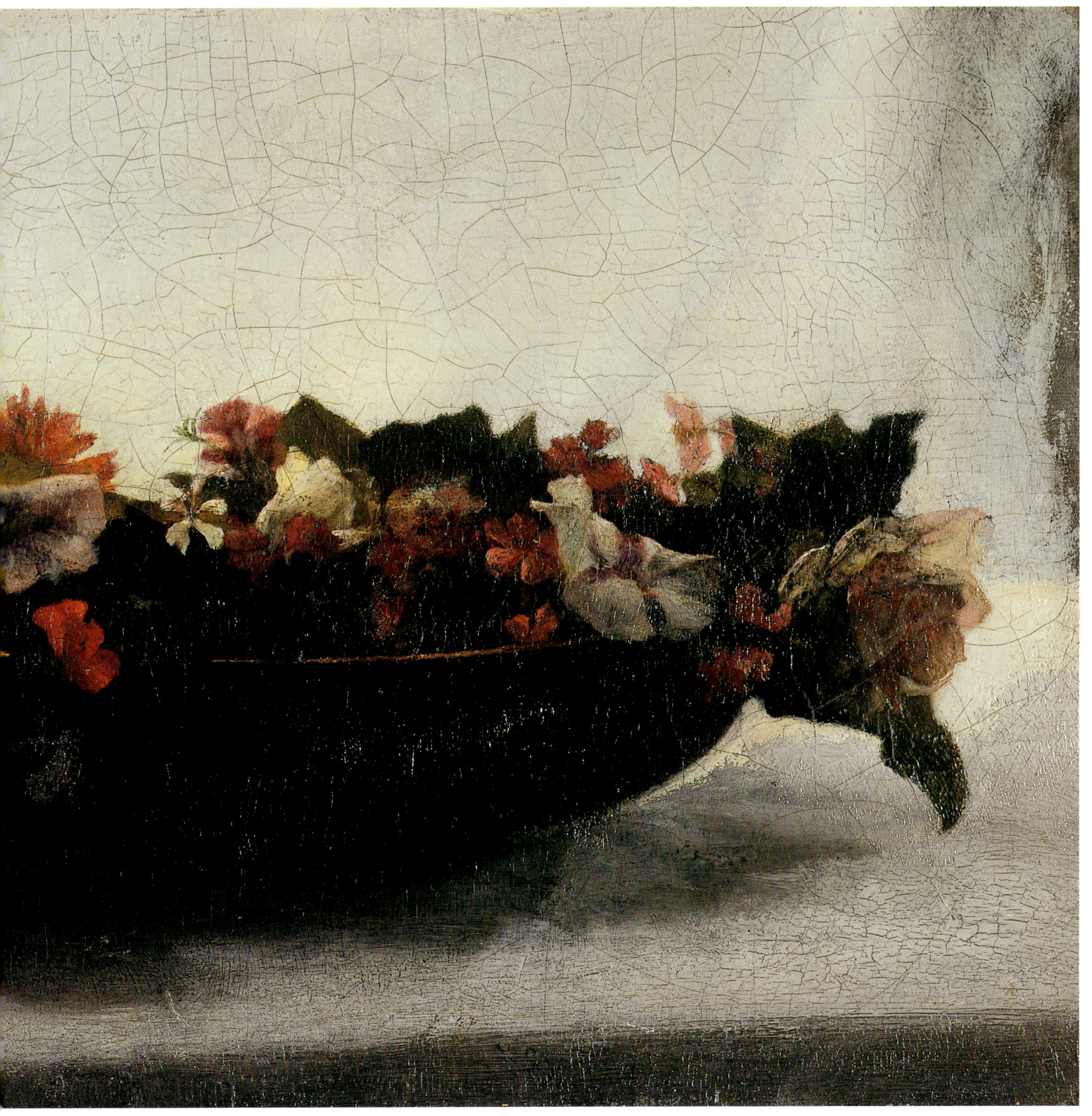

Robert Blum 1857–1903

Robert Blum fell in love with Venice, beginning with his first trip to the city in 1880 when he was associated with "Duveneck's boys," a circle of young artists who studied with Frank Duveneck in America and abroad. Like his fellow artists James McNeill Whistler and John Singer Sargent, Blum was as captivated by the back streets and local inhabitants of Venice as he was charmed by the popular tourist landmarks. *Venetian Bead Stringers* takes the viewer off the beaten path to observe a group of local women stringing pearls, whom Blum referred to in his broken Italian as "Raggazzi" [sic].[1] Blum took great care in arranging this composition, using the posture and position of each of the women, the tilt of their chairs, and the rhythm of their gestures to convey the sociable nature of their work. Their relaxed demeanor and ready smiles speak of long hours spent together in this make-shift workshop in a quintessentially Venetian courtyard.

Such handicrafts as bead stringing and lace making had fallen into decline, until tourism and the Arts and Crafts movement sparked a revival of such traditional skills.[2] Blum's subject is this revival. Here a young girl in a pale blue dress quietly applies herself while her older companions engage in lively conversation. The birdcage above their heads houses five birds arranged in a circle, matching the grouping of the women. Although birdcages traditionally connote confinement, and thereby comment on the inevitability of these women's fate, the songbirds may also allude to the lively chatter of the girls at their tasks. Such scenes were already popular with both native and foreign artists in Italy by the time Blum adopted the theme.

Blum conceived *Venetian Bead Stringers* as a pendant to his successful *Venetian Lacemakers* from the previous year, a composition he painted in both oils and pastel. He sent the pastel version as a gift to his parents, possibly to encourage their somewhat grudging financial support of his frequent trips to Venice.[3] Blum painted the lace makers at work indoors, clustered in small groups along a bank of windows in a long room. For the bead stringers he moved outside, but the November weather turned chilly and gray. In a letter to his parents he confessed, "For the picture which I started out of doors and continued indoors I need a lot of light and when it is gloomy I can't see enough. It is difficult enough on a bright day."[4] Blum arranged to use the studio of his friend and fellow artist Charles Ulrich to continue working on the painting, but he eventually shipped it back to New York and completed it in his studio in time for the National Academy of Design exhibition in March 1888. Its lively brushwork and the vivid colors of the women's dresses caught the

Venetian Bead Stringers

1888, oil on canvas, 30 × 40 in.
Private Collection

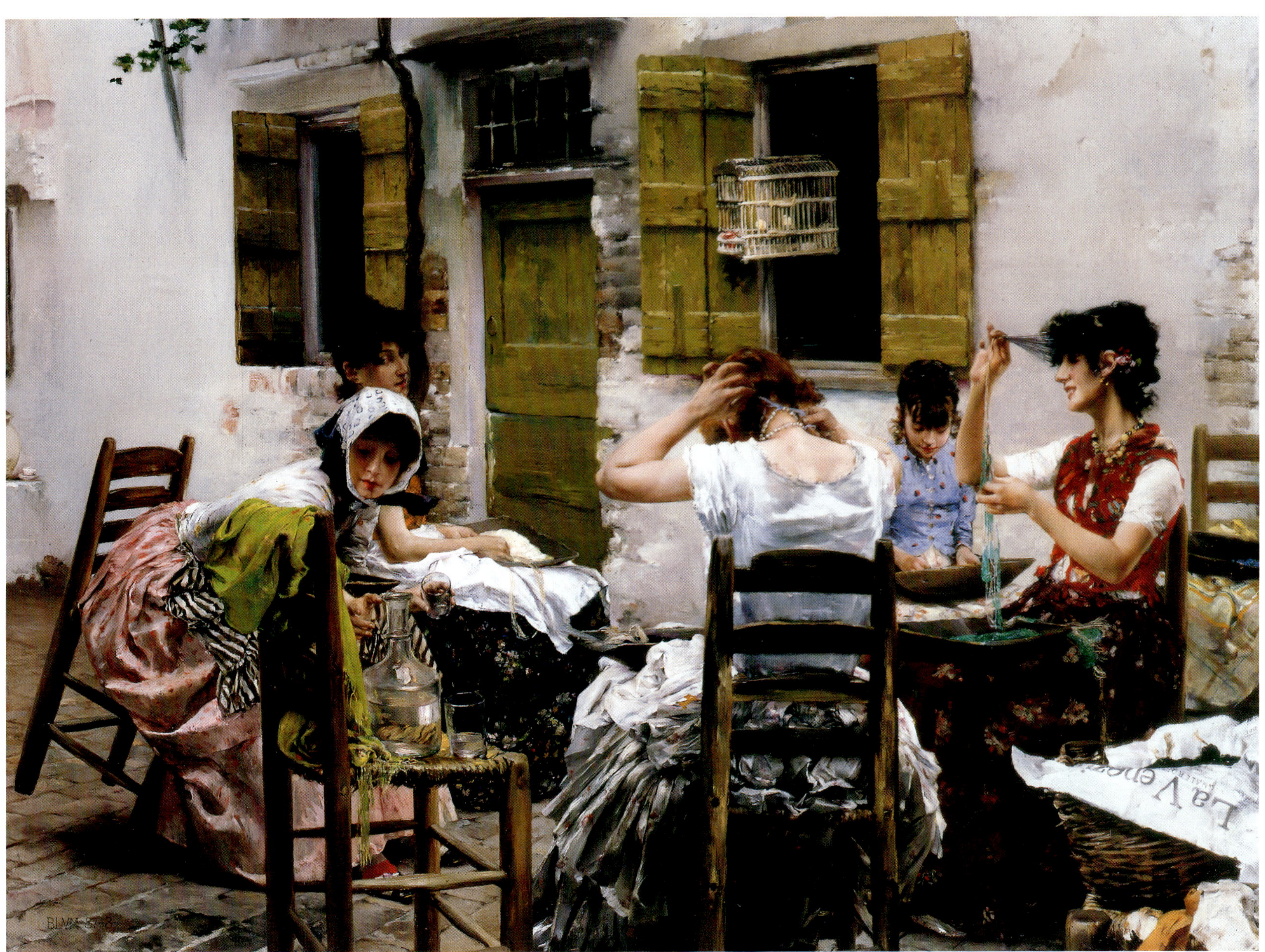

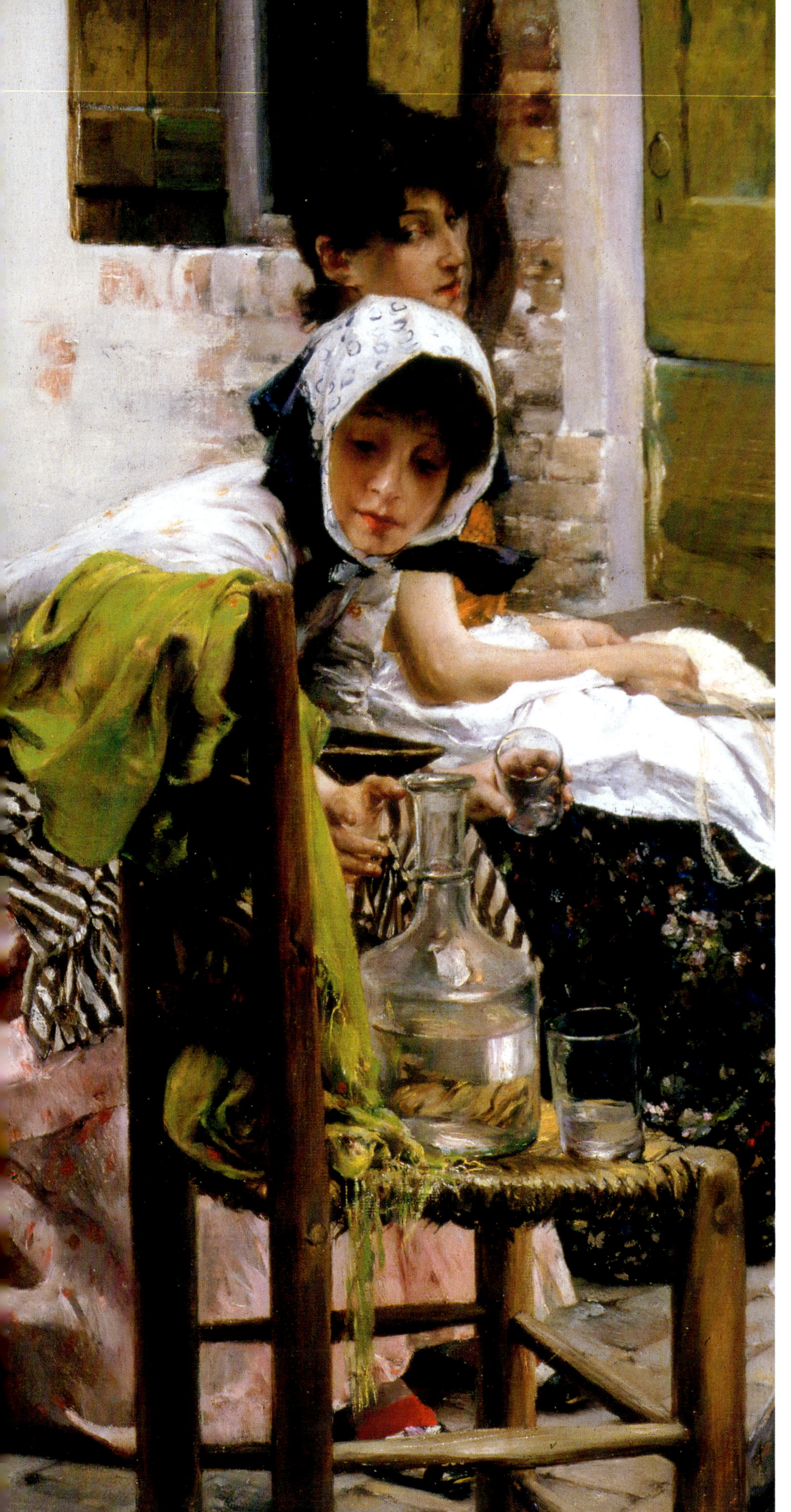

attention of reviewers, and on the strength of *Venetian Bead Stringers* Blum was made an associate member of the academy. [EJH]

---

[1] While working on his *Venetian Lacemakers*, Blum wrote: "[A]fter dinner at the Capellonero which I spin out as long as a cheap dinner can be I saunter forth chewing a toothpick and ogle the Raggazzi for a while up and down the Mercerie then for a cup of Capuchina at the Orientale and then home." See Blum to Otto Bacher, January 1886, quoted in Margaretta Lovell, *Venice: The American View, 1860–1920* (San Francisco: Fine Arts Museums of San Francisco, 1984), p. 26.

[2] Ibid., p. 27.

[3] Blum made trips to Venice in 1880, 1881, 1885, 1886, 1887, and 1889. In 1887, he appealed to his parents for money to fund that summer's trip. Blum Family Correspondence, letter from Blum to his parents, March 28, 1887; cited in Bruce Weber, "Robert Frederick Blum (1857–1903) and his Milieu," PhD diss. (Ann Arbor, MI: University Microfilms International, 1986), p. 296. Blum sent the pastel to his parents in Cincinnati in July 1887. BFC, July 24, 1887; ibid., p. 292.

[4] BFC, November 14, 1887; ibid., p. 298.

Detail:

Venetian Bead Stringers

Mary Cassatt 1844–1926

The year 1877 was pivotal in Mary Cassatt's life. In the fall, her parents came to live with her and her older sister, Lydia, in Paris. The sisters had settled there three years earlier, since Paris afforded Mary access to the heart of the European art world and provided Lydia, ill with Bright's disease, with much-needed medical care. Having both her semi-invalid sister and her aging parents close forced Cassatt to change her routine. The family's apartment was only a few blocks from her studio, and the short walk between them came to symbolize the growing tension between Cassatt's increased responsibilities of looking after her family and her efforts to further her painting career.

Earlier the same year Cassatt had met Edgar Degas, establishing a lasting friendship that enabled her to join the Independents, the group of artists better known now as the impressionists. Encouraged by his response to her work, Cassatt began preparing for the impressionists' 1878 exhibition, possibly intending to include this portrait of her mother reading the morning newspaper. *Reading "Le Figaro"* is a sophisticated blending of Cassatt's domestic and worldly realms. Her mother, Katharine Kelso Cassatt, sits in her morning dress reading *Le Figaro*, a right-of-center newspaper noted for its arts coverage as well as its political news. Cassatt's thick paint lends the painting a tactile quality, her sure strokes emphasizing the corporality of her mother and the solidity of her surroundings.[1] The artist's vigorous hand underscores her mother's strength of character. With her strong hands and severe glasses, Mrs. Cassatt is presented as a matriarchal figure dominating the canvas and absorbed in the affairs of the outside world.

Mrs. Cassatt firmly grasps the newspaper, implying a similar grasp of the news inside it. What the painting does not convey, however, is an intimate sense of her as a person. Even her reflection in the mirror is confined to one hand and part of the paper, with no hint of her profile or body. The artist frequently employed mirrors in her compositions, often using the reflection to expand on her sitters' surroundings, providing context for their actions at the theater or at home. Here the mirror seems to conceal more about Mrs. Cassatt than it reveals, reinforcing her emotional reserve.

Cassatt would have had in mind two groundbreaking portraits of artists' parents as she composed this portrait of her own mother. Paul Cézanne painted *The Artist's Father, Reading "L'Événement"* in 1866, in which he shows his banker father, who adamantly opposed his desire to become an artist, reading the newspaper written by Emile Zola that regularly championed Cézanne's

Reading "Le Figaro"

about 1877–78, oil on canvas, 39 ¾ × 32 in.
Private Collection, Washington, DC

work. Cézanne also included in the painting one of his own still lifes on the wall behind his father, as though hoping to convince himself of his father's eventual support. James McNeill Whistler's canonical portrait of his mother had been the subject of transatlantic criticism at its debut in 1871. She appears seated in profile in the manner of Roman funerary sculptures.[2] One of his etchings hangs on the wall, and a patterned *japonesque* curtain—revealing his interest in Japanese prints—extends the symbolic pairing of mother and son. Cassatt's painting of her mother presents her as a dominant presence in her life, but one wholly supportive of her talents. Still, the emotional distance between mother and daughter in the painting is pronounced. Despite the open newspaper, Mrs. Cassatt appears to the viewer as a closed book.

Cassatt may have intended *Reading "Le Figaro"* to be her debut picture as one of the impressionists, but the planned 1878 exhibition was unexpectedly canceled. Her father noted in a letter to her brother that the painting had been shown in Europe, most likely in Paris, and would be shipped to him in Philadelphia later that fall.[3] In his letter to Alexander, he commented, "I hope you will be pleased with the portrait, in fact I do not allow myself to doubt that you will be.... Here there is but one opinion as to its excellence."[4] Cassatt arranged with the American artist J. Alden Weir to have this painting shown at the 1879 Society of American Artists exhibition in New York. One reviewer admiringly wrote:

> Among the technically best pictures in the entire collection was Miss Cassatt's portrait, a capitally drawn figure of an agreeable looking, middle-aged lady, with a clear skin over her well formed features, and with soft, brown, wavy hair. It is pleasant to see how well an ordinary person dressed in an ordinary way can be made to look; and we think nobody seeing this lady reading a newspaper through her shell "nippers," and seated so composedly in her white morning dress, could have failed to like this well-drawn, well-lighted, well-anatomized, and well-composed painting.[5]

Cassatt may have painted *Reading "Le Figaro"* for her brother Alexander; the two were part of a close-knit family. Mary's portrait of their mother may have helped ease his sense of loss after his parents' departure for Europe. This painting remained in Alexander's family as a cherished heirloom for over a century. The painting also had a lasting impact on Cassatt. Years later, she agreed to let the American architect Theodate Pope take her photograph. Seated in an upholstered armchair, Cassatt holds her lorgnette to her face while she reads a newspaper. Now comfortably ensconced in the same role that once

Reading "Le Figaro"

about 1877–78, oil on canvas, 39 ¾ × 32 in.
Private Collection, Washington, DC

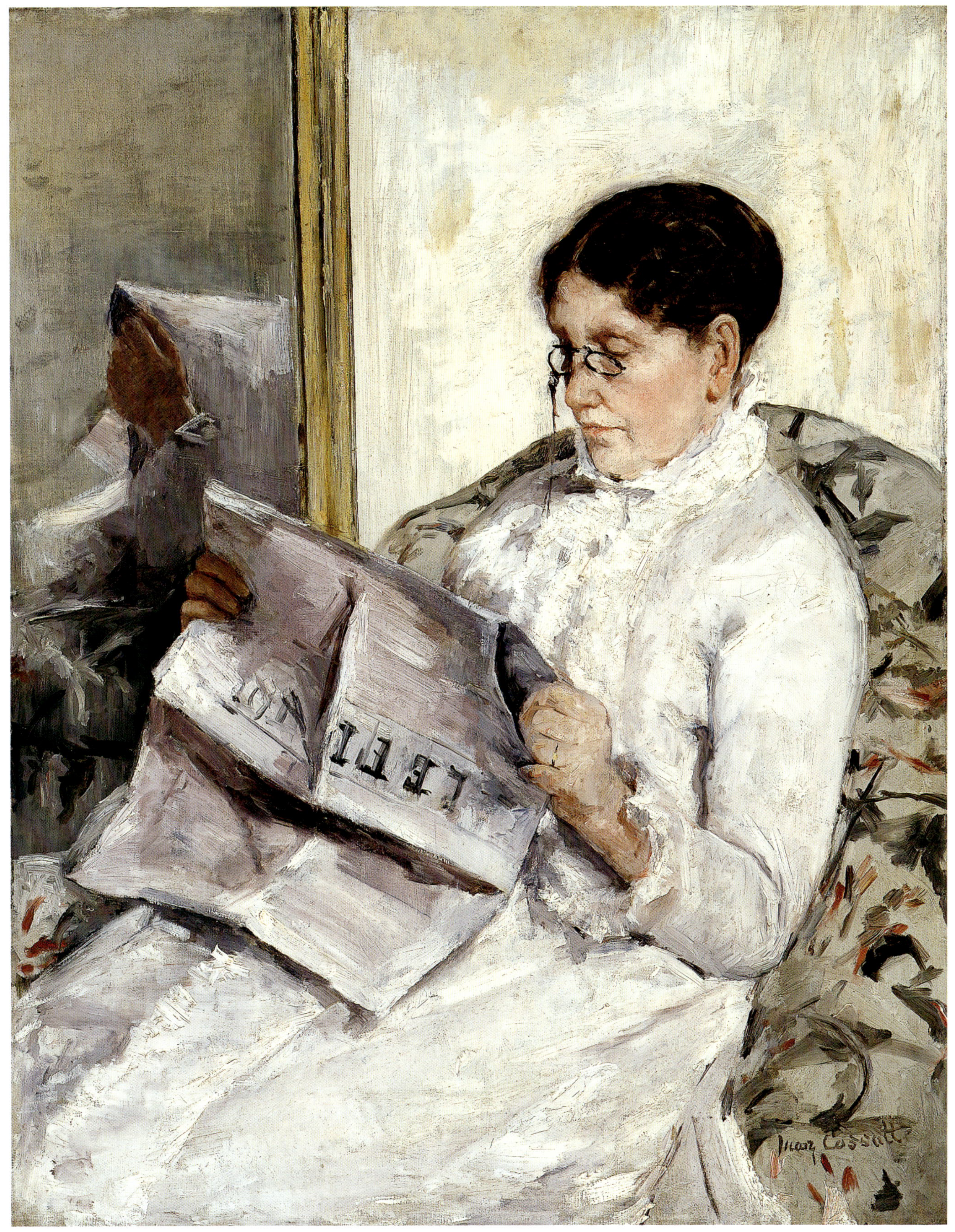
Mary Cassatt

belonged to her mother, she replicated, consciously or not, the composition of *Reading "Le Figaro."* [EJH]

---

[1] "By wise and vigorous painting, with the full strength of her palette and a careful observance of the local variations, she secures the intrinsic quality of her fleshy tones—so that you can well imagine that her rendering would feel under your fingers much as the naked body does in life—and she is much aided in this desirable effect by a free use of that hard outline which the impressionists so generally disregard." See William Walton, "Miss Mary Cassatt," *Scribner's Magazine* 19, no. 3 (March 1896), pp. 358–59.

[2] Elizabeth Broun, "Thoughts That Began with the Gods: The Content of Whistler's Art," *Arts Magazine* 62, no. 2 (October 1987): 42.

[3] In a letter to his son, Cassatt's father, Robert, wrote of the frame for this painting, "Mame [Mary] had a very fine one, bought a bargain in Rome, in which the picture was exhibited here & which suited it admirably." His statement indicates that this painting was exhibited in Paris during 1878. Robert Cassatt to Alexander Cassatt, Friday, October 4, 1878; quoted in Nancy Mowll Mathews, ed., *Cassatt and Her Circle: Selected Letters* (New York: Abbeville Press, 1984), p. 138.

[4] Ibid.

[5] S. N. Carter, "Exhibition of the Society of American Artists," *The Art Journal*, vol. V (1879): 157.

Louis Comfort Tiffany 1848–1933

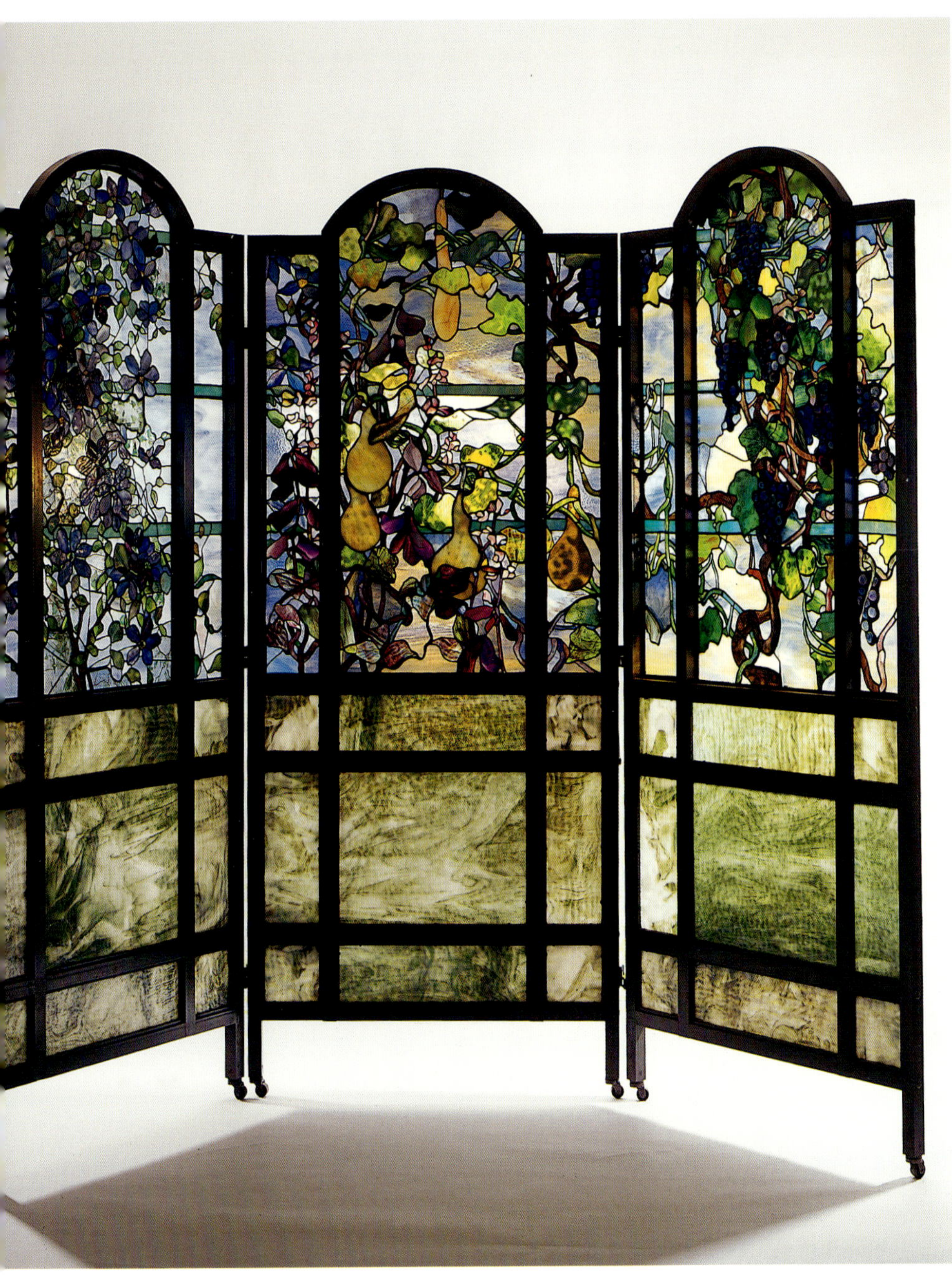

Louis Comfort Tiffany had already established himself as a talented painter when he turned his attention to revolutionizing stained-glass production in America. Throughout the 1890s he threw himself into making the finest glass available for religious and secular windows, experimenting with color and technique, in constant rivalry with fellow artist John La Farge. For the 1893 World's Columbian Exposition, Tiffany had displayed his Byzantine-inspired stone mosaics to announce himself as the leading decorator for church commissions. Not content to rest on those laurels, he turned his attention to stained glass, the medium in which he would make his reputation and his fortune. He began designing religious and secular glass windows, screens, and decorative objects.

For his booth at the 1900 Paris Exposition Internationale, he assembled an impressive array of more than one hundred decorative works, from Zuni-inspired silver bowls to opalescent glass windows. Foremost among the trove was this three-panel screen, made with Tiffany's newly developed opalescent glass, and inventively mounted in a framework that allowed the structural leading to serve as part of the overall design. His efforts won him the grand prize, over competition that included his chief European rivals, René Lalique

Dining Room Screen with Autumnal Fruits

about 1900, leaded opalescent glass in a three-panel screen, 72 ⅜ × 88 ¾ in.
Private Collection, Washington, DC

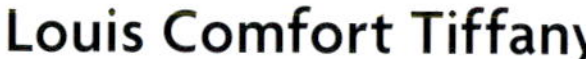

Louis Comfort Tiffany

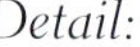

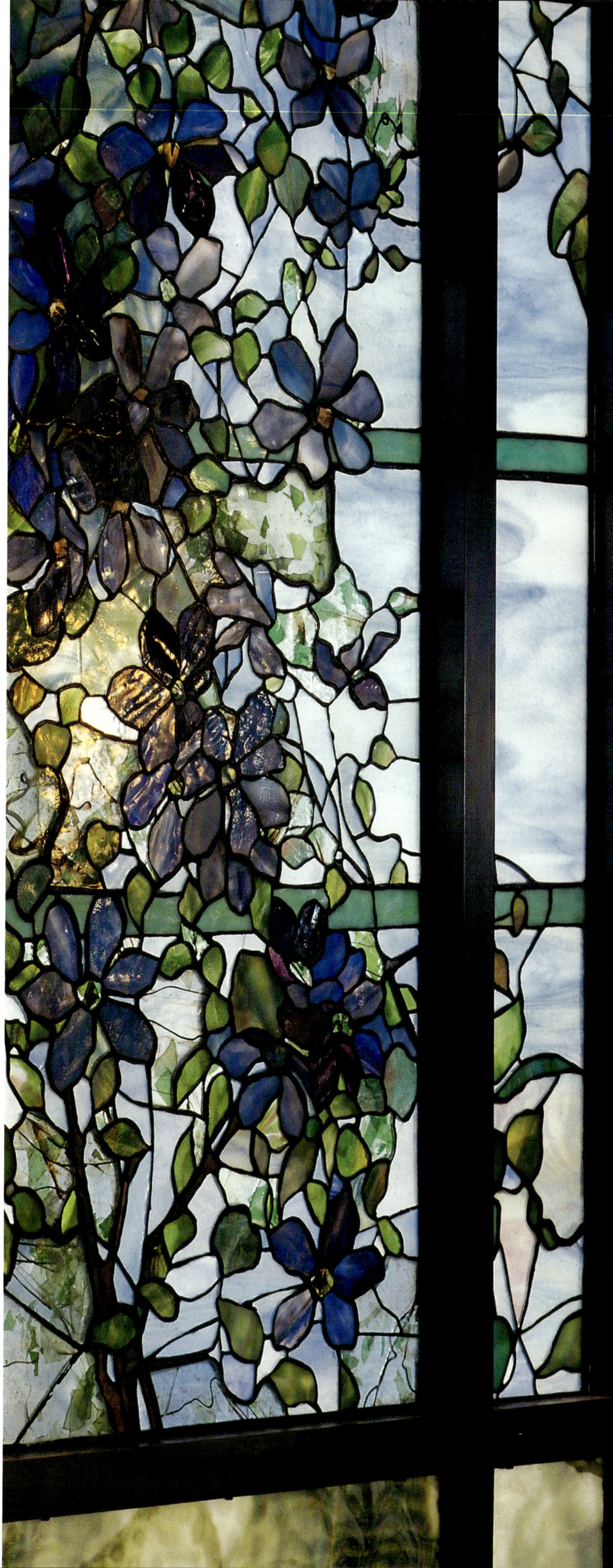

Detail:

Dining Room Screen with Autumnal Fruits

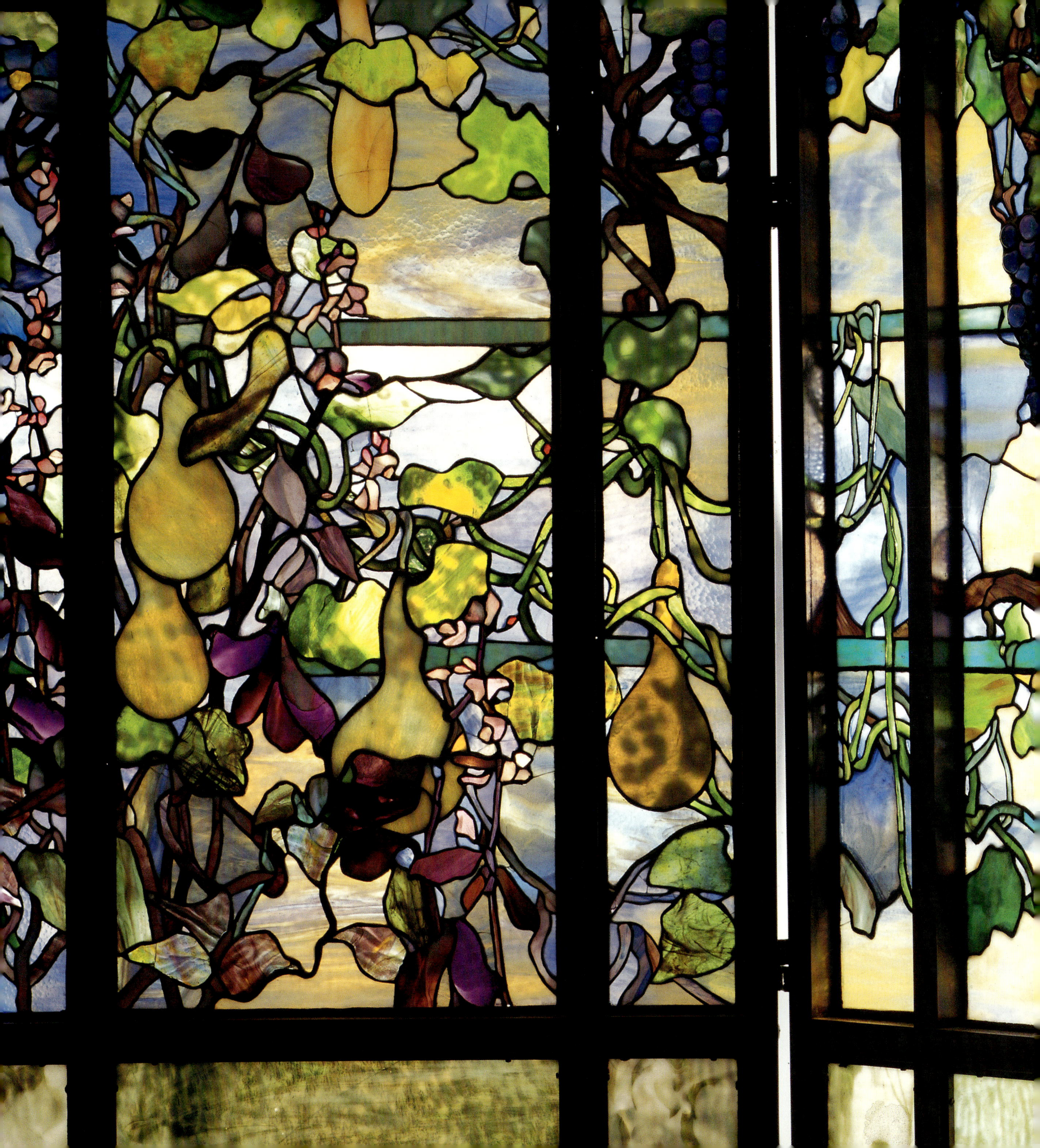

and Émile Gallé. The French government awarded Tiffany the rank of chevalier of the Legion of Honor.

Reviewers praised the screen's decorative scheme that brought together panels depicting blue clematis, yellow squash gourds and purple squash blossoms, and ripe bunches of purple grapes.[1] A dedicated gardener, Tiffany knew that all three plants flourish well into the fall. With the popularity of landscaping and gardening at the turn of the century, his audience too appreciated this invocation of a specific season. Tiffany owned an enormous horticultural library that he consulted as he developed his designs. Clematis, gourd, and grape are all climbers, and Tiffany supported them on a trellis that he worked into both the lead canes and the decorative glass bars that divide the screen into a grid. In a masterful stroke, Tiffany interwove the three plants from one panel into the next, uniting the separate panels into a harmonic whole, much as he did in his large-scale stained-glass windows.

In his passion for making glass, Tiffany blended his fascination with both medieval glass techniques and modern science. For his opalescent glass, he introduced mother-of-pearl into the molten glass, and for his abstract, marbled panels he swirled different metals into the hot liquid, allowing the colors to set as the glass cooled.[2] Tiffany molded his grapes into balls, and used multiple layers of glass fused together—called plating—to achieve unrivaled depth of color. He studied the optical properties of different types of glass to give himself a palette of "five thousand colors and hues... in as many as 200 tons of glass in the form of ovals about three feet long... stored in the bins of the Tiffany Studios."[3]

Both Tiffany and John La Farge developed varieties of decorated glass, but their approaches to the medium differed significantly. Tiffany's preferred innovations allowed metals and other impurities to create vibrant colors that melted into the glass. La Farge's compositions were in many ways stronger than Tiffany's studio productions, which often depended on other artists' designs, but for gloriously beautiful glass, there was no doubt of Tiffany's mastery, and when he personally designed a work, such as this screen, the effect was incomparable. Tiffany described his involvement in making stained glass: "[The artist] is often compelled to superintend and direct the making of the glass itself which he proposes to use, and the glass once obtained, he must stand by the glazier and superintend the selection, cutting, and arrangement as the window is slowly built up. In other words, in the American system the glass window under the hand of the artist is like the picture on the canvas."[4]

His obsessive approach to inventing, supervising, and making his varieties of glass culminated in the experiments he carried out at Laurelton Hall, his Long Island estate where gardens and stained-glass windows merged in a complete aesthetic environment.

Tiffany created this *Dining Room Screen with Autumnal Fruits* at the height of his powers, and the accolades he won in Paris made it clear he eclipsed all of his rivals, in both America and Europe. Tiffany brought this screen home from Paris, and displayed it the following year at the 1901 Pan-American Exhibition in Buffalo. Someone in upstate New York must have delighted in acquiring the screen for a residence, since it disappeared for a half-century before being purchased from an estate sale near Buffalo in the 1950s. During those fifty years, changes in taste brought down the empire Tiffany had built, and the Tiffany Studios glass works ceased production in 1932. With the resurgence of interest in art glass after World War II, this screen, like so many other masterpieces by Tiffany, re-emerged to renewed appreciation for his innovative work in glass. [EJH]

---

[1] In a review of Tiffany's booth, this work was called a "Dining Room Screen Showing Autumnal Fruits." Although the article described the three panels as displaying "wisteria," "gourd," and "grape," it is clear that the floral motif is clematis, a showy vine capable of producing four-, five-, and six-petaled blossoms well into the fall. See "Some Examples of American Glass Work at Paris," *The Art Interchange* (June 1900): 131.

[2] Opalescent glass is described as having "a peculiar richness…given by the varying texture and density of the glass and the insertion of bits of mother-of-pearl." See Cecilia Wearn, "The Industrial Arts in America," *The International Studio* 11, no. 2 (September 1897): 158. Films of metal oxides could be added to the hot glass, or the hot glass exposed to those vapors to produce various colors. Cobalt and copper oxide produced blue; iron oxide produced green; manganese oxide generated purple; gold or copper gave red; and carbon oxides produced amber. See the introduction in Harold Jaffe, *The Age of Tiffany: Glass, Paintings, Bronzes, Furniture: February 6–March 15, 1981*, C. W. Post Art Gallery (Greenvale, NY: Gallery, 1981).

[3] Hugh F. McKean, *The "Lost" Treasures of Louis Comfort Tiffany* (New York: Doubleday, 1980), p. 237; cited in Donald L. Stover, *The Art of Louis Comfort Tiffany: An Exhibition Organized by the Fine Arts Museums of San Francisco from the Collection of the Charles Hosmer Morse Foundation, M. H. de Young Memorial Museum, 25 April through 8 August, 1981* (San Francisco: Fine Arts Museums of San Francisco, 1981), p. 46.

[4] Louis Comfort Tiffany, "American Art Supreme in Colored Glass," *The Forum*, vol. 15 (1893): 624.

Thomas Moran 1837–1926

On July 4th, 1871, Thomas Moran entered the remote Yellowstone region as part of Ferdinand Hayden's U.S. Geological Survey. Almost three weeks later, Moran, Hayden, and photographer William Henry Jackson became the first Anglo-Americans to record the Mammoth Hot Springs. The scenery was stunning, with geothermal formations towering up to two hundred feet high, and stretching over a mile wide, described as resembling "a vast frozen cascade."[1] Moran made several watercolor field sketches of the impressive polychrome features over the next three days, and often appeared in Jackson's photographs as the only evidence of human scale in this hauntingly beautiful, if alien, landscape. On the face of one watercolor, Moran wrote, "The Basins graduate from White to yellow to Brown to Orange to Red to Gray/ Water in Great Spring pure Blue," evocative color notes that would guide him once he was back in the studio.[2]

The trip to Yellowstone changed Moran's life, propelling him from relative obscurity as a Philadelphia-based landscape painter to the artist so closely identified with the West that he carried the nickname Thomas "Yellowstone" Moran. Early in 1872, Hayden's survey report, presented with a suite of Moran's watercolor sketches and William Henry Jackson's photographs, spurred Congress to enact legislation proclaiming Yellowstone as America's first national park. Building on that enthusiasm, Moran swiftly completed his first monumental oil painting from the trip, *The Grand Canyon of the Yellowstone*, which was purchased by Congress in June 1872 and installed in the House of Representatives' chamber.

Moran did not rest on his laurels. That fall he turned his attention to *Hot Springs of Gardiner's River*, his largest and most impressive Yellowstone watercolor. Moran knew well the importance of large-scale "presentation" watercolors in England and, given his fluency in this difficult medium, set out to rival them. Moran's friendship with John Ruskin, and their mutual admiration of J. M. W. Turner's early watercolors, fueled the American artist's desire to live up to Turner's legacy. In a breathtaking burst of creativity, Moran spent only four days in early November 1872 painting and perfecting this watercolor, which he then placed on view in Washington, DC, near his monumental oil painting of Yellowstone.[3]

Scribner's magazine reviewed Moran's watercolors in January 1873, declaring them "the most brilliant and poetic pictures that have been done in America thus far... with all his senses alive for rich and strange and tender shimmering color, rainbow and mist, with fleeting cloud, and more hues than Iris herself with her purple

Hot Springs of Gardiner's River, Yellowstone National Park, Wyoming

1872, watercolor on tan paper, 20 1/4 × 28 5/8 in.
Private Collection, Washington, DC

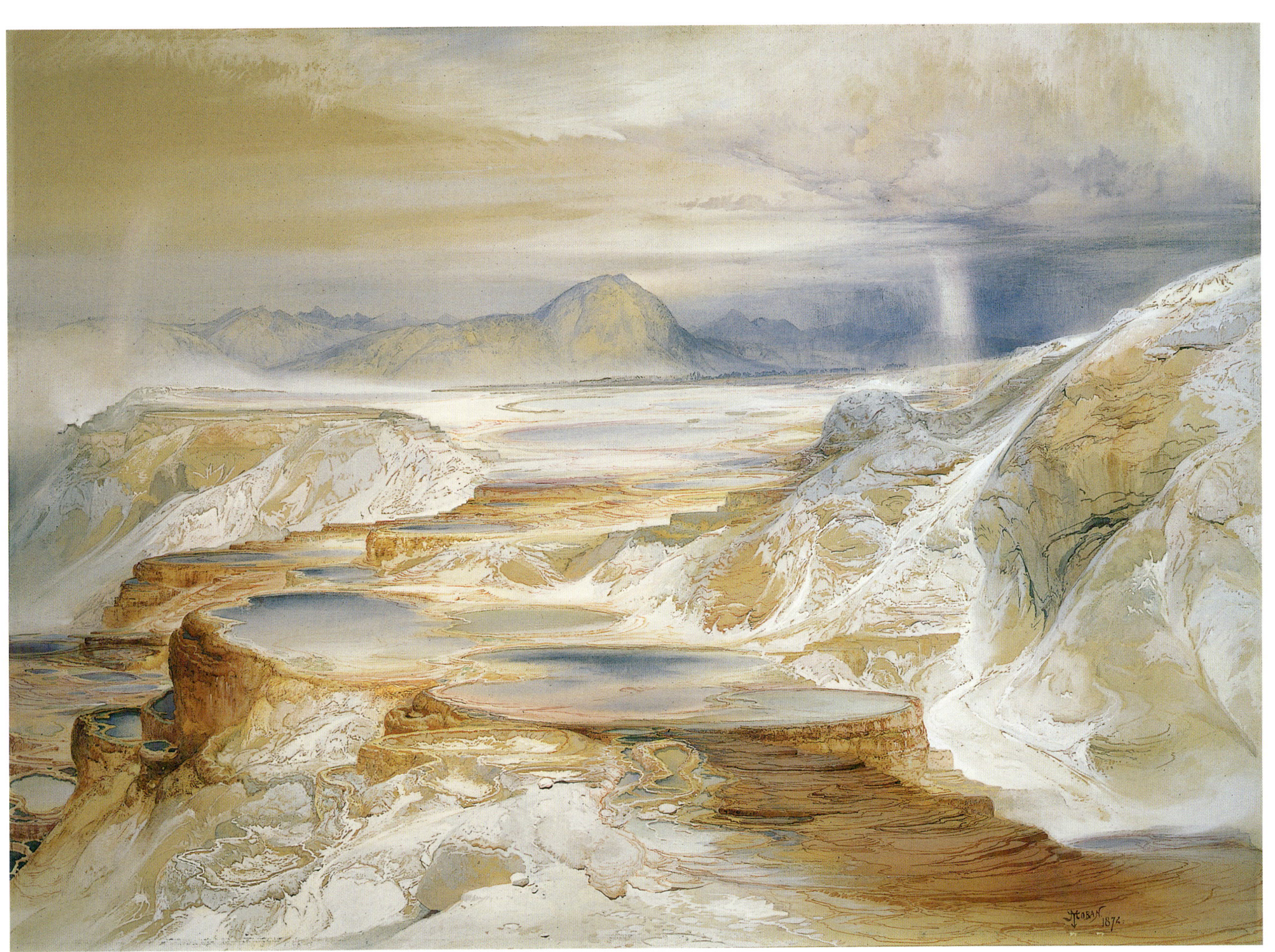

scarf can show. His love of form is as strong as his love of color, and his lines betray the same innate grace of spirit, the same delicately moving mind."[4] Moran kept this monumental watercolor until 1884, when he and Arthur Renshaw, British representative to the Mexican National Railroad, gave it to the Geological Society of London, where it remained for over a century. [EJH]

---

[1] R. W. Raymond, "The Heart of the Continent: The Hot Springs and Geysers of the Yellow Stone Region," *Harper's Weekly*, April 5, 1873, p. 274.

[2] Inscription on a watercolor sketch of the Great Blue Spring of the Lower Geyser Basin of Fire Hole River, Yellowstone (1871); cited by Carol Clark, *Thomas Moran, Watercolors of the American West: Text and Catalogue Raisonné* (Austin, TX: University of Texas Press and the Amon Carter Museum of Western Art, Forth Worth, 1980), p. 19.

[3] Moran recorded the creation of this work, writing "Lg wc rwg of the Hot Springs of Gardiner's River 22 × 29 made in 4 days Nov 8th 1872. Exhibited at Shaw's & in Washington & it is there yet Feb 28. 1874/have it still 1878." Thomas Moran's "Notebook"(unpublished mss, Thomas Gilcrease Institute of American History and Art, Tulsa, Oklahoma, 1874–82).

[4] Alexander Drake?, "Thomas Moran's Water-Color Drawings," *Scribner's Monthly* 5, no. 3 (January 1873), p. 394.

Arthur Wesley Dow 1857–1922

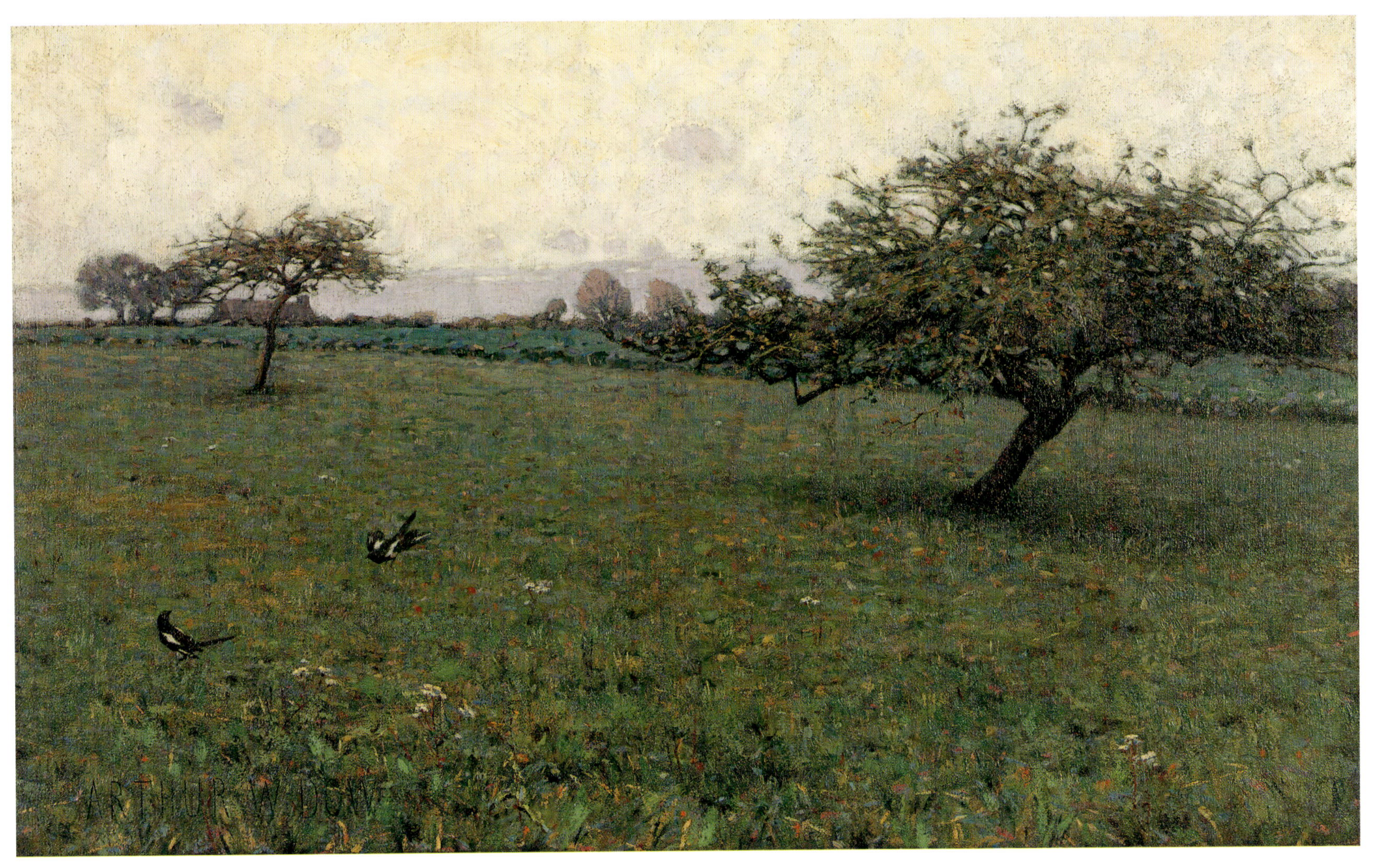

A Field, Kerlaouen

1885, oil on canvas, 32 × 53 in.
The Dicke Collection

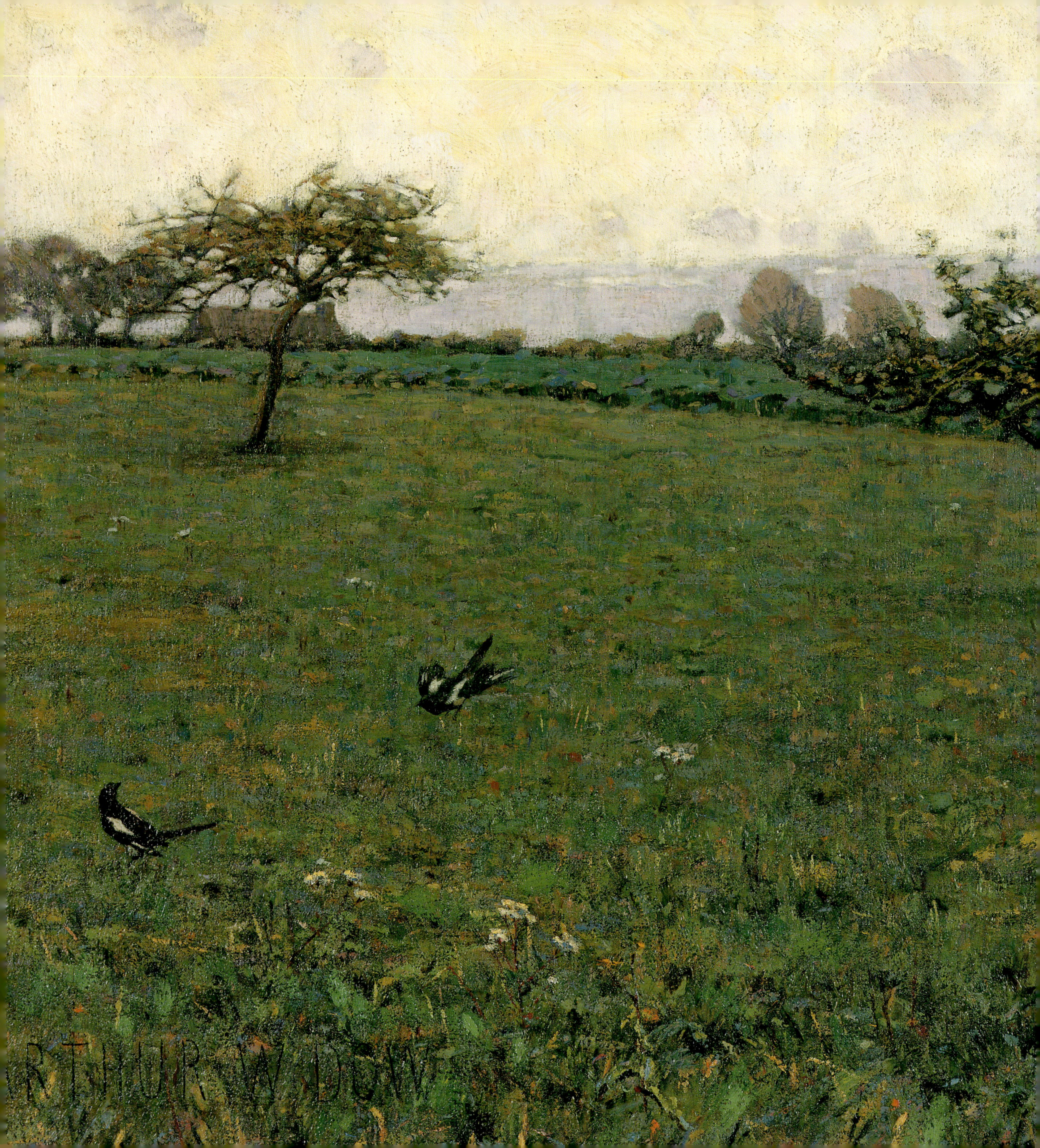
RTHUR W DOW

Arthur Wesley Dow

As early as 1860, southwest Brittany had attracted many American artists hoping to learn from the French masters who worked there. Arthur Wesley Dow arrived in Pont-Aven in May 1885, took sketching trips to nearby towns and villages, and also traveled north to Kerlaouen to paint this scene. The jurors of the Paris salon, the most renowned international art show, accepted *A Field, Kerlaouen* for exhibition in 1887.[1]

This painting reveals Dow's early interest in the plein-air landscapes of the French Barbizon school, a style that suited his early habits of observing the surroundings of his native Ipswich, Massachusetts. With its muted palette of greens and ochres warmed by the pink glow of twilight, and enlivened by two magpies in the foreground, the work captures the serene passing of a day. Its rusticity and elegiac mood is similar in feeling to the works of two artists whom Dow admired—French painter Jules Bastien-Lepage and American artist Alexander Harrison.

Although Dow's subject matter was conventional and popular in the late nineteenth century, the flatness of the picture plane in *A Field, Kerlaouen* reveals his interest in composition and design. A blue green wedge cleanly divides the broad field from the sky at a high horizon. The axes connecting the birds with the trees form several interlocking triangles that help the eye move over the canvas.

Dow's emphasis on design took on greater significance shortly after he returned to the United States in 1887. Despite the artistic validation of the French Academy, he became disillusioned by his own academic training and by the lukewarm response to his work from the Ipswich community. He soon felt "caught in some net of artistic futility."[2] He would later find liberation and renewed energy by experimenting with composition and decorative effect, inspired by the principles of Japanese aesthetics. "If a few elements can be united harmoniously," Dow wrote in the introduction to his seminal book *Composition*, first published in 1899, "a step has been taken toward further creation."[3] [EY]

---

[1] For details about jury selection, see Lois Marie Fink's *American Art at the Nineteenth-Century Paris Salons* (Washington, DC: National Museum of American Art, Smithsonian Institution, and Cambridge University Press, 1990), pp. 81, 114–5.

[2] Arthur Warren Johnson, *Arthur Wesley Dow: Historian, Artist, Teacher* (Ipswich, MA: Ipswich Historical Society, 1934), p. 52.

[3] Dow, Arthur Wesley, "Beginnings," in *Composition: A Series of Exercises in Art Structure for the Use of Students and Teachers*, 13th ed. (1920; repr., Berkeley, CA: University of California Press, 1997), p. 63.

Detail:

A Field, Kerlaouen

Adolph Alexander Weinman 1870–1952

Adolph Alexander Weinman first portrayed Chief Blackbird in *The Destiny of the Red Man*, a monumental sculptural group created for the St. Louis World's Fair of 1904. The fair commemorated the one hundredth anniversary of President Thomas Jefferson's Louisiana Purchase, which opened the continent to republican expansion. Weinman's ensemble portrayed Chief Blackbird and his people driven across the Great Plains by the momentum of Manifest Destiny. For the fairgoers in St. Louis, which was famed as the "gateway to the West," *The Destiny of the Red Man* suggested nothing controversial in the establishment of a nation dominated by Anglo-Europeans. In fact, Weinman's sculpture was dwarfed by the fair's neoclassical architecture, which announced the realization of Jefferson's hopes for a nation modeled after Greece and Rome and grounded in the ideals of the Enlightenment.

Weinman hired Chief Blackbird and other Sioux Indians to pose for him while they were performing in "Colonel Cumming's Wild West Show" at Coney Island, and he referred to the warrior as a "stoic, if ever there was one."[1] In *Chief Blackbird—Ogalalla Sioux*, the chief's wind-blown war bonnet emphasizes the sense of being buffeted by an irresistible force. His strong features remain, but his eyes are haunted, as if he had withdrawn into his memories and doubted his own leadership. At the turn of the twentieth century, there was little self-consciousness in Weinman's intention to symbolize "the passing of an heroic race," which was "but a matter of time."[2] Nevertheless, this portrait conveys an elegiac and sympathetic understanding that was rare among Weinman's contemporaries. Born in Germany but raised in New York City where he studied sculpture, Weinman obtained a thorough indoctrination in the Beaux-Arts tradition as an assistant in the studios of Philip Martiny, Olin Warner, Augustus Saint-Gaudens, and Daniel Chester French. In 1904, he opened his own studio and won his first acclaim with *The Destiny of the Red Man* at the world's fair. Weinman went on to have a successful career as an architectural sculptor and monument maker. On a smaller scale he is remembered as participating with Saint-Gaudens and James Earl Fraser in redesigning the United States coinage and was responsible for the designs of the Winged Head dime and Walking Liberty half dollar of 1916.[3] [GS]

---

[1] Quoted in Patricia Janis Broder, *Bronzes of the American West* (New York: Harry N. Abrams, 1974), p. 197.

[2] Weinman is quoted in Broder, *Bronzes*, p. 193.

[3] George Gurney, *Sculpture and the Federal Triangle* (Washington, DC: Smithsonian Institution Press, 1985), p. 134.

Chief Blackbird—Ogalalla Sioux

Modeled 1903, cast after 1907, bronze,
18 ½ × 16 ½ × 12 in.
Inscribed: *Chief Blackbird Ogalalla Sioux*
A. A. *Weinman* and *Roman Bronze Works* NY
Collection of Gerald and Kathleen Peters

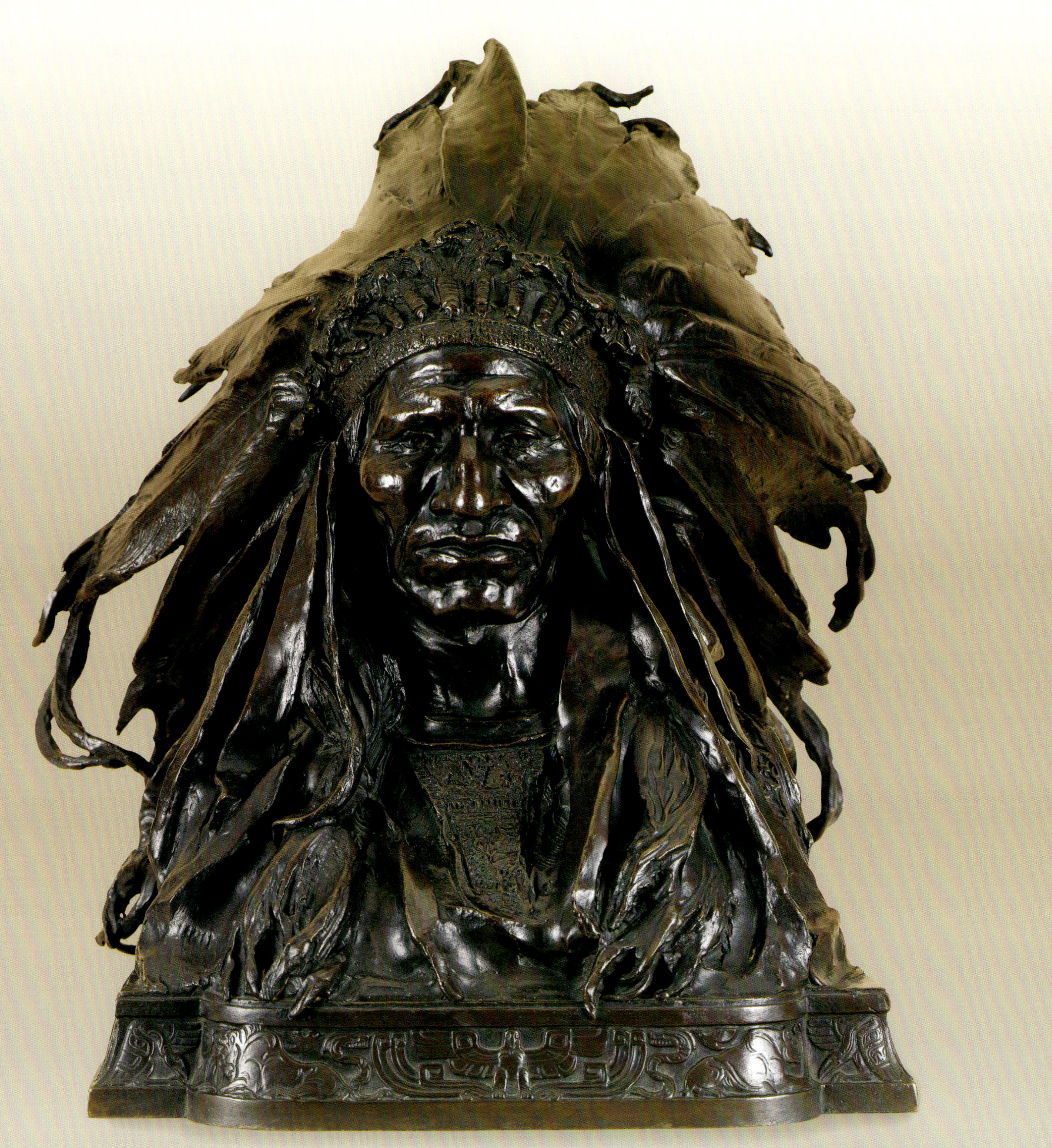

James Earle Fraser 1876–1953

The trail is lost, the path is hid, and the winds that blow from out the ages sweep me onto that chill borderland where Time's spent sands engulf lost peoples and lost trails. Marion Manville Pope[1]

Marion Manville Pope's words inspired sculptor James Earle Fraser's most important sculpture, *End of the Trail*. The artist had grown up in the Dakota territory in what is now Minnesota, and spent his childhood on the frontier near trappers and the local Sioux tribes who came and went with the seasons. In numerous interviews and in his unpublished memoirs, Fraser recalled the genesis of *End of the Trail*:

> I was brought up on the plains of Dakota when it really was a plain. My father was a railroad builder, and with others was building a railroad through Dakota and the Black Hills. Of course, he brought his family along. The Indians were constantly around our ranch house. I got to know the Indian children—played with them, and liked them very much. Often trappers, friends of my grandfather, came to visit us and I often heard them speak about the Indians . . . and where they would end up. They all thought that would be in the Pacific Ocean. Being a small boy, and rather impressionable, I felt badly about it. It stuck in my mind. Finally, after I had seen other sculptures, the idea occurred to me of making an Indian which represented his race reaching the end of the trail, at the edge of the Pacific.[2]

Fraser's iconic sculpture epitomizes the resignation and pathos associated with the impact of the closing of the frontier on Native American tribes. Slumped atop his weary pony, Fraser's brave cradles his lance with the point facing the ground, its position emphasizing his own. With the raw wind at their backs, neither man nor horse seems capable of fighting either the weather or the pressures of westward expansion. At the 1893 World's Columbian Exposition in Chicago, Frederick Jackson Turner had delivered his seminal lecture announcing the closing of the American frontier and its importance in shaping the American character.[3] Images of the vanishing West, and in particular depictions of American Indians as a vanquished race, proliferated at the turn of the century largely due to the impact of Turner's frontier thesis.

End of the Trail became the centerpiece of Fraser's career. He first began work on this sculpture after visiting the World's Columbian Exposition, finishing his first model for it in 1894. He took the maquette with him to Paris two years later, and his finished model took first prize at the 1898 American Art Association competition. There it attracted the attention of Augustus Saint-Gaudens, who asked Fraser to apprentice with him when Fraser returned to America. Under Saint-Gaudens's tutelage, Fraser continued refining the sculpture, and in 1915

End of the Trail

1918, bronze, 33 × 26 × 9½ in.
Inscribed: © *Fraser* and *Roman Bronze Works* N.Y.
and stamped underneath *RB8*
Collection of Gerald and Kathleen Peters

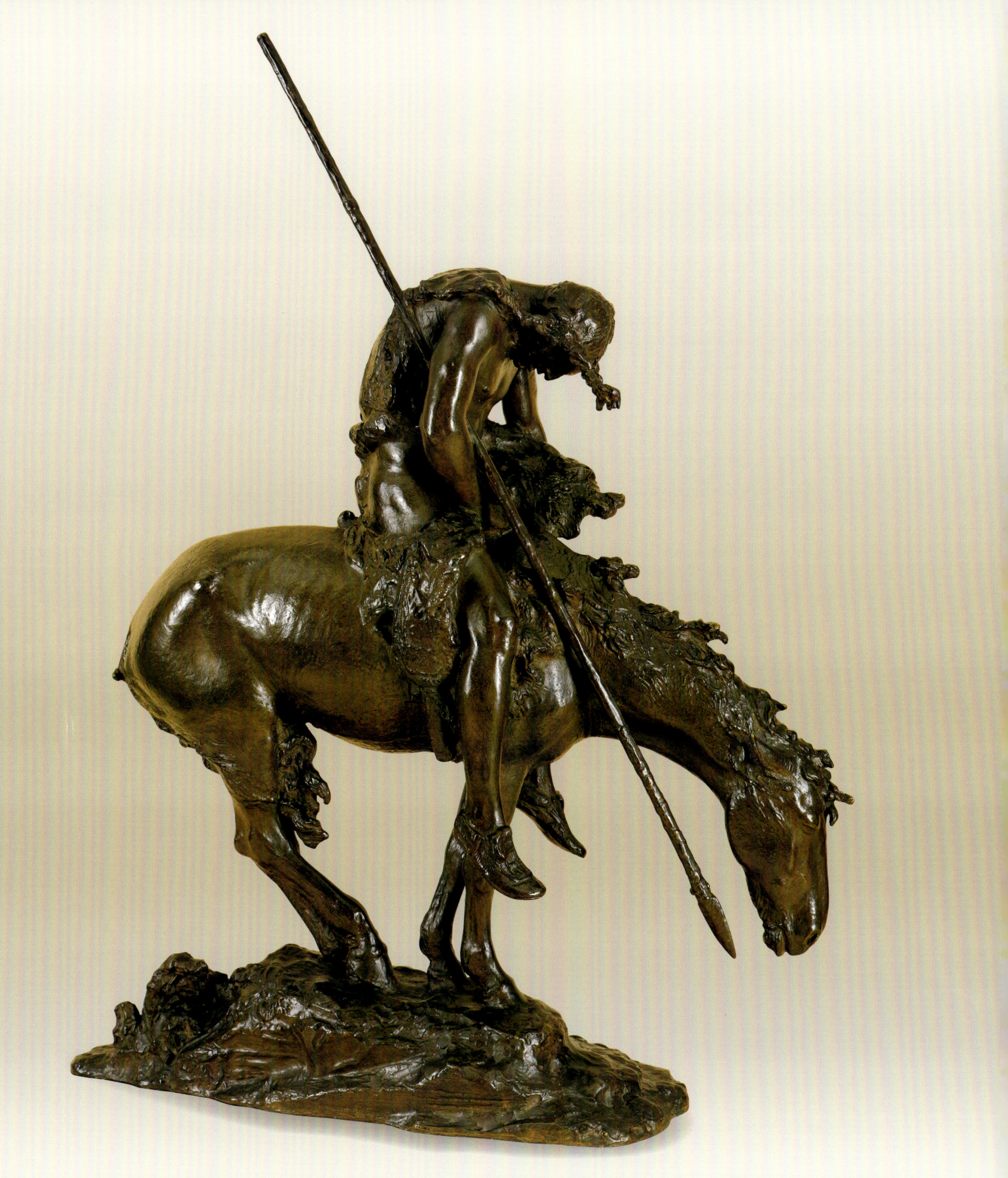

he displayed a life-size plaster model of *End of the Trail* at the San Francisco Exposition, where it won a gold medal. The sculpture became so popular that Fraser made several different smaller-scale versions cast in bronze. This sculpture of *End of the Trail* is number eight and was cast by the Roman Bronze Works in New York and sold in May 1918.[4] [EJH]

---

[1] The quotation is taken from Marion Manville Pope, quoted in Wayne Craven, *Sculpture in America* (New York: Thomas Y. Crowell, 1968), p. 493.

[2] Transcript of an interview with Julie Haggeman, "Spotlight on Youth," August 8, 1947, p. 6; James Earle Fraser Papers, reel 2548: 0563–0564, Archives of American Art, Washington, DC.

[3] "The frontier has gone, and with its going has closed the first period of American history." Frederick Jackson Turner, "The Significance of the Frontier in American History," an address read at a meeting of the American Historical Association on July 12, 1893, in Chicago.

[4] Roman Bronze Works' ledger page for James E. Fraser, p. 287. Roman Bronze Works Archives, Amon Carter Museum, Fort Worth, Texas. This work appears to be what Roman Bronze Works referred to as its "small" version; it began selling this version in January 1918. It also lists a "large" version, one cast of which is at the Amon Carter Museum.

Cyrus Edwin Dallin 1861–1944

Cyrus E. Dallin created four major statues to dramatize the Native Americans' unsuccessful struggle against whites for their land and way of life. *Appeal to the Great Spirit* is the last of these. His three earlier figures depict the Indians' first friendly meeting with whites, the medicine man who foresees the threat to his people, and the militant warrior fighting the encroachment on his civilization. Having exhausted both peace gestures and protests, the Lakota chief in *Appeal to the Great Spirit* turns to a higher power for deliverance.[1]

Appeal to the Great Spirit was by far the most popular of all of Dallin's sculptures. The original life-size bronze was given by donors to the Museum of Fine Arts in Boston in 1912, and the sculptor transferred the title to the statue to the museum. However, he retained the right to sell reductions not in excess of three feet. P. P. Caproni and Brother of Boston began selling plaster casts in 1915, and the following year the Gorham foundry in Providence, Rhode Island, started casting reproductions in three sizes: nine inches, twenty inches, and thirty-six inches. The latter quarter-scale-size model, of which this sculpture is one of nine casts, would be closer to forty inches than thirty-six inches.[2]

Dallin's Native American poses dramatically with arms outstretched, palms facing the sky, and face upturned. His figure is powerful and composed, even as he succumbs to his own helplessness and asks the Great Spirit for assistance. He sits upright and his muscles are taunt and defined. As he raises his head, the tendons in his strong neck are visible. The sculptor captured both horse and rider in a moment of absolute stillness. Apart from the horse's mane and the Indian's headdress, Dallin created little surface texture. The simplicity of his rendering augments the figure's stoicism.[3]

Dallin was one of a number of turn-of-the-century sculptors, including Hermon MacNeil, Alexander Phimister Proctor, Frederic Remington, and Solon H. Borglum, whose nostalgic images of Indians reflected a bygone era. Dallin's sensitivity to his subjects arose from his childhood spent in the frontier settlement of Springville, Utah, near the Ute and Paiute tribes. The artist's firsthand experience with Indians enabled him to depict them compassionately and distinguished him from many of his contemporaries from the East who visited the West briefly or not at all before creating their images of Native Americans.[4] [GG]

Appeal to the Great Spirit

modeled 1912, cast about 1919, bronze, 39 × 26 ½ × 39 in.
Inscribed: *C. E. Dallin 1912* and *GORHAM CO FOUNDERS / QAPU / GAC #2*
The Dicke Collection

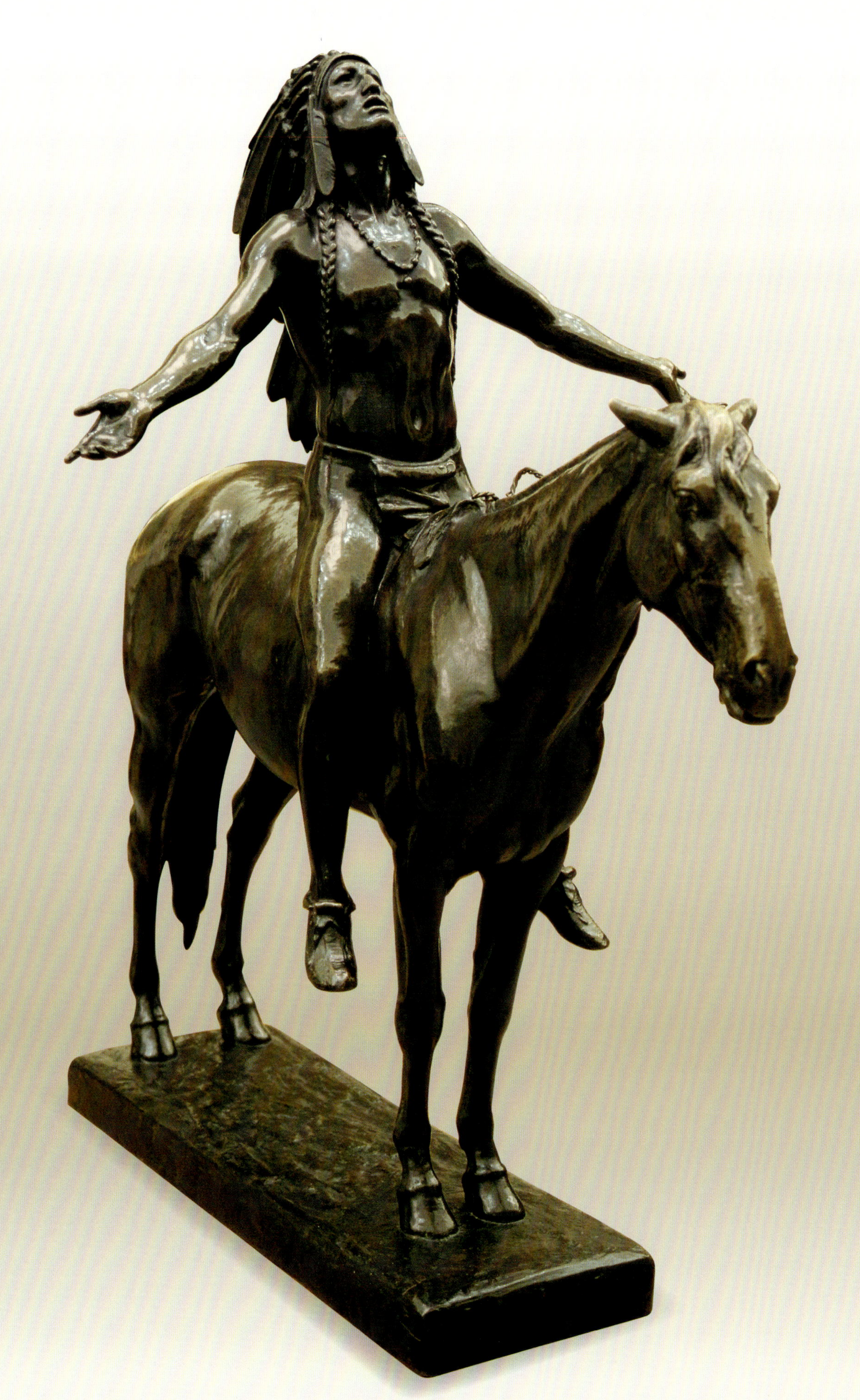

Cyrus Edwin Dallin

---

[1] John Ewers, "Cyrus E. Dallin: Master Sculptor of the Plains Indians," *Montana Magazine of Western History* 18, no. 1 (January 1968), pp. 38–40.

[2] Museum of Fine Arts, Boston, and Kathryn Greenthal et al., *American Figurative Sculpture in the Museum of Fine Arts Boston* (Boston: Museum of Fine Arts, 1986), pp. 276–78. Kent Ahrens, *Cyrus E. Dallin: His Small Bronzes and Plasters* (Corning, NY: Rockwell Museum, 1995), pp. 50–52.

[3] Ewers, "Cyrus E. Dallin," p. 98.

[4] Patricia Janis Broder, *Bronzes of the American West* (New York: Harry N. Abrams, 1974), p. 92.

For information on the modeling and casting of the sculpture, see Gorham Manufacturing Company, Bronze Division Records, 5. "Records of Royalties Paid to Sculptors for Casting of Their Works," Archives of American Art, Washington, DC, Reel 3680, frames 96, 229. Gorham ledgers record the first casting of the forty-inch version as February 2, 1917, and the Gorham royalty ledgers show that it was shipped February 13, 1918. No listing appears for the casting date of number #2, but it was shipped May 27, 1919.

Appeal to the Great Spirit

modeled 1912, cast about 1919, bronze, 39 × 26 ½ × 39 in.
Inscribed: *C. E. Dallin 1912* and *GORHAM CO FOUNDERS / QAPU / GAC #2*
The Dicke Collection

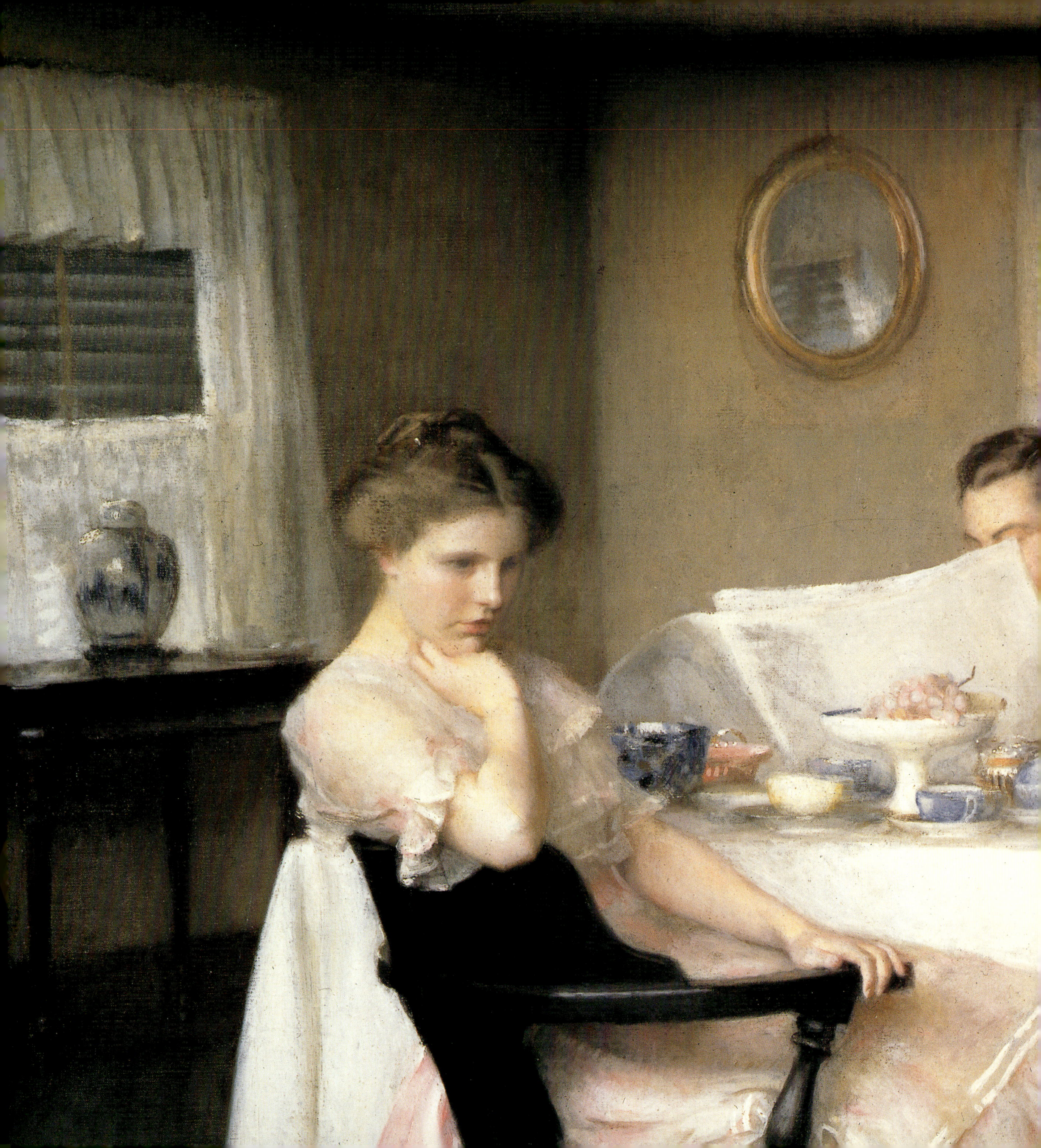

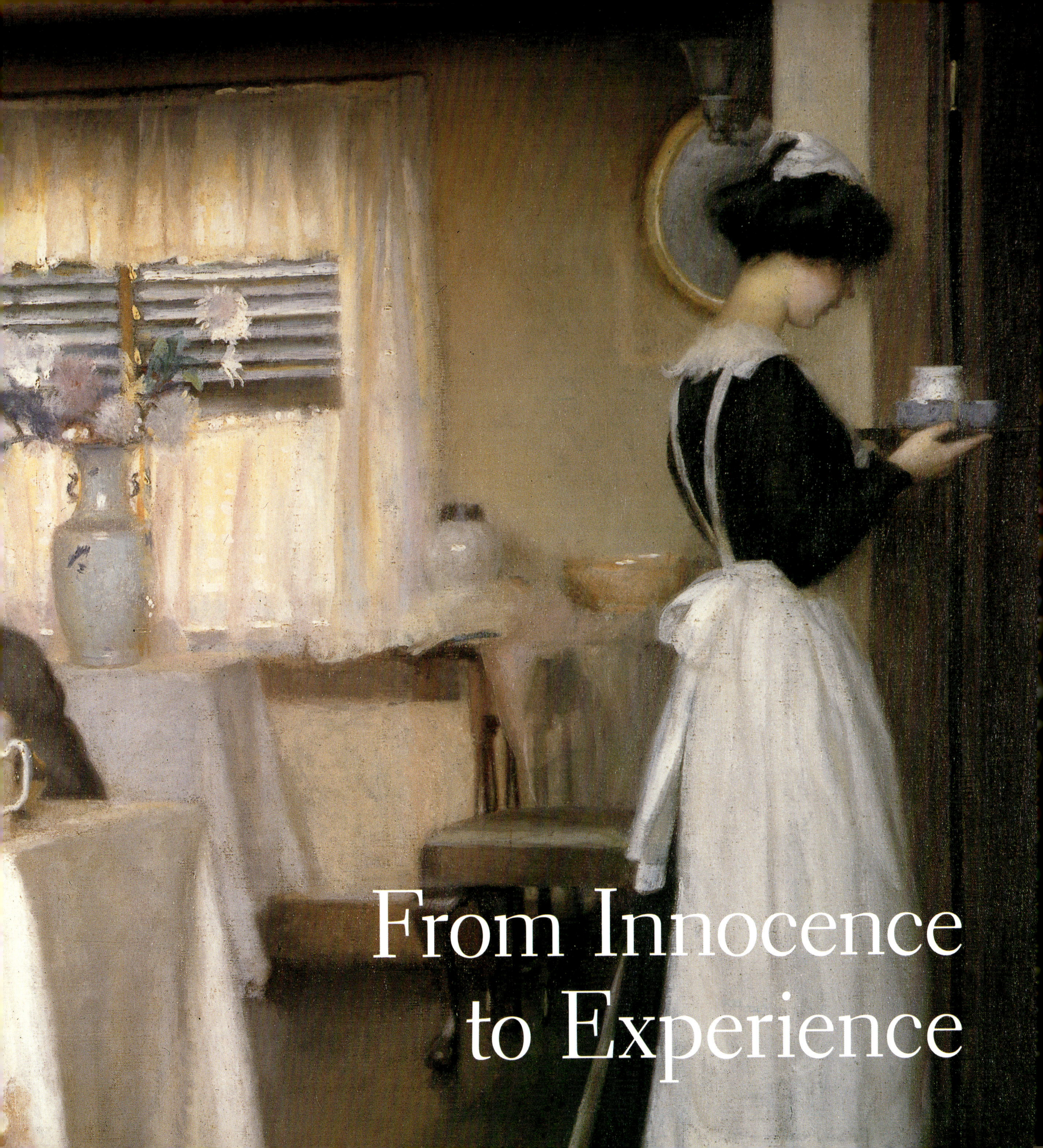
From Innocence
to Experience

Dennis Miller Bunker 1861–1890

In 1886, Dennis Miller Bunker fled his teaching job in Boston to spend the summer with the painter Abbott Handerson Thayer in Woodstock, Connecticut. "I'm having a bully time here," he wrote, "and I don't want to go away."[1] Yet, despite his pleasure at being there, Bunker complained to his friend Anne Page that "the days are distressingly bright for me, and I long for a solemn sky and a grey world."[2] In *Pines beyond the Fence*, he captured a time of day more suited to his temperament and skills. Hemlocks and oaks grow dark against the evening sky while wildflowers in the foreground glow like fireflies. This intimate landscape acknowledges Bunker's debt to the Barbizon painters of France and to the tonalism of fellow American artists, including George Inness, who recorded such transcendent moments among the settled farmlands of the eastern seaboard. Bunker's impressionistic washes of color in the foreground play against the tighter brushwork of the trees in the middle distance, reflecting the mix of French and American techniques he was still assimilating.

After his sojourn in Woodstock, Bunker wrote to Page that "the love, the simple love of the beautiful things of nature ... is enough to give anyone the right to be a painter."[3] *Pines beyond the Fence* is one of three canvases that survive from that summer, when Bunker painted under the eye of Thayer, whom he idolized not only for his talent but for his exuberant embrace of life. But Bunker shared the older artist's moody nature, veering between excitement and depression. Bunker disparaged his own work as "thin and deadly," and wrote to Isabella Stewart Gardner, the Boston collector, that he was only "rehearsing" to be a great artist. "I might be a painter if I could live again and begin fresh," he wrote. "We ought to be given three tries—like the baseball men."[4] *Pines beyond the Fence* captures a moment after the light of day, when darkness begins to absorb the colors of the landscape. It evokes the passing of New England's brief warm season and, in retrospect, seems to signal how little time Bunker would have to rehearse. The painter died unexpectedly from heart failure on December 28, 1890, at the age of twenty-nine. [GS]

---

[1] Bunker to Joseph Evans, June 20, 1886. Dennis Miller Bunker Papers, Archives of American Art, Reel 1201, Washington, DC.

[2] Bunker to Anne Page, September 1, 1886. Dennis Miller Bunker Papers, Archives of American Art, Reel 1201, Washington, DC.

[3] Bunker to Anne Page, September 11, 1886. Dennis Miller Bunker Papers, Archives of American Art, Reel 1201, Washington, DC.

[4] Quoted in Nelson C. White, *Abbott H. Thayer, Painter and Naturalist* (Hartford: Connecticut Printers, 1951), p. 48; quoted in Efrat Adler Porat, "Dennis Miller Bunker: A Tribute to an American Impressionist," *American Art Review* 7, no. 2 (April–May 1995): 113.

Pines beyond the Fence

1886, oil on canvas, 28 ¾ × 21 ¼ in.
Private Collection

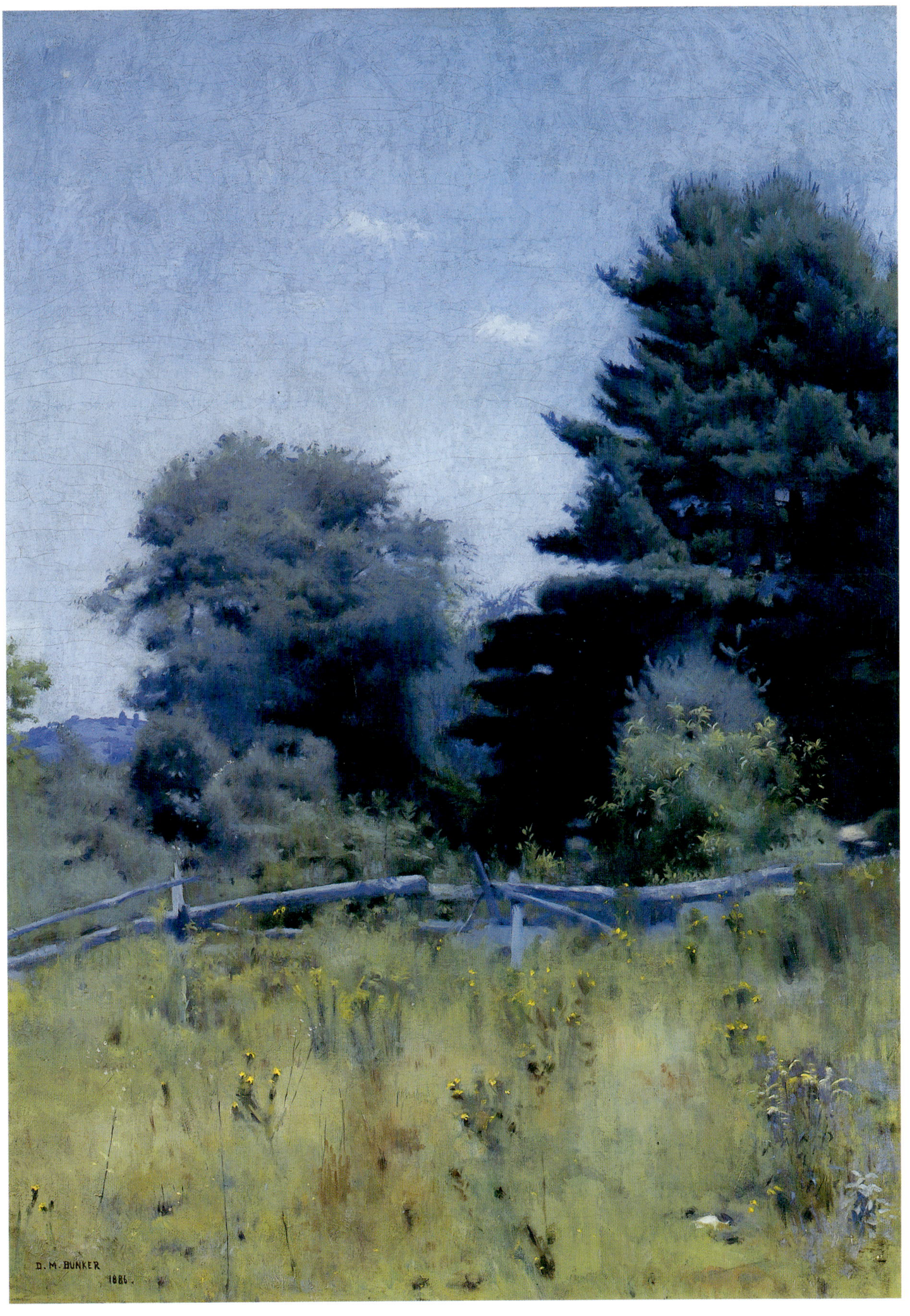
D. M. BUNKER
1886.

Theodore Robinson 1852–1896

Theodore Robinson's paintings of Cos Cob, Connecticut, provide a lyrical view of a once-thriving port town that was rapidly becoming a summer resort for wealthy New Yorkers. In 1890, Robinson's close friend and colleague John Twachtman had founded an art colony there, adopting the nearby Holley House as the artists' home. Blending his interest in Japanese prints with lessons he learned from Claude Monet in Giverny, Robinson painted a suite of works with a view across the Mianus River, looking toward the Riverside Yacht Club. Robinson often worked from photographs, but this summer he chose to take his sketchbook and his paints outdoors. His vantage point was the pedestrian walkway on the railroad bridge. While working on *The Anchorage, Cos Cob* in June of 1894, Robinson noted his favorite time to paint was in the "late afternoon, the club house and little yachts at anchor, low-tide, patches of sea grass. It is particularly brilliant at about 5 p.m."[1] Four days later he added, "charming in effect—especially at 6:30—richer and fuller in color than before."[2]

Like so many of his colleagues, Robinson was fascinated by the pictorial potential of Japanese prints, in particular their emphasis on planes of color, abstracted forms, and strong patterns. In *The Anchorage, Cos Cob*, Robinson invoked these lessons by adopting a high horizon in which the sky, sea, and shoreline create spare, yet powerful, horizontal bands of color. The slim, tall masts of the anchored boats punctuate these flat planes, instilling a sense of harmony not unlike the rhythm of the tides.[3]

The small boats in Robinson's Cos Cob paintings speak to the town's shift from a colonial-era fishing and farming village to an affluent suburb of New York, with oyster boats still plying the beds sharing the coastline with recreational catboats and yachts.[4] In that sense, Cos Cob made its peace with progress, embracing both its seafaring past and its newfound popularity as a resort community. Robinson's paintings evince a similar adaptability, incorporating both his study of Japanese prints and modern lessons learned in France. As one admirer wrote, "Out of little, he made much. He painted light, air, and colour. The purest lyric talent we have thus far produced, he sang a song steeped in outdoor brightness and objective tranquility."[5] [EJH]

The Anchorage, Cos Cob

about 1894, oil on canvas, 18 × 22 in.
Collection of Marie and Hugh Halff

[1] Theodore Robinson diary entry for June 19, 1894; quoted in John I. H. Baur, *Theodore Robinson, 1852–1896* (New York: Brooklyn Museum of Art, 1946), p. 41. Theodore Robinson Diaries: 1892–1896. Manuscript is in the Frick Art Reference Library, New York.

[2] Theodore Robinson diary entry for June 23, 1894; quoted in Susan Larkin, *The Cos Cob Art Colony: Impressionists on the Connecticut Shore* (New Haven, CT: Yale University Press, 2001), p. 97.

[3] In his diary, Robinson noted, "My Japanese print points in a direction I must try and take: an aim for refinement and a kind of precision.... The Japanese work ought to open one's eyes to certain things in nature, before almost invisible and a new enjoyment, their infinite variety of compositions, and their extraordinary combination of the convention and the reality." Theodore Robinson's diary entry for February 17, 1894; quoted in Susan Larkin, "Light, Time, and Tide: Theodore Robinson at Cos Cob," *The American Art Journal* 23, no. 2 (1991): 85.

[4] Larkin, *The Cos Cob Art Colony*, p. 96.

[5] Christian Brinton, "American Painting at the Panama-Pacific Exposition," *International Studio* (August 1915): 30; quoted in Baur, *Theodore Robinson*, p. 52.

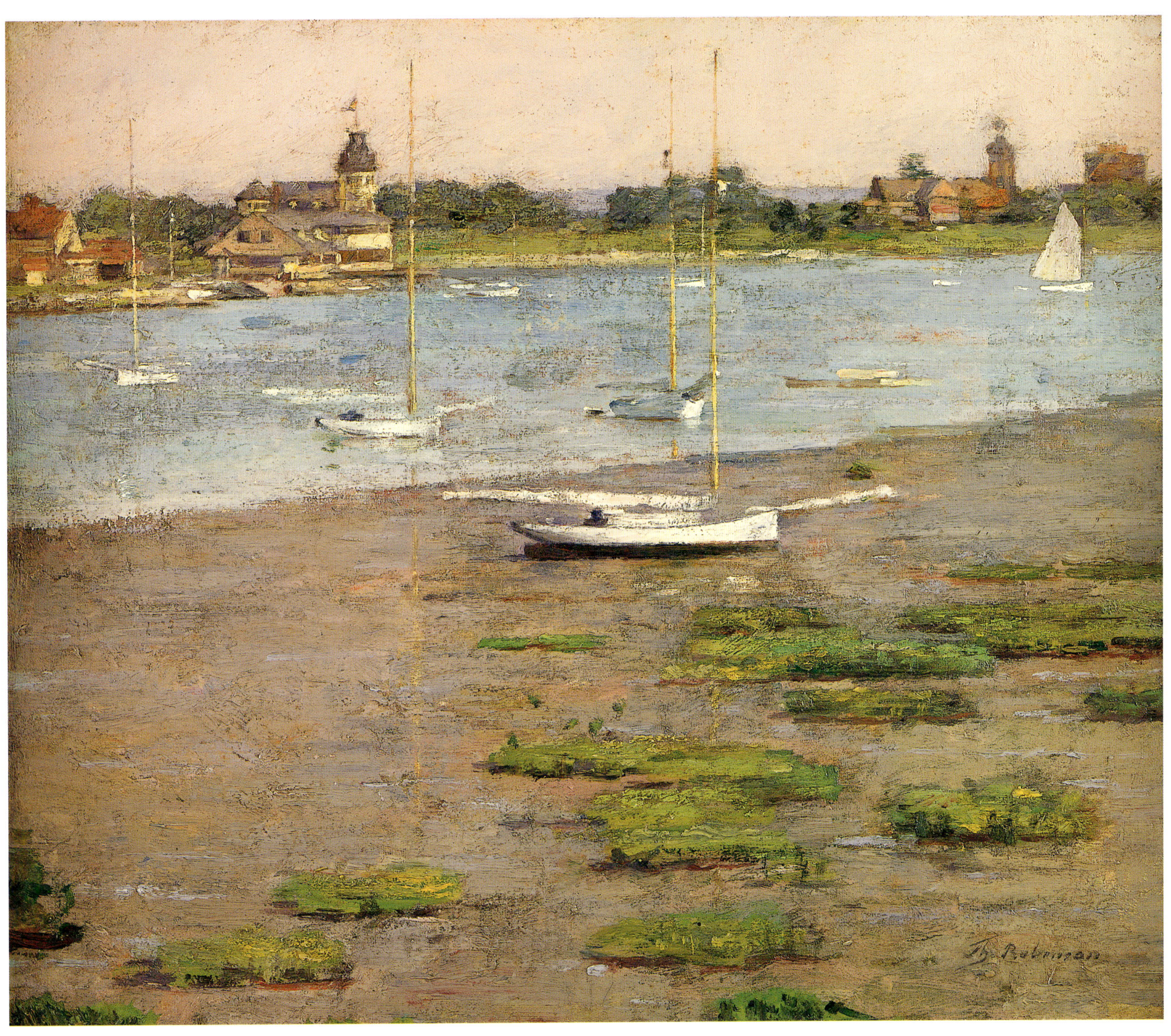

Winslow Homer 1836–1910

In 1873, Winslow Homer traveled to Gloucester, Massachusetts, thirty miles northeast of Boston on the Cape Ann peninsula. The *Gloucester Telegraph* noted on August 20 that "Winslow Homer, the artist, has been spending the summer at the Atlantic House, and the pages of 'Harper's Weekly' have been heightened by his seaside sketches."[1] Homer sent ten sheets from that first summer's work to the 1874 exhibition of the American Society of Painters in Water Colors. Critics praised these forthright images, in which Homer looked to nature rather than to "some other man's pictures." His "memorandum blots and exclamation points" of color left his critics "almost content not to ask Mr. Homer for a finished piece."[2] In subsequent seasons at Gloucester, the tight drawing of his magazine illustrations loosened considerably, and he painted confidently with large washes and bold strokes.

Transparent colors and bright areas of white gouache in *Watching Ships, Gloucester* capture the effervescent atmosphere of the coast and the spontaneity and freedom of the barefoot boys who look out to sea. Still, there is a sense in this painting of a brief moment that passes, perhaps too quickly. Soon enough, the sun will cast longer shadows, and the ships will pass out of the harbor and beyond the horizon. The boys will wait, as families of fishermen always did, for their fathers' safe return.[3]

Watching Ships, Gloucester represents an ideal of childhood that resonated after the Civil War. These boys represent a younger America, a more innocent time before the flaws in society grew too great to negotiate peacefully. In the decades to come, the Gilded Age would present its own difficulties, when the "hollowness of heart" that Walt Whitman mourned in modern culture led many Americans to look back to the more comforting moment Homer immortalized here.[4] [GS]

---

[1] Quoted in D. Scott Atkinson, "Introduction," *Winslow Homer in Gloucester*, Sue Taylor, ed. (Chicago: Terra Museum of American Art, 1990), p. 10.

[2] Quoted in Helen A. Cooper, *Winslow Homer Watercolors* (New Haven, CT: Yale University Press and the National Gallery of Art, Washington, DC, 1986), p. 24.

[3] Nicolai Cikovsky Jr. and Franklin Kelly, *Winslow Homer* (New Haven, CT: Yale University Press and the National Gallery of Art, Washington, DC, 1995), p. 136.

[4] Cited in Cooper, *Winslow Homer*, p. 26. "Hollowness of heart" is excerpted from Whitman's *Democratic Vistas* (1892).

Watching Ships, Gloucester

1875, watercolor and gouache on paper, 8 1/2 × 14 in.
Collection of Nan Tucker McEvoy

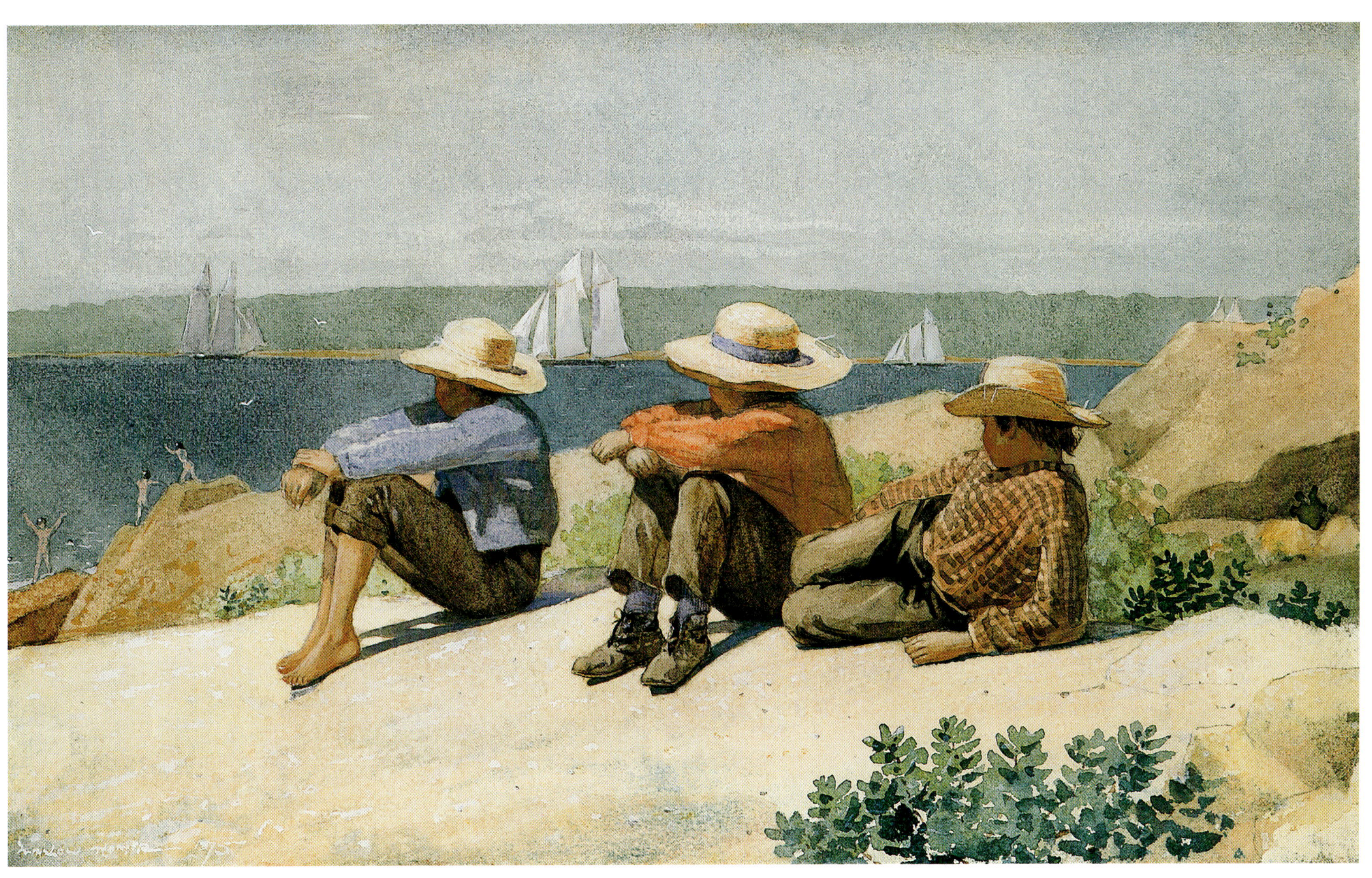

Thomas Anshutz 1851–1912

In November of 1893, Thomas Anshutz was sharing a drafty studio in Philadelphia with two other artists. He wrote to his wife, Effie, complaining about the distractions and describing his hopes for the home and studio they planned to buy in Holly Beach, New Jersey: "[T]he afternoons [in Philadelphia] are so short, and one dark the next bright, that there is but little time. It makes the prospect of long quiet uninterrupted days at Holly Beach seem quite the best thing in view."[1]

Thomas and Effie were settled on the coast by the following summer, and Anshutz began taking photographs of bathers, fishermen, and boys playing among the boats pulled ashore. *Sand Burr* employs elements of one photograph, *Two Boys by a Boat*, and a more freely painted watercolor with the same title, both from 1894. For this painting Anshutz eliminated many of the photograph's details but repeated the oblique angle of the dory, as well as the ropes trailing over gunwales and into the grass. The transparency of the watercolor medium and the bright paper beneath capture the luminous atmosphere of the coast in summer.[2]

The boys in this painting represent an ideal of childhood innocence that had been popularized in American art and literature after the Civil War. Mark Twain's *Huckleberry Finn* and *Tom Sawyer* and Winslow Homer's famous paintings of boys sailing dories off the Atlantic coast presaged Anshutz's works, as did his teacher Thomas Eakins's arcadian images of nude figures in natural settings. The boats that appear in many of these scenes suggest the adult responsibilities that lie in the future for these children. At Holly Beach, the days of swimming and exploring ended quickly. At the close of the season, Anshutz related to a friend in Philadelphia that he had "been making some pictures of kids lately," and lamented that "as they all have to start school next week, my occupation is gone."[3] [GS]

---

[1] Thomas Anshutz to Effie Anshutz, November 11, 1893, Reel 140, Archives of American Art, Washington, DC.

[2] Randall Griffin, *Thomas Anshutz: Artist and Teacher* (Huntington, NY: Heckscher Museum and the University of Washington Press, Seattle, 1994), p. 65.

[3] Ibid., p. 64.

Sand Burr

about 1894, watercolor on paper, 22 × 28 in.
Ann and Tom Barwick Family Collection

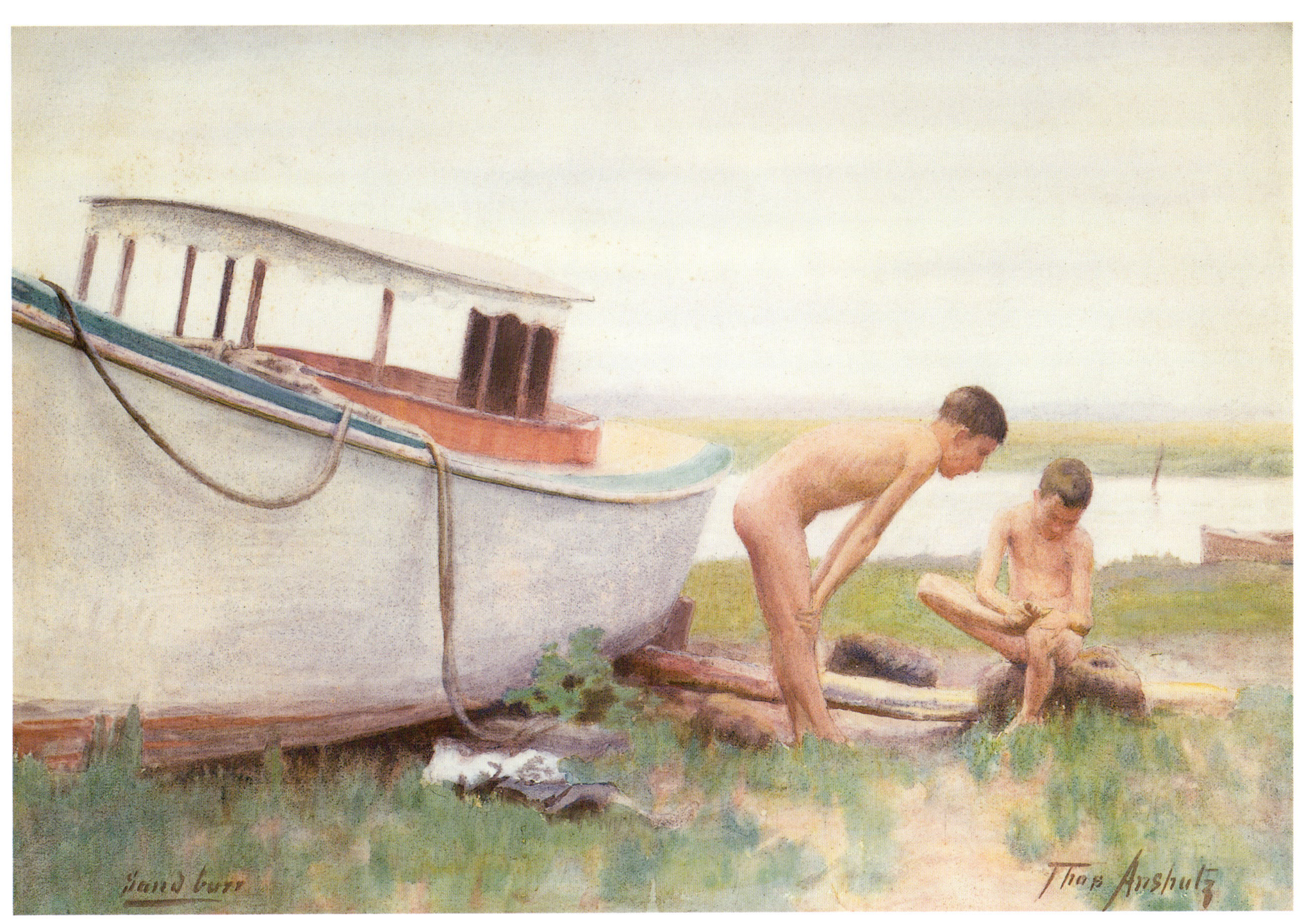
Sand burr
Thos Anshutz

Maurice Prendergast 1858–1924

Summer Visitors is one of the liveliest and most complex compositions that Maurice Prendergast painted after his return to Boston from Paris in 1895, where he was exposed to the work of the impressionists and postimpressionists. At Nantasket Beach, south of Boston, two women with parasols step precariously on the rocks (in the foreground), as does a young girl slightly farther back at the left. The twisting movement of their dresses, hiked above their feet, enhances the sense of bustling activity. Figures bend, stoop, sit, lean, stand, and walk at various angles, leading the viewer's eye to zigzag across the beach. The sand itself disappears intermittently under pools of water. Solidly modeled rocks anchor the foreground, while the hazy edges of clouds, created by painting wet-on-wet, enhance the feeling of a breeze that inflates the sails in the middle ground.

Prendergast's mastery of watercolor is evident in the subtle reflections in the shallow pools on the beach. With concise brushstrokes and minimal detail, he captured the various postures of people relaxing and playing on a sunny summer day. He also suggested the silhouette of the Massachusetts state capitol building in the Boston skyline. Touches of pink in the sky and the lavender cityscape in the distance evoke late afternoon when the sun is just beginning to set and the air is cooler. Prendergast created deep, airy space, but unified the composition on the picture plane with the harmonious blues of the sky, the water of Boston Harbor, and the pools on the beach, revealing his familiarity with these spatial concepts of European modernism.

Prendergast depicted the beaches, promenades, and harbors of Boston's south shore in large part because he wanted to create an American counterpart to the seascapes and shore scenes of European art. In the 1890s, Nantasket and the surrounding areas were cleaned up and transformed into places for Bostonians to spend their leisure time. Prendergast's shore scenes celebrated the improvements his home city had made. When shown in Boston, his works inspired civic pride, and when shown in other cities, they boasted of Boston's picturesque environs and modernization.[1] [JM]

---

[1] Nancy Mowll Mathews, *The Art of Leisure: Maurice Prendergast in the Williams College Museum of Art* (Williamstown, MA: Williams College Museum of Art, 1999), p. 22; and Richard J. Wattenmaker, *Maurice Prendergast* (New York: Harry N. Abrams and the National Museum of American Art, Smithsonian Institution, 1994).

Summer Visitors

1896, watercolor and pencil on paper, 19 × 15 in.
Collection of Ted Slavin

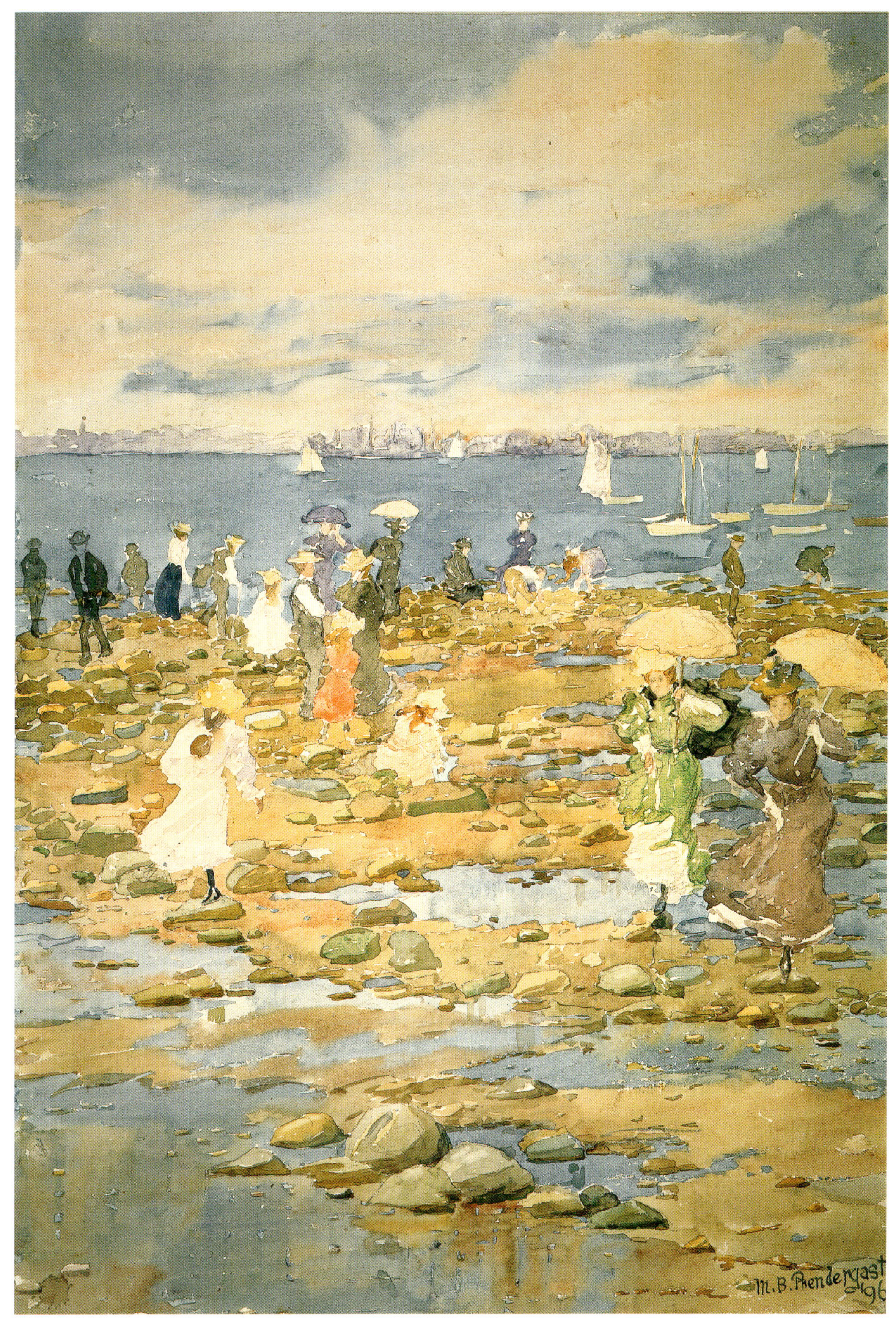
M.B. Prendergast
96

Edward Hopper 1882–1967

The summer of 1923 proved to be the turning point of Edward Hopper's life. He met his future wife, Jo Nivison, another Robert Henri student, and began painting in watercolor, a medium he had rarely used since his art school days. Hopper had been working in oil for twenty years, but had sold only a single canvas, ten years earlier. Although his etchings were in demand, his paintings were repeatedly rejected for exhibitions, and he resigned himself to making his living as a skilled but reluctant illustrator.

Hopper was within weeks of his forty-first birthday when he left New York City for Gloucester, a commercial fishing community and lively tourist destination on the Massachusetts coast just north of Boston. Rather than the seascapes and rural scenes popular among many summering artists—Milton Avery and Stuart Davis were regulars there—Hopper and Nivison explored sandy beaches and rocky shorelines and wandered the back streets, looking at the houses of ship captains and immigrant fishermen.

House in Italian Quarter is a tour de force of color. Brilliant in the midday sun, the orange façade, blue steps, and lavender shadows reveal a chromatic virtuosity never before apparent in Hopper's work. His use of watercolor, too, showed remarkable, if unforeseen, skill. Using a light pencil to trace in the basic forms of the house and yard, he then applied thin glazes of color, allowing puddles of translucent wash to form the rocks and grass. Drier pigment defines the slope of the hillside, and paper left unpainted captures the effects of light.

Hopper finished a dozen or more watercolors that summer, six of which were exhibited at the Brooklyn Museum's annual watercolor extravaganza in the fall. The real triumph, though, came when the museum purchased a watercolor called *The Mansard Roof* for its permanent collection. In July 1924, looking forward to another productive summer, Hopper and Nivison married and returned to Gloucester. By the fall, with several dozen works in hand, Hopper approached Frank Rehn, whose gallery featured contemporary American artists. Rehn immediately offered Hopper a show in a small back room. Critics raved and collectors bought. George Bellows, another brilliant colorist, chose *House in Italian Quarter* for his own collection. Hopper's career as America's best-known realist was launched. [VMM]

House in Italian Quarter

1923, watercolor on paper, 14 × 20 in.
Private Collection, Washington, DC

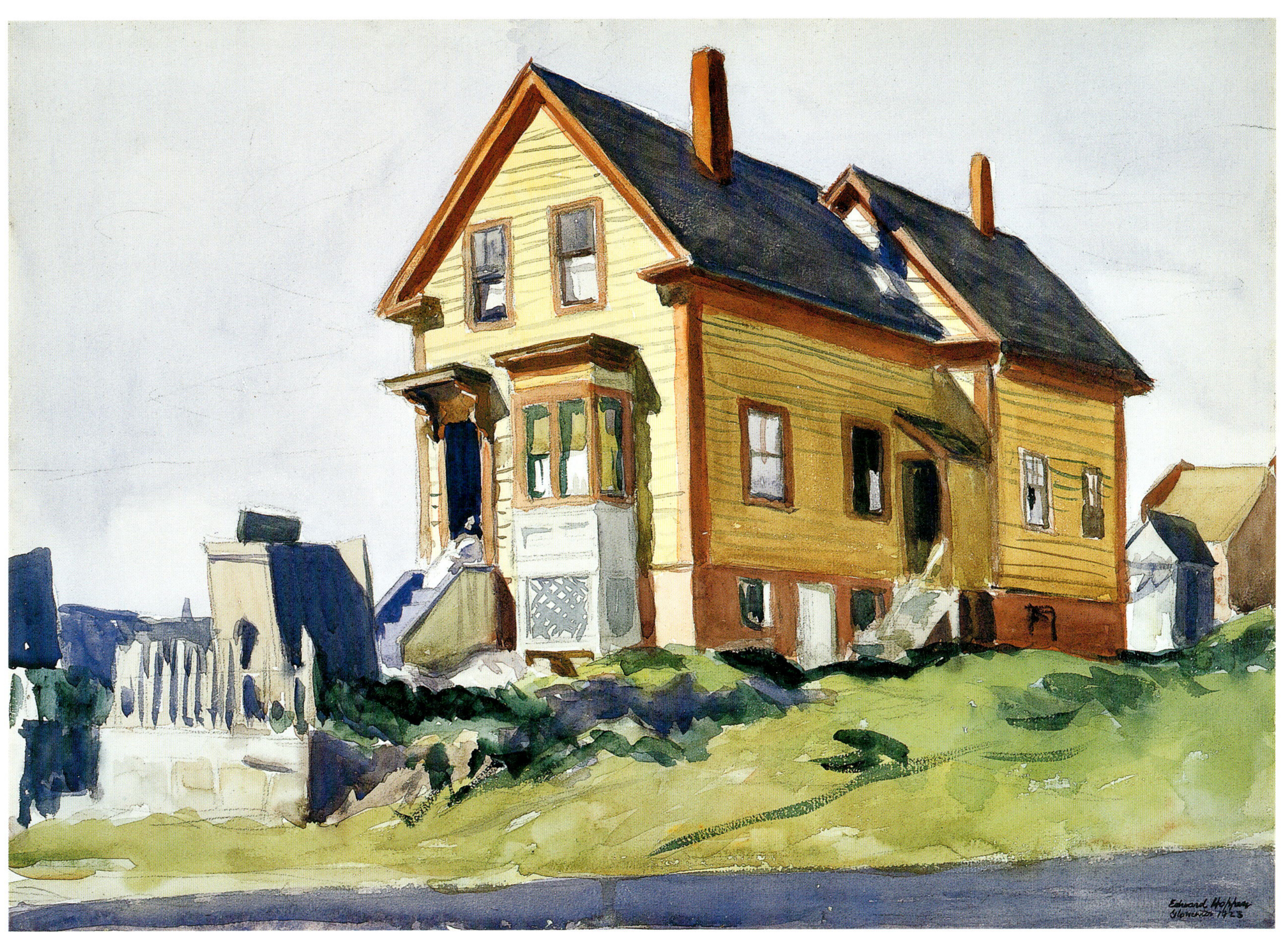
Edward Hopper
Gloucester 1923

William McGregor Paxton 1869–1941

William Paxton's portrait of fellow artist Ernest Fosbery is a graceful study of arrested motion. Palette and brushes in hand, Fosbery turns to acknowledge the viewer just as he is about to begin work on his own painting. His palette is prepared, his colors mixed, his medium cup in place. Along with the palette, he holds between his left thumb and forefinger a mahlstick and two brushes, loaded with yellow ochre and fleshy pink. He holds a third brush in his lowered right hand and appears ready to make the first strokes on his canvas. Everything speaks to careful preparation for embarking on a major painting, down to the carefully sketched design on the blank canvas, complete with penciled notes to guide his progress.

Fosbery looks at the viewer, and by extension at Paxton, with an air of self-possession. Paxton artfully framed his friend's profile against the blank canvas as though he were already its subject, with only the missing background needing to be painted. This picture-within-a-picture is a particularly apt device for one artist's portrait of another, but it ultimately pays homage to one of Paxton's favorite artists, Jan Vermeer. Fellow Boston school artist Philip Leslie Hale introduced Vermeer to his American colleagues in his 1904 publication *Masters in Art*, and Paxton responded with such enthusiasm that he helped write the first American monograph on the Dutch artist, published in 1913.[1] Paxton's interiors display a strong affinity with Vermeer's work, and in this portrait the ambiguous space, soft, warm light, and gentle expression recall *The Girl with a Pearl Earring*.

Paxton and Fosbery shared space in the Harcourt Studio Building in Boston from 1902 until 1903, when this portrait was probably painted.[2] Fosbery, a Canadian, studied with Paxton and remained in Boston from 1900 until 1910, where he became an established portraitist and illustrator. In November of 1904, Paxton exhibited this painting at the St. Botolph Club in a one-man exhibition of his work.[3] On November 11, fire destroyed the Harcourt Studios, then home to many of Boston's leading artists, and with it much of the work in their studios. Thanks to the exhibition, most of Paxton's finished work was safely on view less than a mile away. Paxton kept this portrait of his friend and pupil the rest of his life.[4] Fosbery later returned to Canada, where he became president of the Canadian Royal Academy. [EJH]

[1] Philip Leslie Hale, "Vermeer," *Masters in Art: A Series of Illustrated Monographs.* (Boston: Bates and Guild, 1904), pp. 211–52.

[2] Janice H. Chabourne, Karl Gabosh, and Charles O. Vogel, eds., *The Boston Art Club, Exhibition Record 1873–1909* (Madison, CT: Sound View Press, 1991), pp. 172, 302.

[3] St. Botolph Club, *Paintings by Mr. William M. Paxton* (Boston: 1904). This work is listed as no. 1 in the exhibition brochure.

[4] A card in Paxton's papers lists this painting as owned by Paxton's widow: "Ernest Fosbery The Painter, holding a palette 1904 owned by Mrs. W. M. P. 30 × 40." William Paxton Papers, Archives of American Art, Reel 3714, frame 1260, Washington, DC.

Ernest Fosbery, Esquire

about 1902–03, oil on canvas, 40 × 30 in.
Private Collection

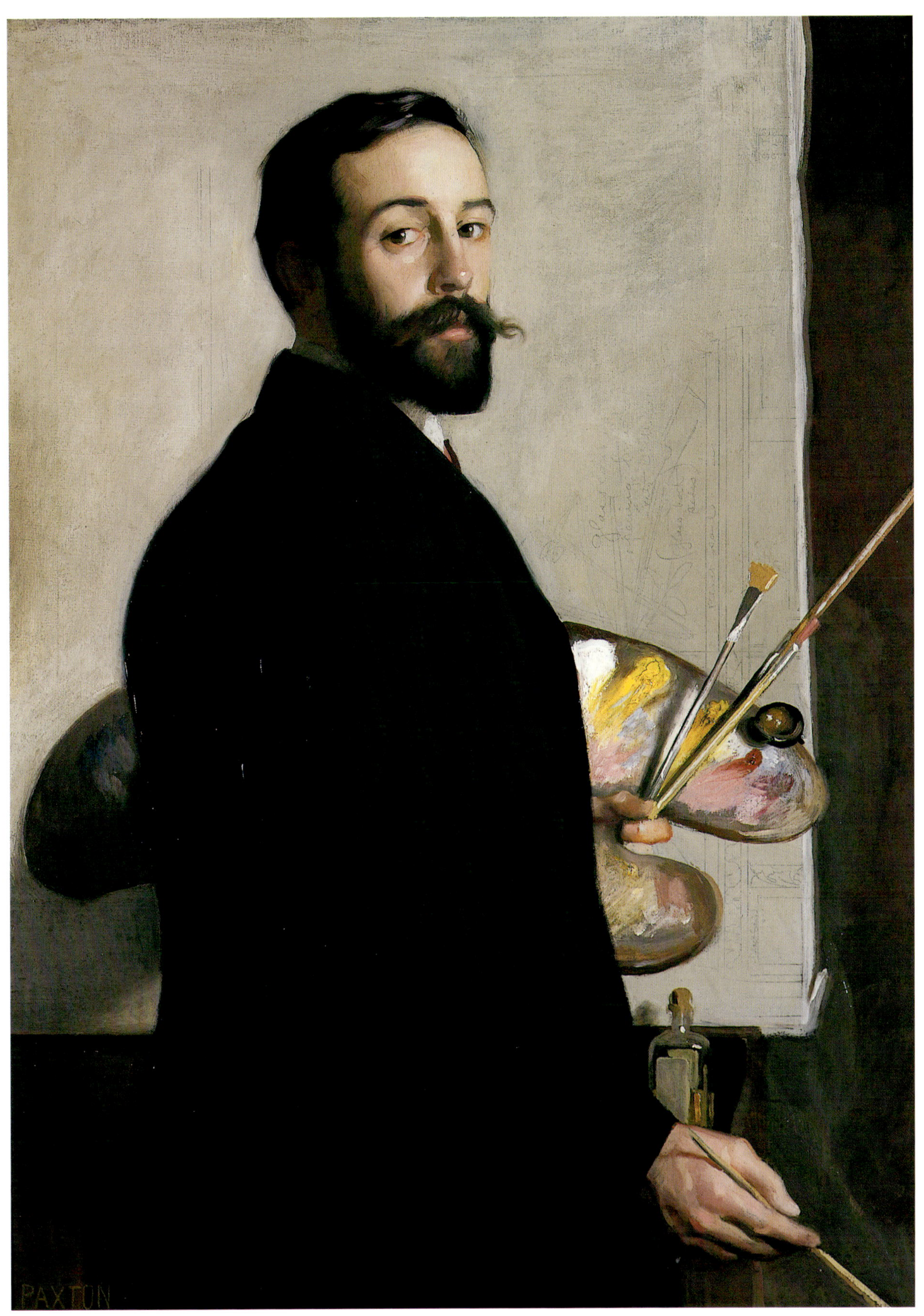
PAXTON

William McGregor Paxton 1869–1941

There is, in all too many married lives, what is called "the newspaper-at-breakfast stage."[1]

William Paxton's painting of a newly married couple at breakfast provides a telling glimpse into the unresolved aspects of domestic life for a modern Boston woman. The elegant yet spare breakfast room, ornamented with cut flowers, Asian ceramic jars and tea service, and the spacious, polished wood floor attest to the refined taste and ample income of the newlyweds. Yet all is not well on this sunny morning. The husband is absorbed in the morning paper while his wife sits opposite him, her presence all but overlooked. The reviewer in 1913 continued his observations: "It is often, as this picture indicates, the first intimation that comes to the bride that the days of her husband's courtesy to her are over. It is the first awakening, and a sad one."[2]

This domestic interior is painted in opalescent tones that suggest tranquility, but the mood in the room is decidedly darker. Her chair turned sideways, away from the table and her husband, the young wife is clearly unhappy with her current state of affairs. The glowing hues of her dress match those of the flowers, rendered in a flurry of silky brushstrokes, suggesting that both are decorative accessories to this young married couple's well-ordered world. Equally complementary are the white curtains and tablecloths that in their opaque color and severe brushwork resemble the starched white apron of the household serving girl. Both of the women in this painting have downcast eyes—the maid responding to her tasks and the wife to the realization that relinquishing household chores is no guarantee of domestic bliss.

The element of dismay in the painting underscores the tension intrinsic to the gradual liberation of women from menial household tasks, especially in turn-of-the-century Boston. There, as literacy rates rose, women found meaningful work outside the home, and there was a general celebration of women's intelligence as well as their beauty. But if the newspaper in the painting represents the pressing matters of the outside world, the husband's absorption in it speaks to the lingering expectation that the domestic realm is the woman's purview, and the external world primarily the man's. It will take more than marriage and a lovely home to make this new wife feel fulfilled. Clearly she is reviewing her options rather than settling for her present circumstances. [EJH]

---

[1] The quotation is taken from "*Breakfast:* Painted by William M. Paxton," *Ladies Home Journal*, vol. 30 (March 1913), p. 17.

[2] Ibid.

The Breakfast

1911, oil on canvas, 28 × 34 in.
Collection of Ted Slavin

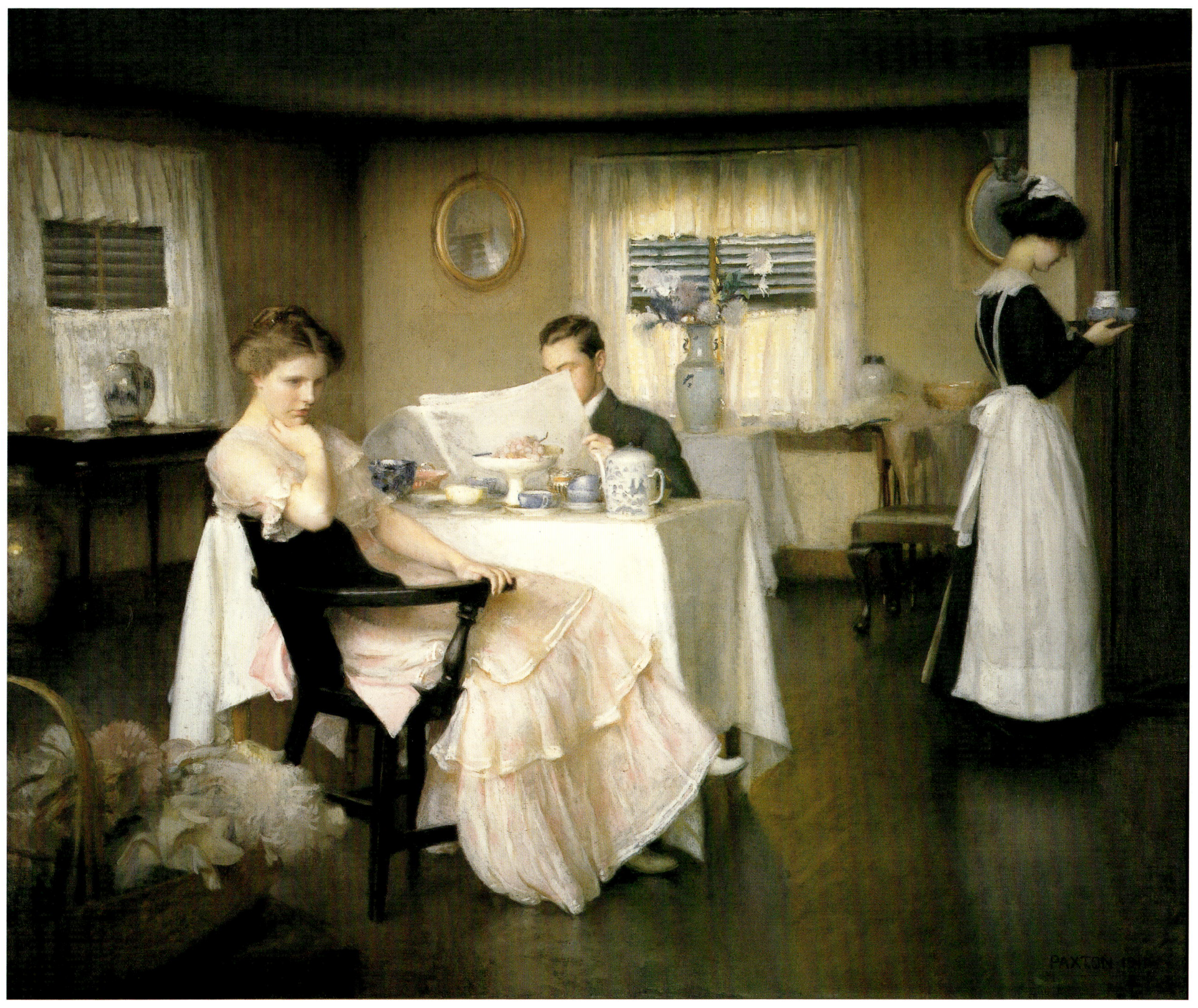
PAXTON

Edmund C. Tarbell 1862–1938

When Edmund Tarbell painted *Girl Cutting Patterns*, America was enthralled by its renewed exposure to Japanese art and culture. Called *japonisme*, the term was coined by a French critic to describe the broad array of Western borrowings from Japanese art. These borrowings often took the form of compositions inflected by the study of Japanese prints or the inclusion of Asian decorative accents in American interiors. In *Girl Cutting Patterns* a young woman in a Japanese print skirt and Western blouse and jacket sits on the floor, in Japanese custom. Her head is bent in concentration as she cuts *kirigami* patterns. A Japanese folding screen and Asian-inspired carpet soften the dark wood interior, creating an intimate setting that implies a high level of cultural sophistication.

The paintings of James McNeill Whistler had a profound influence on Tarbell's adoption of *japonesque* elements in his own work. In many of Whistler's paintings, Western women appear dressed in Asian kimonos, some examining Japanese prints, others carrying fans or painting porcelain jars. Tarbell had ample opportunity to absorb Whistler's influence, especially during the memorial exhibition for Whistler organized by the Copley Society in Boston in 1904. On view was *La Princesse du pays de la porcelaine* (Freer Gallery of Art), the artist's first major japonesque painting. Boston proved especially receptive to the Japanese taste, and merchants made Asian wares readily accessible to their sophisticated clientele.[1] Tarbell was among those ready buyers, and his personal collection included the Chinese porcelain jar that appears in this painting.[2]

In *Girl Cutting Patterns*, Tarbell presented his subject as a kind of girl in a gilded cage, a self-contained environment in which her absorption at her task mirrors her removal from the modern aspects of Boston society. During the early twentieth century, the genteel aspects of proper Boston society clashed with the more modern view of women entering the work force and asserting their rights as individuals. The supernal calm of Tarbell's dark interior also recalls the tranquility of Jan Vermeer's depictions of young women, an influence the artist acknowledged and the critics praised, lending this painting the air of a refuge from an increasingly complicated world.[3] [EJH]

---

[1] Maurice Baldwin, "The Whistler Memorial Exhibition," *New England Magazine* (May 1904): 292. The exhibition was organized by the Copley Society of Boston, and prominent guests at the opening were listed in the *Boston Evening Transcript* for February 24, 1904. See Trevor Fairbrother, "Edmund C. Tarbell's Paintings of Interiors," *Antiques* (January 1987): 234.

[2] A photograph of the jar is reproduced in Trevor Fairbrother, "Edmund C. Tarbell's Paintings of Interiors," *Antiques* (January 1987): 232–33, 234, n. 11.

[3] Kenyon Cox invoked Vermeer, drawing parallels in their arrangement of forms in their interiors, and the soft quality of light. Kenyon Cox, "The Recent Work of Edmund C. Tarbell," *Art in America* 14, no. 70 (January 15, 1909): 254–60.

Girl Cutting Patterns

1907–08, oil on canvas, 25 × 30 in.
Collection of Marie and Hugh Halff

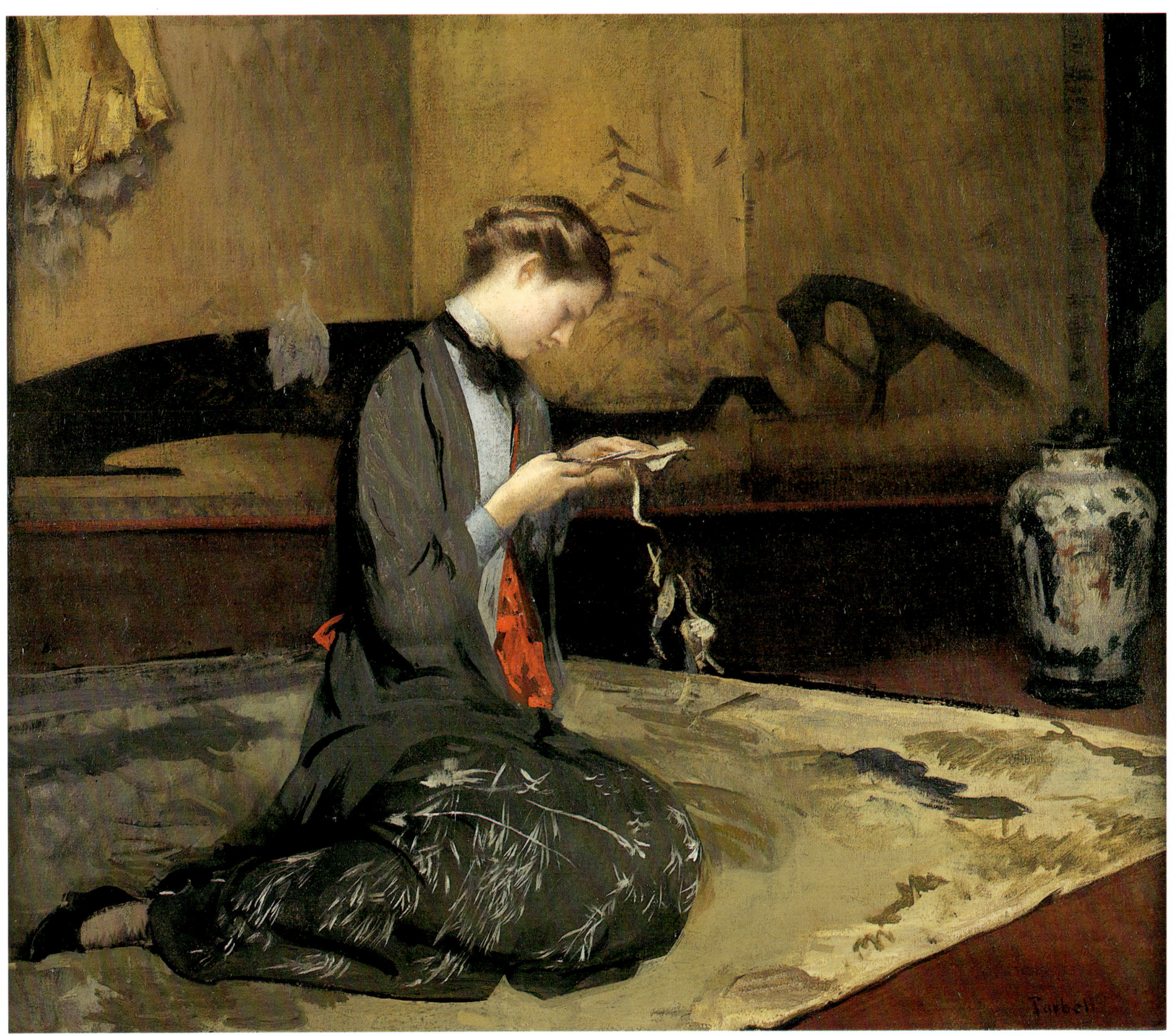
Tarbell

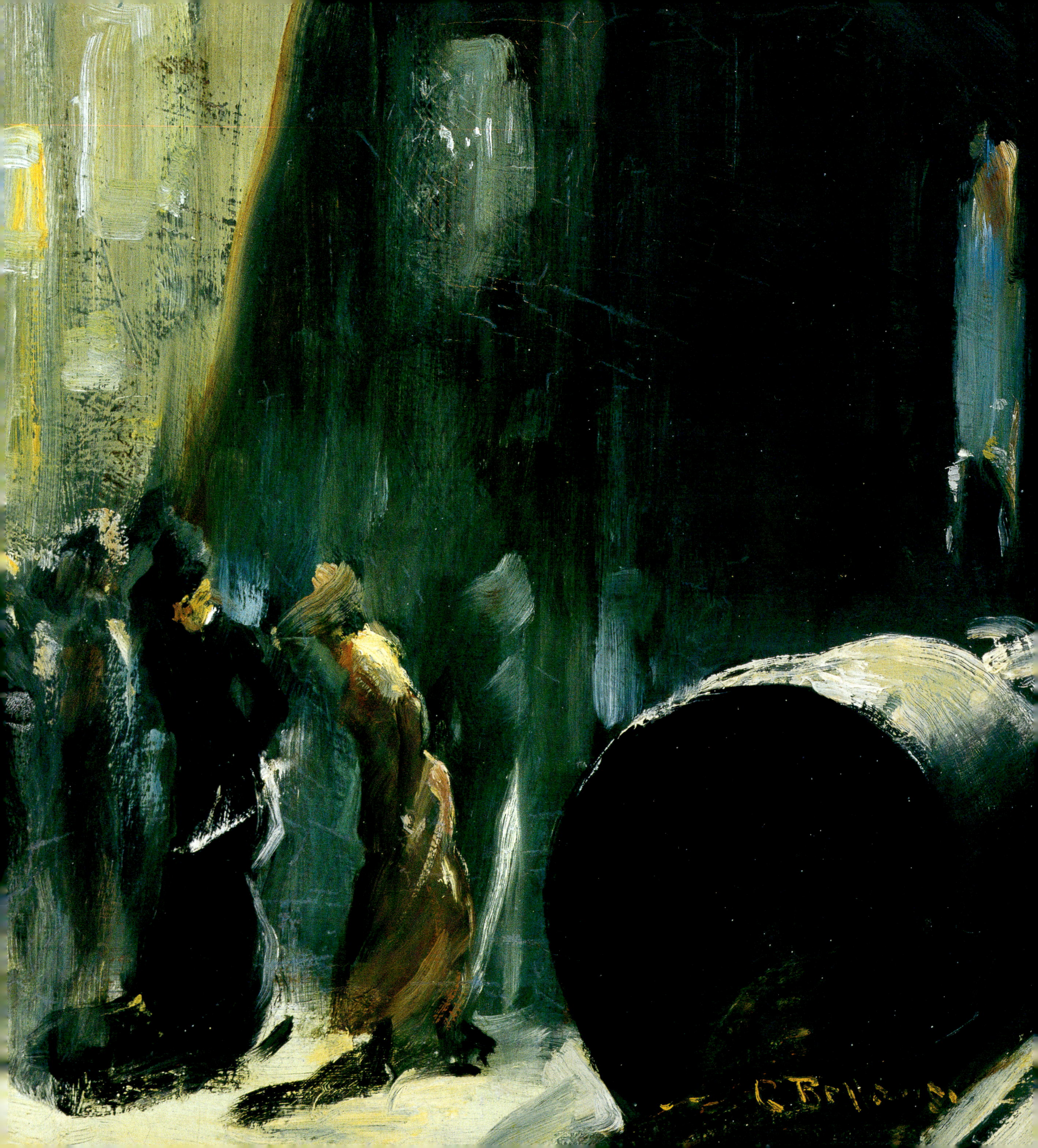

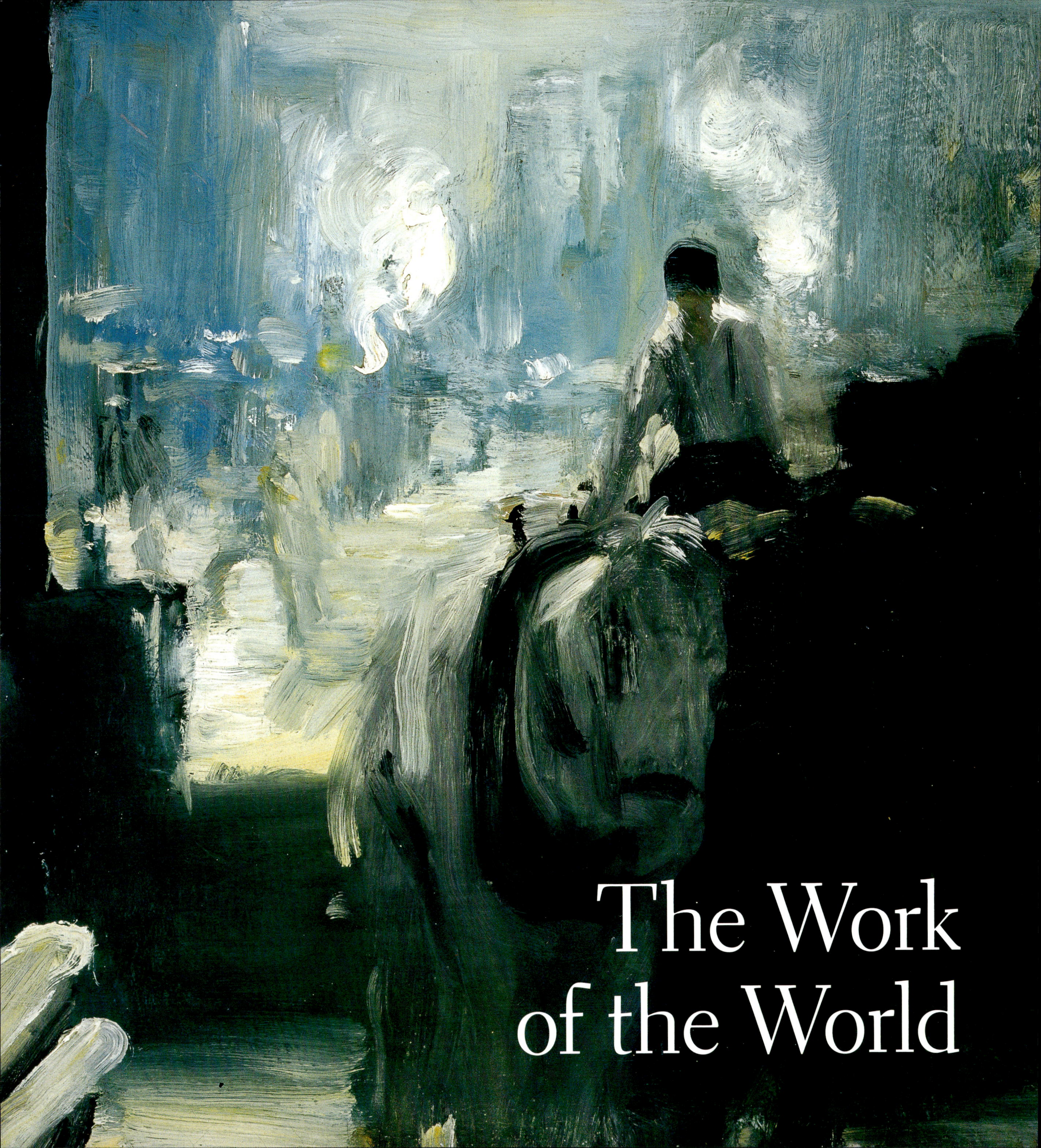

The Work of the World

Rockwell Kent 1882–1971

Rockwell Kent painted *Tugboat on the Hudson* during a pivotal year in New York when the artist's professional recognition and budding political awareness coalesced into a sense of mission. In 1904, two key oils, *Dublin Pond* and *Mount Monadnock*, both created the year before, sold at the Society of American Artists show and established Kent as a young artist to watch.[1] He had painted the works in New Hampshire as a guest of Abbott Handerson Thayer, with whom he had long conversations on art, nature, and the importance of the "strenuous" life.

In *Tugboat on the Hudson*, Kent made the transition from the New Hampshire hills to the city and its working class. Boatmen clamber between the tug and the barges to secure lines and cargo, dangerous work that sometimes pulled the deck hands under the barges or crushed them between the hulls. The painting foreshadows Kent's travels to Newfoundland and Greenland, where he worked as a longshoreman, among other trades. "Getting to know working people . . . was more to me than anything else in my life," he later recalled. "It came over me, my God what would people like myself be if people like that didn't do the work of the world for them."[2]

In its fluid paint and assertive brushwork, *Tugboat on the Hudson* is less studied than the New Hampshire pictures, and the anecdotal scene of labor signals the artist's convictions. His sense of social injustice led Kent, the son of a genteel but impoverished widow, to join the Socialist Party that year.[3] The party attracted many reform-minded artists and writers whose marginal careers helped them to identify with the working class. Kent's teacher, Robert Henri, and other Ashcan painters worked to capture the messy beauty of the modern world, motivated by reformist politics as well as by the spectacle of urban life.[4] By 1904, depicting nature alone was no longer sufficient for Kent, and *Tugboat on the Hudson* led directly to such works as *Afternoon on the Sea, Monhegan* (1907) and *The Road Roller* (1909), paintings that capture the uncertain balance of power between brave men and an often hostile world. [GS]

---

1 Jake Milgram Wien, *Rockwell Kent: The Mythic and the Modern* (New York: Hudson Hills Press and the Portland Museum of Art, 2005), p. 9.

2 "An Interview with Rockwell Kent . . .," conducted by Paul Cummings at Au Sable Forks, New York, February 26–7, 1969, *Archives of American Art Journal* 12, no. 1 (January 1972): 13.

3 Gemey Kelly, *Rockwell Kent: The Newfoundland Work* (Halifax, NS: Dalhousie Art Gallery, 1987), p. 13.

4 See Robert W. Snyder, "City in Transition," in *Metropolitan Lives: The Ashcan Artists and Their New York* by Rebecca Zurier, Robert W. Snyder, and Virginia M. Mecklenburg (New York: W. W. Norton and the National Museum of American Art, 1995), pp. 29–58.

Tugboat on the Hudson

1904, oil on canvas, 20 × 30 in.
Private Collection

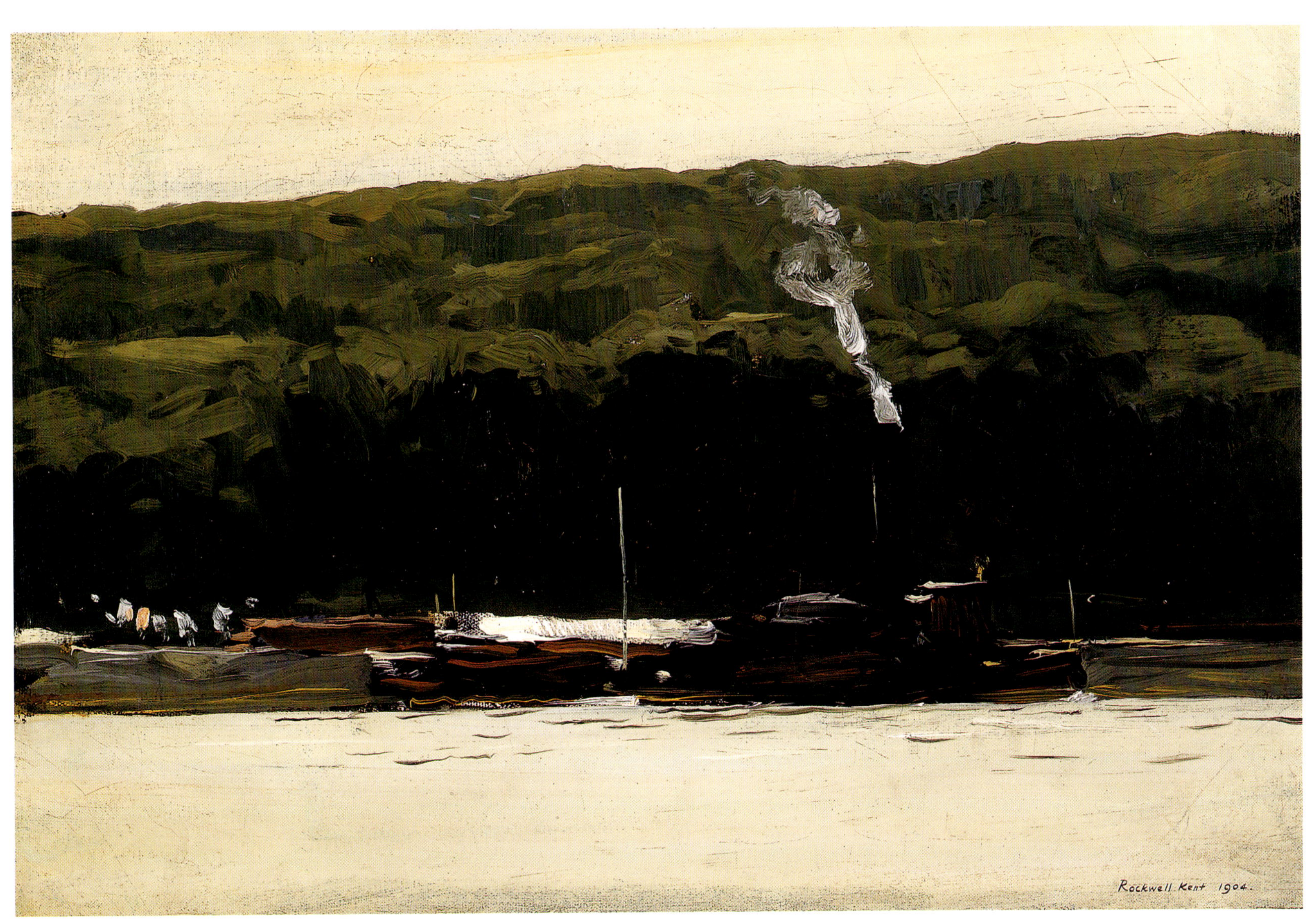
Rockwell Kent 1904.

George Bellows 1882–1925

For avant-garde artists New York was a city of icons. Max Weber, John Marin, Joseph Stella, Georgia O'Keeffe, and other abstract artists portrayed skyscrapers, the Brooklyn Bridge, the Flatiron Building, and other towering landmarks as symbols of progress and futurity.[1] For George Bellows, life in the streets, building sites, and commercial activity along the rivers that separated Manhattan from surrounding natural spaces were the "real" New York.

Bellows had come to the city from Columbus, Ohio, to study painting, after deciding against a career in professional baseball. When he arrived in 1904, he enrolled with Robert Henri, and took his teacher's advice to head to the streets for his subjects. Although critics derided his friend John Sloan for painting "ugly" aspects of urban life, Bellows was able to successfully negotiate the contentious New York art world. *River Rats,* the canvas he submitted to the 1906 annual exhibition at the National Academy of Design, easily passed the jury's muster.

As a newcomer to New York, Bellows was fascinated with the tumultuous transformations overtaking the city. *Noon* is full of contrasts that juxtapose older ways and new. The dark structure of the elevated bridge surrounds dray horses that pull an unseen load. An elevated train rumbles overhead. Cylindrical drainage pipes resting on a skid attest to the disruption caused by construction throughout the city. Bellows also provided a few clues about the time of year. The snowy street and steam indicate that the air is crisp, but the boy atop the horses is in shirtsleeves and the women wear light street clothes, so it is probably early spring.

Noon is a view New Yorkers might have seen on almost any day in almost any part of the city. It has the hallmarks of impressionist painting—light breaking though the clouds and billowing steam are classic impressionist motifs. But Bellows introduced an up-to-the-minute quality in the incident at the left. Passersby look down at an unidentifiable something on the sidewalk. It is the kind of vignette that prompted William Dean Howells to describe New York as an ongoing spectacle: "It [is] better than the theater. . . . What drama!"[2] [VMM]

---

[1] Wanda Corn, "The New New York," *Art in America* 61 (July–August 1973): 59.

[2] William Dean Howells, *A Hazard of New Fortunes* (1890; repr., New York: Signet Classics, 1965), p. 66.

Noon

1908, oil on canvas, 22 × 28 in.
Private Collection, Washington, DC

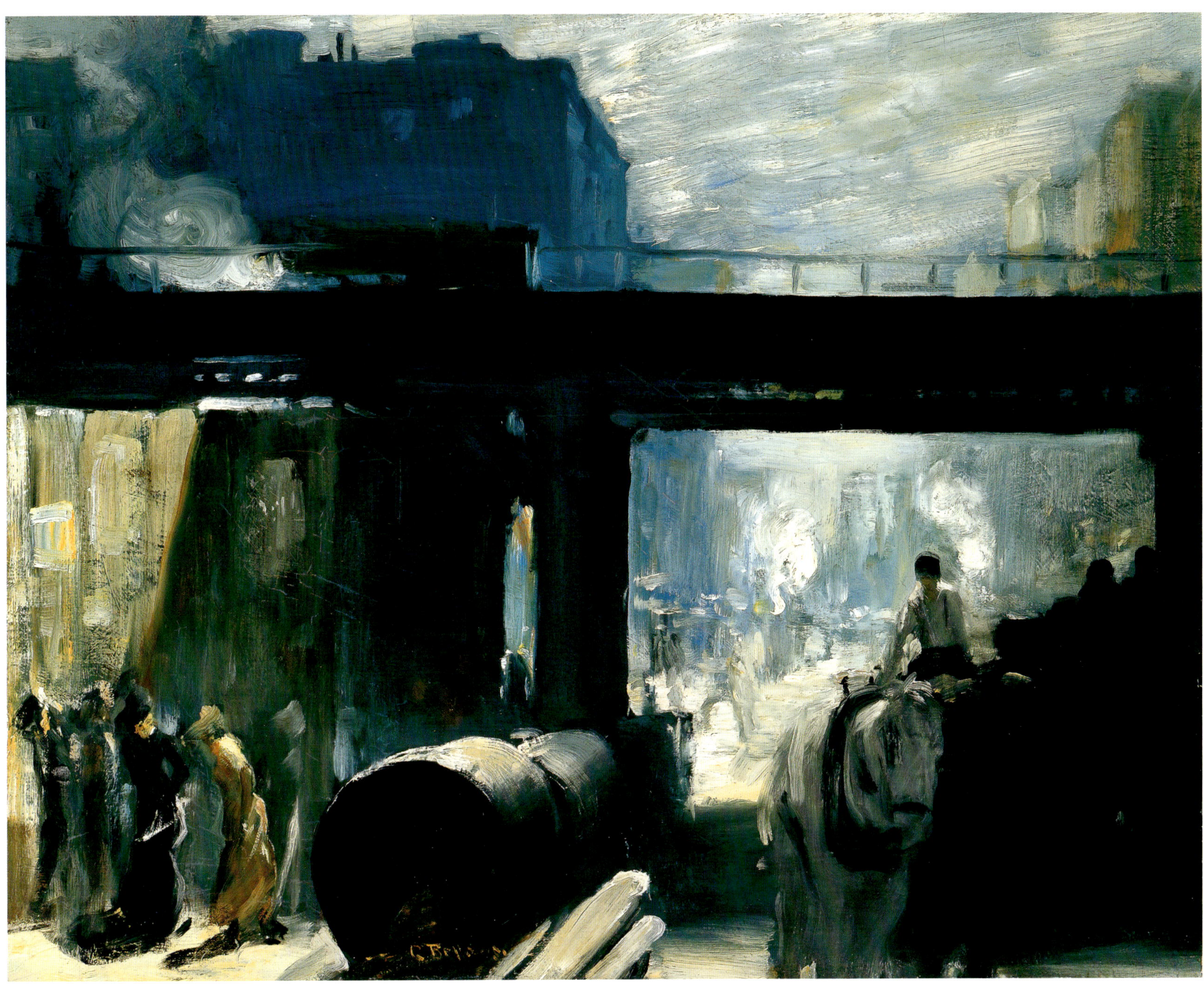

Everett Shinn 1876–1953

At the intersection of Broadway and Fifth Avenue, Madison Square in the late 1890s was one of New York's busiest and most glamorous public spaces. The square was home to elegant hotels and private residences, as well as the new Stanford White-designed Madison Square Garden, a magnificent Beaux-Arts building crowned with Augustus Saint-Gaudens's gilded sculpture *Diana*.[1] In 1898, the square was selected as the site for the city's triumphal celebration of Admiral George Dewey's recent victory over Spanish naval forces at Manila Bay. The Dewey Arch was a temporary structure, built as a backdrop for parades, troop maneuvers, and other festivities held for three days in late September.[2] Made of staff, a combination of lath and plaster reinforced with straw, the arch was dismantled just eighteen months later.

The arch was a perfect subject for Everett Shinn, who lived just a few blocks from the square. Having recently arrived from Philadelphia, where he worked as a newspaper sketch artist, he was fascinated by the contrasts he saw on the streets of New York. *Madison Square, Dewey Arch* is itself a study in contrasts. The arch gleams white against the subdued tones of surrounding buildings, and bright touches of red briefly delineate figures on a gray New York day. The real subjects of the pastel, though, are workers trudging along the path, some carrying lunch pails, some with hands in pockets, who are hunched against the cold. Behind them, boldly sketched in white, are imposing sculptures of American naval heroes, among them Captains John Paul Jones and Stephen Decatur and Admirals Matthew C. Perry and David G. Farragut that, with the arch, commemorated America's commanding power at sea.

The skill Shinn developed as a sketch artist for the *Philadelphia Press* newspaper served him well, especially when he worked in pastel. In the years before newspapers began using photographs to illustrate stories, Shinn worked on assignment, rushing to fires, accidents, and other newsworthy events to create images that appeared in the next day's paper. For Shinn, this meant capturing the character of people, a place, or an event at a particular moment. He became adept at rendering telling details—here lunch pails, body language, and bright white structures—that communicate the remarkable activities that played out in New York's public spaces. [VMM]

---

[1] Janay Wong, *Everett Shinn: The Spectacle of Life* (New York: Berry-Hill Galleries, 2000), pp. 23–24.

[2] "The Dewey Arch," *New York Times*, August 27, 1899.

Madison Square, Dewey Arch

1899, pastel, 20 ½ × 28 ½ in.
Private Collection

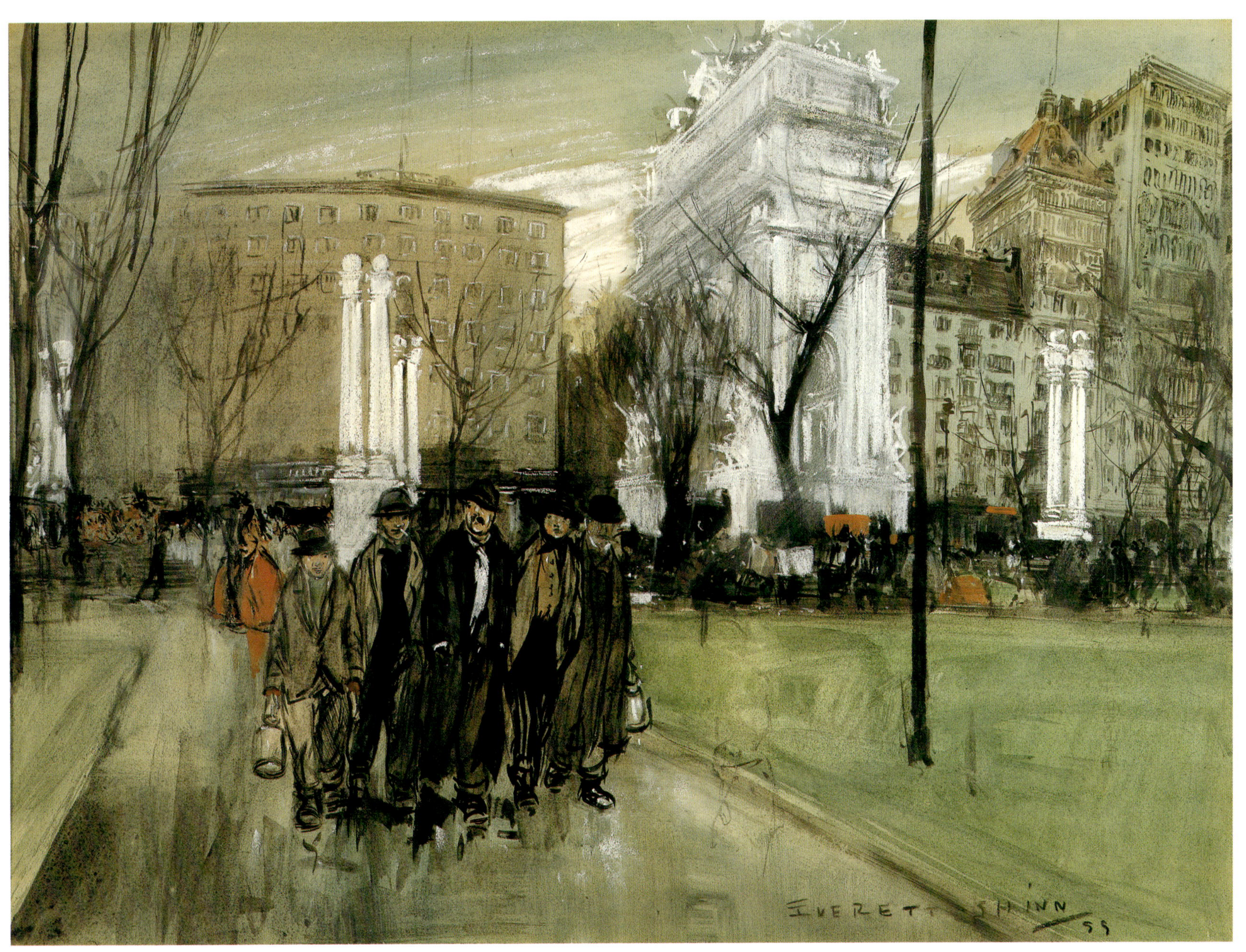
EVERETT SHINN

Everett Shinn 1876–1953

When I want to be sure to find beauty, I go to Washington Square. . . . That north side of [the] Square with the Washington Arch is fine. . . . The architecture of the row houses is the best—it is the only mark to be found in New York of a fine old city. Everett Shinn[1]

Washington Square had been designated a public park in 1827, and in 1835 was the site of the first public demonstration of the telegraph by Samuel F. B. Morse. The original wooden arch was erected in 1889 to commemorate the hundredth anniversary of George Washington's inauguration. It was replaced in the early 1890s with a marble arch, modeled after the Arc de Triomphe in Paris by Shinn's friend and patron, the noted architect Stanford White.

Shinn, who could see Washington Square from his home on Waverly Place, portrayed the effects of changing weather and light on the parklike space in at least twenty pastels and oils. Like the weather, his points of view varied. Sometimes he emphasized the design of the arch, so it seems as much a monument to White as to the country's first president. On other occasions the square functions as a backdrop for figures hurrying across a windy or snowy expanse. In still others he emphasized "the Row," the nineteenth-century homes on the north side of the square that have long been acknowledged as the finest Greek revival residences in New York.[2] This focus on historic buildings serves as a subtle reminder of their original owners—the statesmen, judges, and merchants who shaped the course of the city and the nation.

In *Washington Arch, After the Rain* Shinn highlighted the arch, the white columns and oriel windows of the corner house on the Row, and the more sketchily defined tower of Judson Church.[3] The church, which had added the tower in 1895 to house the poor, served the immigrants who lived in the run-down neighborhoods surrounding the square.[4] Shinn was acutely conscious of the economic and architectural contrasts. In *Washington Arch, After the Rain* he visually acknowledged the dramatic changes taking place in turn-of-the century New York. [VMM]

---

[1] The quotation is drawn from "What is the Most Beautiful Spot in New York?" *New York Times*, June 18, 1911, p. SM4.

[1] Bruce Weber, *Homage to the Square: Picturing Washington Square, 1890–1965* (New York: Berry-Hill Galleries, 2001), pp. 18–19.

[3] I am grateful to Bruce Weber for assisting with the geography of Washington Square and for identifying the building at the right as Judson Church.

[4] For information about the history and architectural design of the church, see http://www.nyu.edu/classes/finearts/nyc/westvil/judson.html (accessed March 24, 2006).

Washington Arch, After the Rain

1902, pastel, 19 × 23 in.
Private Collection

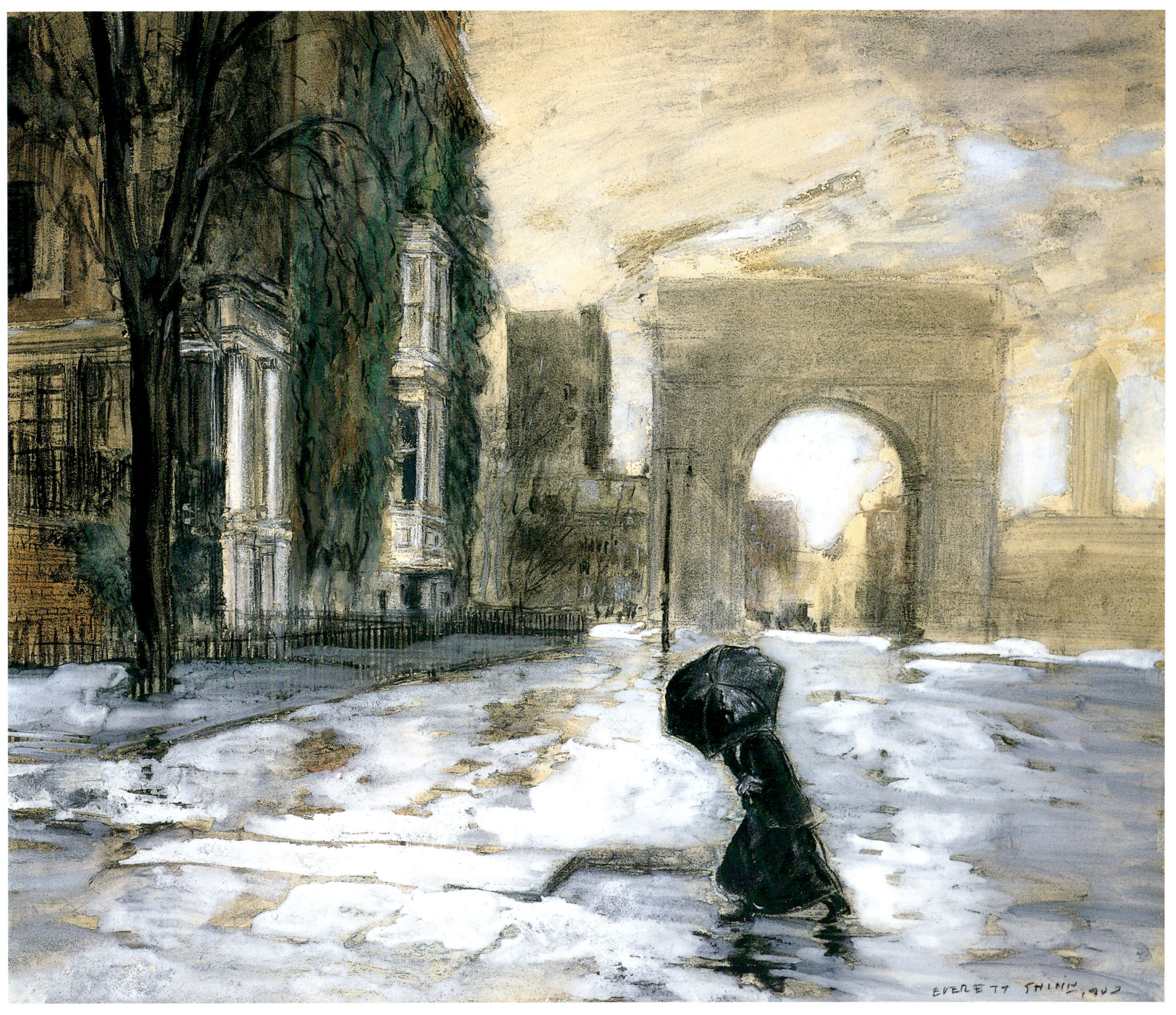
EVERETT SHINN

John Sloan 1871–1951

On March 28, 1907, after working all day on a painting of the fountain in Madison Square, John Sloan looked out his window, then noted in his diary: "Rained in the late evening and I saw an idea for a picture in the Flower Shop across the way. Stock out in front and open all night on account of Easter."[1] He started the painting the next day. A year later he selected *Easter Eve* to be one of just seven paintings to represent him in the now famous exhibition of The Eight at Macbeth Galleries in New York.

Sloan was an inveterate people watcher, who constantly roamed the streets and rode the elevated trains, observing New Yorkers in the parks, outside the theaters, and through the windows of their apartments. The amusing moments and telling interactions that played out in public and private spaces were his favored subjects, and he was attuned to the ordinary episodes of life in the nation's most populous city. Described by critics of the day as an impressionist, Sloan was sensitive to the way light transformed color, and he used atmospheric effects to define the character of his scenes.

In *Easter Eve*, a flower seller shows lilies to a couple who share an umbrella. Focused on the flowers, they take no note of a man who has just passed by or a woman who watches the potential transaction. The painting is a study in sightlines. The glances of the shadowy florist hoping to make a sale, of the couple examining the lilies, and of the woman who watches them create a web of human interaction. Sloan, too, participates as the unseen observer who records the scene. The focus on the foreground space and the shallow visual depth reinforce the sense of "you-are-there" immediacy. The contrast between the lighted interior shop and the dark night outside was a new subject for art in the early twentieth century, as electrification made night shopping not only possible, but exciting.

Of the seven paintings Sloan sent to The Eight exhibition, *Easter Eve* was the most appealing. Others, including a canvas showing a buxom blond hairdresser at work, another of an inebriated woman tottering across a street with beer bucket in hand, and a third depicting a raucous crowd in Herald Square on election night, featured subjects that transgressed the bounds of good taste. With its flurry of soft color, intimate grouping, and well-dressed protagonists, *Easter Eve* shows a gentler side of New York. [VMM]

---

[1] Bruce St. John, ed., *John Sloan's New York Scene: From Diaries, Notes and Correspondence, 1906–1913* (New York: Harper & Row, 1965), p. 116.

Easter Eve

1907, oil on canvas, 31 ¾ × 26 in.
Private Collection, Washington, DC

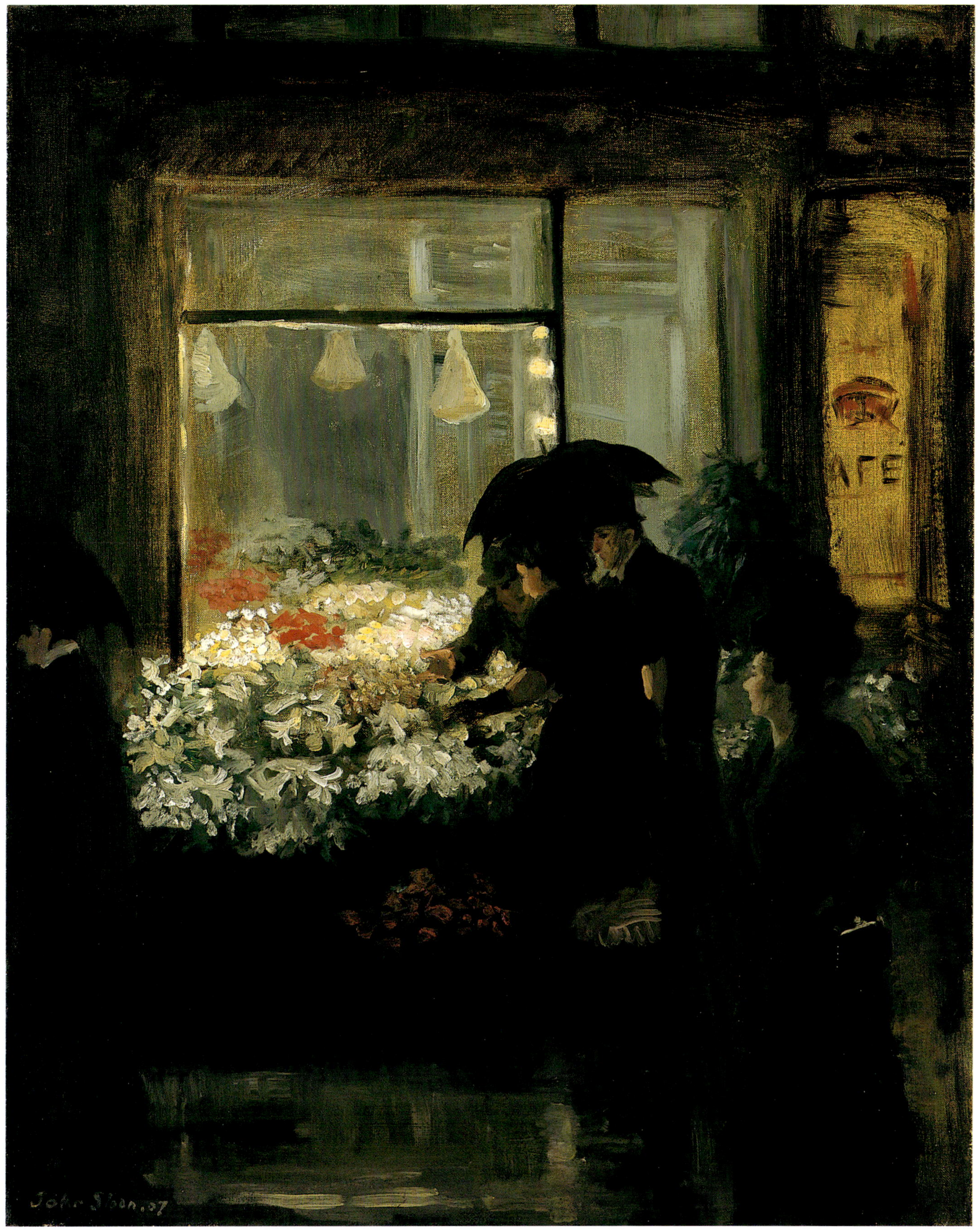

Guy Pène du Bois 1884–1958

Guy Pène du Bois led a double life. He was a skilled artist trained in Paris and New York who took on the role of reviewer and critic just after art school. It proved a productive combination. He was a steadfast voice supporting progressive art causes and, as editor, devoted an entire issue of *Arts and Decoration* to the 1913 Armory Show. Edward Hopper was just one of many struggling artists whose work came to public attention in stories that carried Pène du Bois's byline.

Pène du Bois was hired by the *New York American* in 1906, to replace his recently deceased father. He worked the police beat and had a short stint as a music critic before landing a job reviewing art exhibitions. He sometimes chafed at having insufficient time to paint, but the newspaper assignments put him in touch with con men, prostitutes, art collectors, socialites, and other "types" who provided an unending source of subject matter. He considered himself an observer of social interaction who highlighted the "manners [and] voluntary discrepancies" that convey human foible and pretension.[1] His figures are stylized, sometimes to the point of caricature, and are often shown in pairs with titles that suggest a pungent point.

Intellect and Intuition is more enigmatic than most of Pène du Bois's canvases. The women are less stylized than many of his figures, and the setting gives no clue about their identities or roles. Like other Pène du Bois paintings, the title is telling. The phrase "intellect and intuition" comes from French philosopher Henri Bergson, who presented a highly publicized series of lectures at Columbia University in 1913.[2] Bergson described the intellect as the pragmatic or utilitarian faculty, the seat of scientific and mathematical thought. Intuition, he wrote, deals with life itself and is the source of vitality and creativity. Bergson's book *Creative Evolution* came out in English in 1911 and was excerpted in *Camera Work*. Along with Wassily Kandinsky's *Concerning the Spiritual in Art* that appeared the following year, it provoked spirited debate among artists about the nature of art and abstraction.

In Bergsonian terms, the women in *Intellect and Intuition* can be understood as allegories. The figure with the shadowy face probably represents intellect, with the more voluptuous figure signifying creativity. The similarity of their appearances, though, invites speculation about how different they really are. It is likely that Pène du Bois, like so many of his contemporaries, viewed intellect and intuition as inseparable components within the artistic personality. [VMM]

---

[1] Guy Pène du Bois, "Caricatures Are Difficult to Draw, Because They Must Be Devoid of Malice," *New York American*, August 8, 1910, quoted in Betsy Fahlman, *Guy Pène du Bois, Painter of Modern Life* (New York: James Graham and Sons, 2004), p. 23.

[2] Louis Levine, "The Philosophy of Henry Bergson and Syndicalism," *New York Times*, January 16, 1913, p. SM4.

Intellect and Intuition

1918, oil on panel, 20 × 15 in.
Private Collection, St. Louis

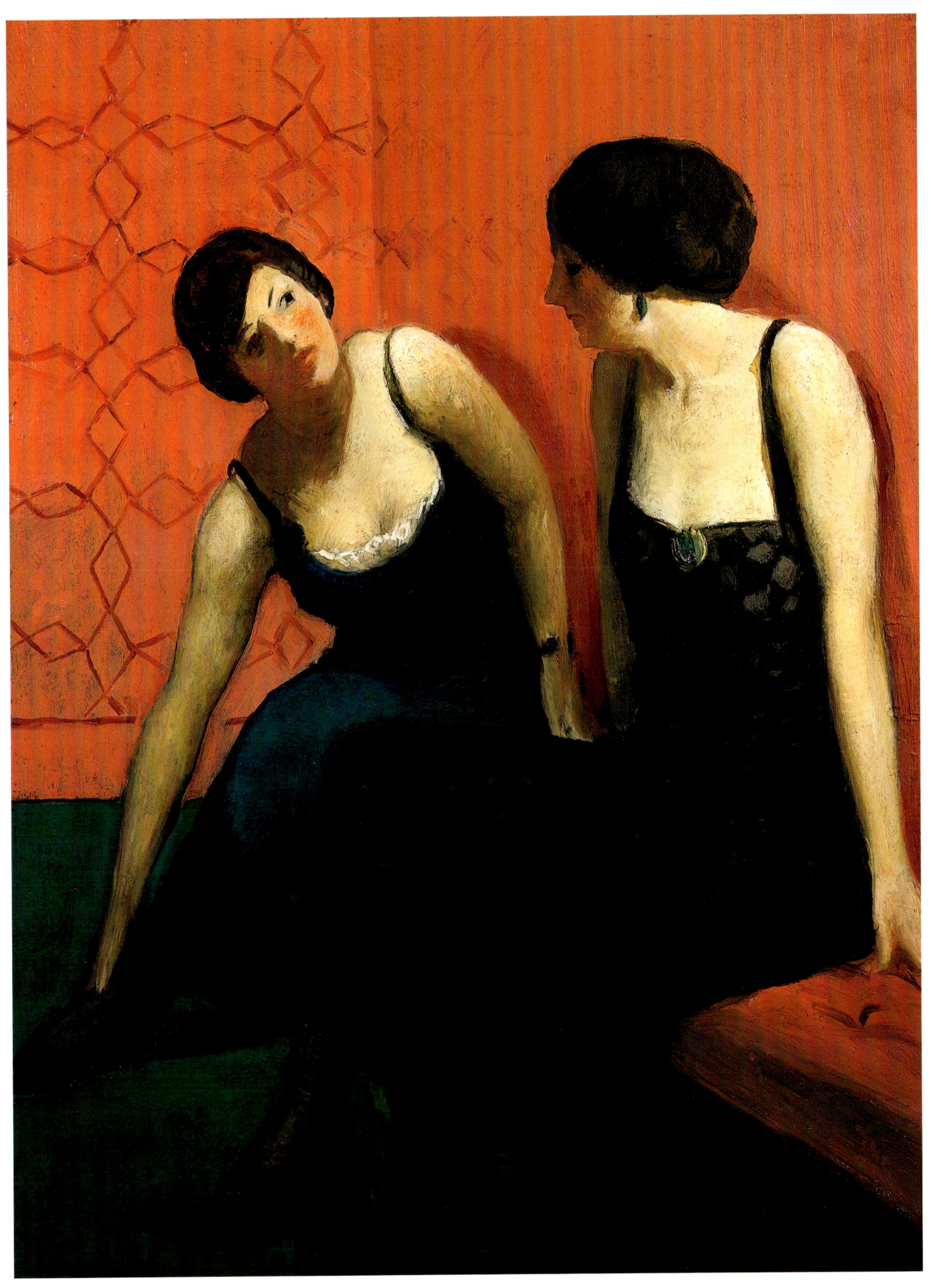

William Glackens 1870–1938

The odalisque tradition of portraying a female figure reclining on a couch is long and distinguished in the history of art. Titian, Ingres, Delacroix, Cézanne, Manet, Matisse, Renoir—for each the motif served different ends. The word odalisque means chambermaid, female slave, or concubine in an oriental harem. For Ingres, whose odalisques wear turbans and look directly at the viewer, the definition seems apt, although critics often ignored the invitation implicit in their gaze and discussed instead the beautiful, sinuous line of their forms. For others, notably Cézanne and Matisse, the odalisque offered a way to explore light, color, and pattern without the distraction of narrative subject matter.

William Glackens conceived *The Purple Dress* as a contemporary odalisque. The reclining figure projects a saucy air. Fully clothed and wearing shoes and a hat, she seems poised to leave as soon as the artist has finished his work. The brushstrokes are loose throughout the canvas, and especially so along the wall at the lower left, as if the painter has hurried to accommodate her quick departure. Neither the spatial configuration nor the psychological impact of the woman's gaze is the result of accident. The wallpaper pattern and crosshatched surfaces fill the interior space, and the Victorian couch (a prop that appears in a number of Glackens's figure paintings) defies the third dimension by casting no shadow on the wall.

The work's combination of historical pose and modern surface reflects Glackens's own changing artistic concerns. He painted it just as Alfred Stieglitz was introducing vanguard European art at 291, his Fifth Avenue gallery. In France in 1895 and again in 1906, Glackens became intrigued with the way Manet, Degas, Renoir, and other late-nineteenth-century artists manipulated space and reinterpreted traditional subject matter. With *The Purple Dress*, Glackens took his initial plunge into modernism, so he was the ideal choice when his high school chum Albert C. Barnes asked him to travel to France in 1912 to buy art. The canvases Glackens purchased—by Manet, Degas, Renoir, Cézanne, van Gogh, Gauguin, and Matisse—launched the now world-famous Barnes collection in Merion, Pennsylvania. [VMM]

The Purple Dress

1908–10, oil on canvas, 25 1/4 × 30 1/4 in.
Collection of Ann and Tom Cousins

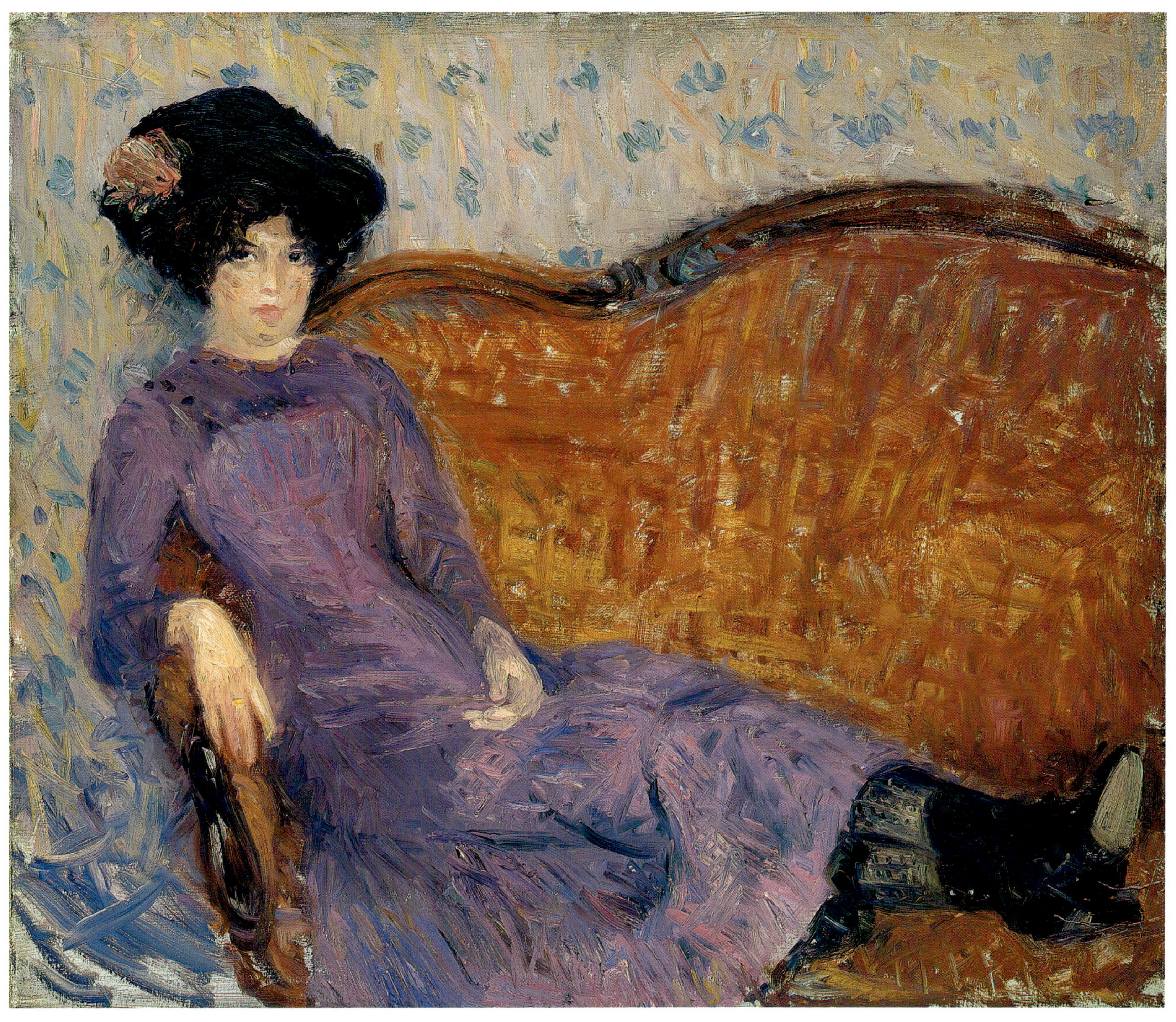

Robert Henri 1865–1929

The River Marne was sparkling that day in 1896 when Robert Henri watched a boatman pulling a skiff ashore. He stood across the river, observing the water and the people in the crowded, darkened structure that served as a pavilion at Joinville-le-Pont, just outside Paris. Parallel boats seen from the side, a man and child descending steps to the water's edge, and a woman holding a parasol angled against the sun—each element in the painting plays a distinctive role in this quiet scene.

Henri was in France for the second time. He had first come as a student in 1888 and stayed for three years. The second trip, begun in June 1895, marked his emergence as a fully fledged, if still young, painter of portraits and plein-air landscapes. Within days of arriving, he had visited the huge salon exhibition. The "miles and miles of pictures" encouraged him: "There is," he wrote his parents, "lots of room at the top in art."[1] Determined to depend no longer on his parents for financial support, Henri, on this second trip, organized an art school, painted, and spent long hours in the Louvre, the Durand-Ruel Gallery, and the annual salon exhibitions. He examined canvases by Manet and Degas at the Luxembourg Museum, and, on a trip to the Low Countries, studied paintings by Rembrandt and Hals.

At Joinville is evidence of lessons well learned. Henri stroked a paint-laden brush fluidly across the canvas and blocked spatial depth, à la Manet, by darkening the pavilion interior. Complementary colors laid down side-by-side and quick touches of paint on the water energize the palette and attest to his growing modernism. On Henri's return to the United States, this painting and eighty-six others featured in a solo show at the Pennsylvania Academy of the Fine Arts in Philadelphia impressed critics and public alike. Henri's "sense of color is rich and individual and his feeling for the beauty of masses is extraordinary," declared the reviewer for the *Philadelphia Item*. Henri, he concluded, had spent a "profitable" three years.[2] [VMM]

---

[1] Robert Henri letter, June 16, 1895, quoted in William Innes Homer, *Robert Henri and His Circle* (Ithaca, NY: Cornell University Press, 1969), p. 85.

[2] "Special Exhibition by Robert Henri," *Philadelphia Item*, October 22, 1897, Robert Henri Papers, 887: 65, Archives of American Art, Washington, DC.

At Joinville

1896, oil on canvas, 30 × 36 in.
Collection of Ted Slavin

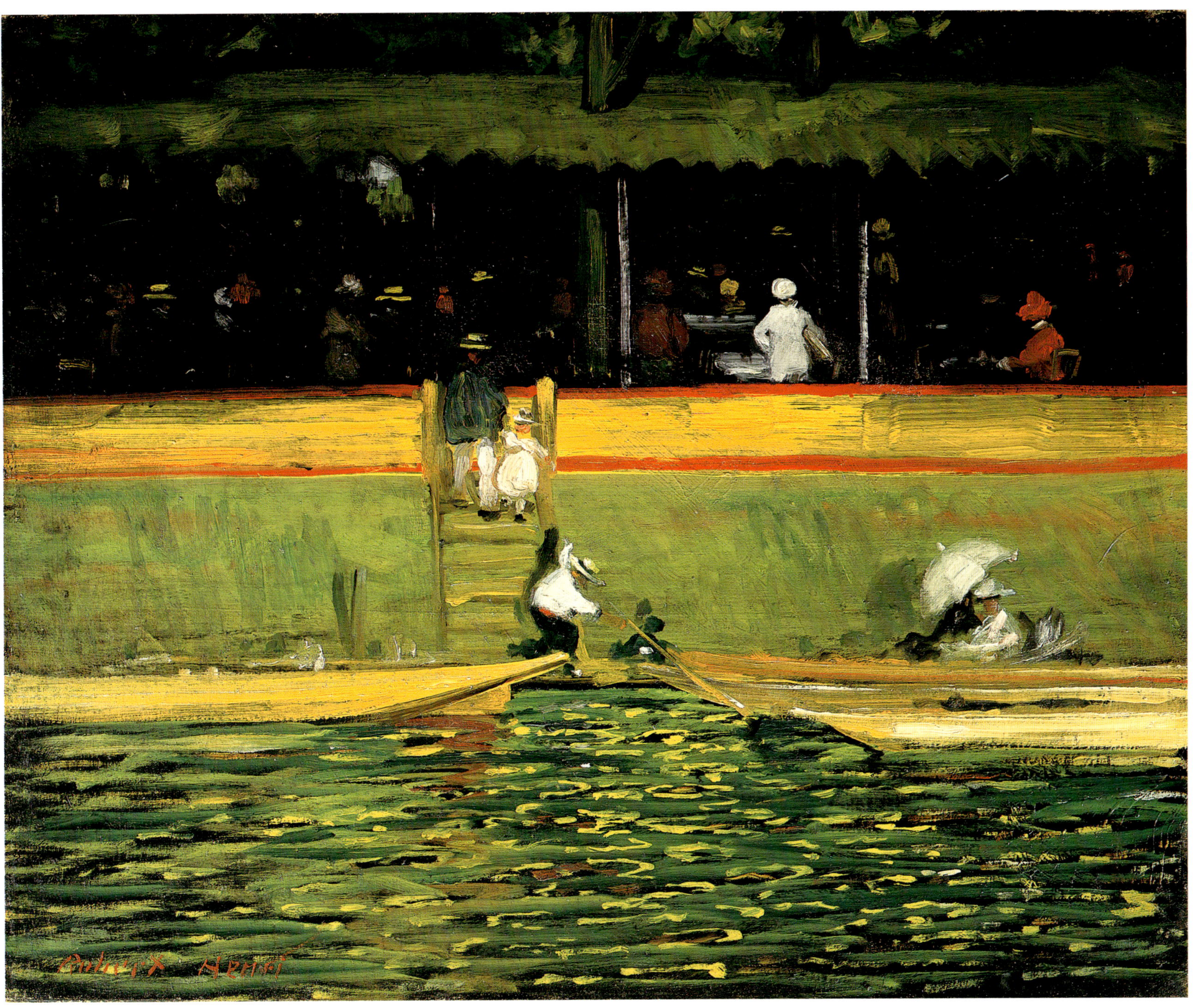

Robert Henri 1865–1929

No. 25. blue sky. sun yellow pavilion... tel-pole... brilliant colors of people on beach walk & in pavillion. blue strip of sea. Robert Henri, July 14, 1902[1]

With these few brief lines, Robert Henri noted his observations the day he painted *Far Rockaway.* He had come to Long Island to visit his parents, after a busy but productive spring. A portrait he had sent to a prestigious exhibition at the Society of American Artists in New York was singled out by a critic as "graceful...simple in coloring... powerfully marked out upon its background," and his April show at Macbeth Galleries was warmly received.[2] Among the seventeen paintings in the exhibition were canvases showing a blizzard blanketing Manhattan brownstones, figures racing for cover during a sudden rain shower, and clouds scudding across a clear sky. These works attracted critical attention, and reviewers described him as an impressionist adept at showing the effects of weather and atmosphere. His own words, though, reflect a compelling interest in the color of that serene summer day at Far Rockaway Beach.

Henri had traveled to Paris several times in the 1890s and, on returning from his latest trip, moved from Philadelphia to New York. In Paris he painted landscapes and street scenes, balancing concerns of color, structure, place, and people and worked out a philosophy of art that would guide not only his own work but also that of hundreds of students who flocked to this charismatic artist's classes. In just a few years he would be as well known for sending his students to the streets to find their subjects as for the portraits and increasingly fewer landscapes he exhibited in New York's galleries and the independent exhibitions he championed.

At first glance, *Far Rockaway* describes a gentle summer day at a beachside resort. On closer examination, the painting communicates a sense of a specific place through a few telling cues. American flags over the pavilion are whipped by a sea breeze (wind that blows from the water when the land heats up on a warm day). Women in bright dresses holding striped parasols and the crowd gathered in the shadows of the beach pavilion attest to the bright sun. Always attuned to structure, Henri balanced the inert forms of ramp railings, the "tel-pole," and waterside buildings with color patterns that evoke casual life on a carefree day. [VMM]

---

[1] The quotation is taken from Robert Henri's *Diary*, July 14, 1902, 885:871, Archives of American Art, Washington, DC.

[2] "Pictures by Robert Henri," *New York Times*, April 9, 1902.

Far Rockaway

1902, oil on canvas, 26 × 32 in.
Private Collection

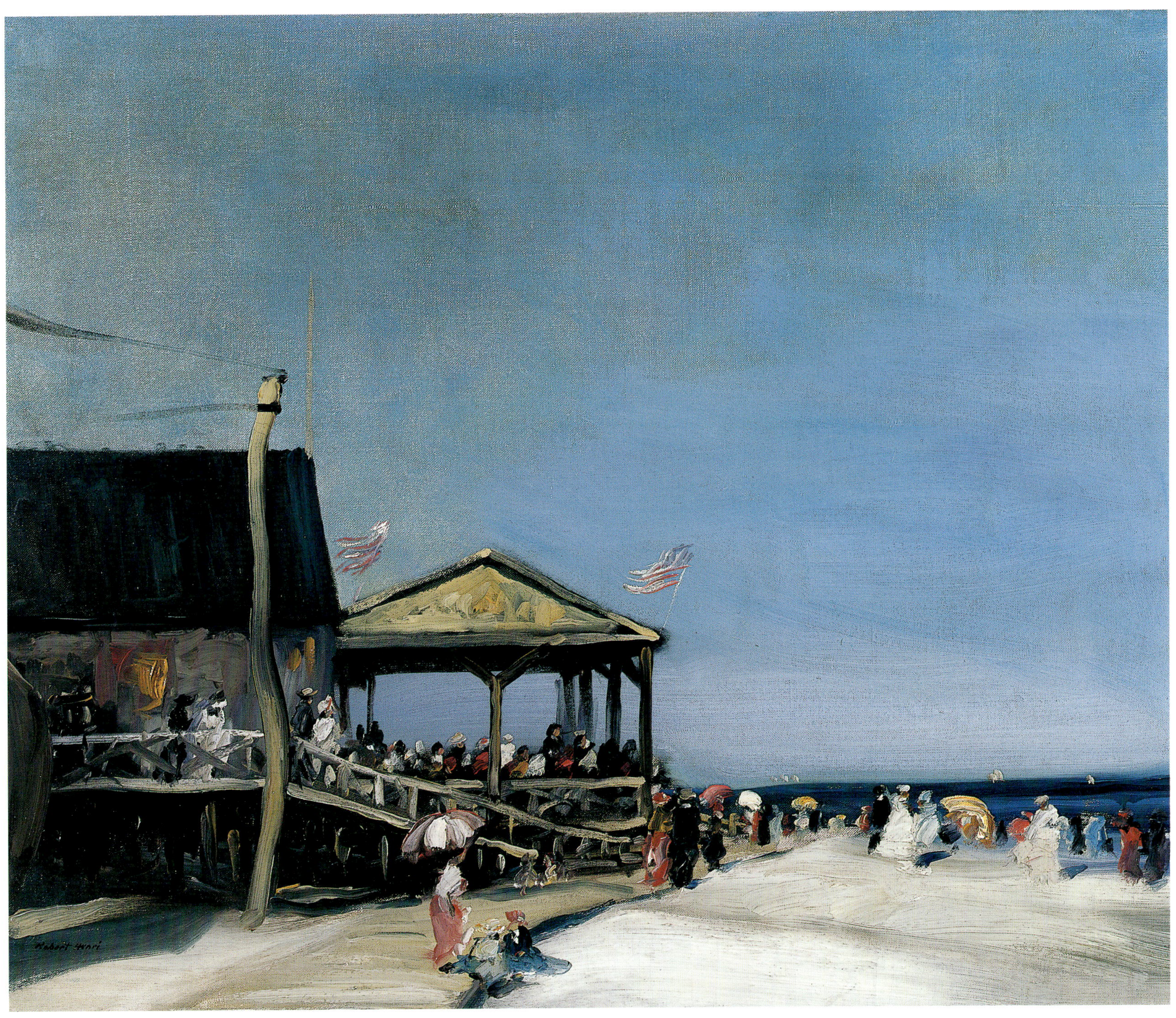
Robert Henri

Howard White McLean 1879–1952

Arms held high, a white-garbed conductor alerts musicians seated in a bandstand. Sunlight strikes pastel-colored parasols and a sea of flamboyant hats. The scene—a concert in Central Park—celebrates people on a glorious afternoon in New York. For those who knew the city well around 1908, Howard White McLean's *Central Park* would also have served as a reminder of social shifts taking place in the nation's largest city.

Until the 1870s, Central Park was the domain of the well-to-do, who paraded in elegant carriages in the late afternoon. By the 1890s, after a successful lobbying campaign on the part of the city's reform movement, concerts on Sundays (the only day of rest for many) attracted New York's working- and middle-class residents. Shop girls, factory workers, office employees, and immigrants congregated in the city's parks to enjoy the music and fine weather. Adorned in inexpensive, ready-wear finery, they came as much to see as to be seen and were walking advertisements for another urban innovation—the department store—that made shopping accessible and exciting to all.

McLean, like his contemporaries John Sloan, Everett Shinn, and William Glackens, roamed the city's streets in search of subject matter. He was drawn especially to scenes of people at leisure. Paintings of women strolling alone or in pairs during the evening hours suggest that he, like Sloan, was fascinated by the increasing freedoms enjoyed by young women in the city. Little is known of McLean's life or career, but the subjects of his paintings reflect the teachings of Robert Henri. The resemblance of several existing oil sketches to the early work of George Bellows and Edward Hopper implies that, like them, McLean knew the work of Sloan, Glackens, Henri, and the other artists now known as the Ashcan group. [VMM]

Central Park

1908, oil on canvas, 34 × 36 in.
Collection of the Honorable Marilyn Logston Mennello and Michael A. Mennello

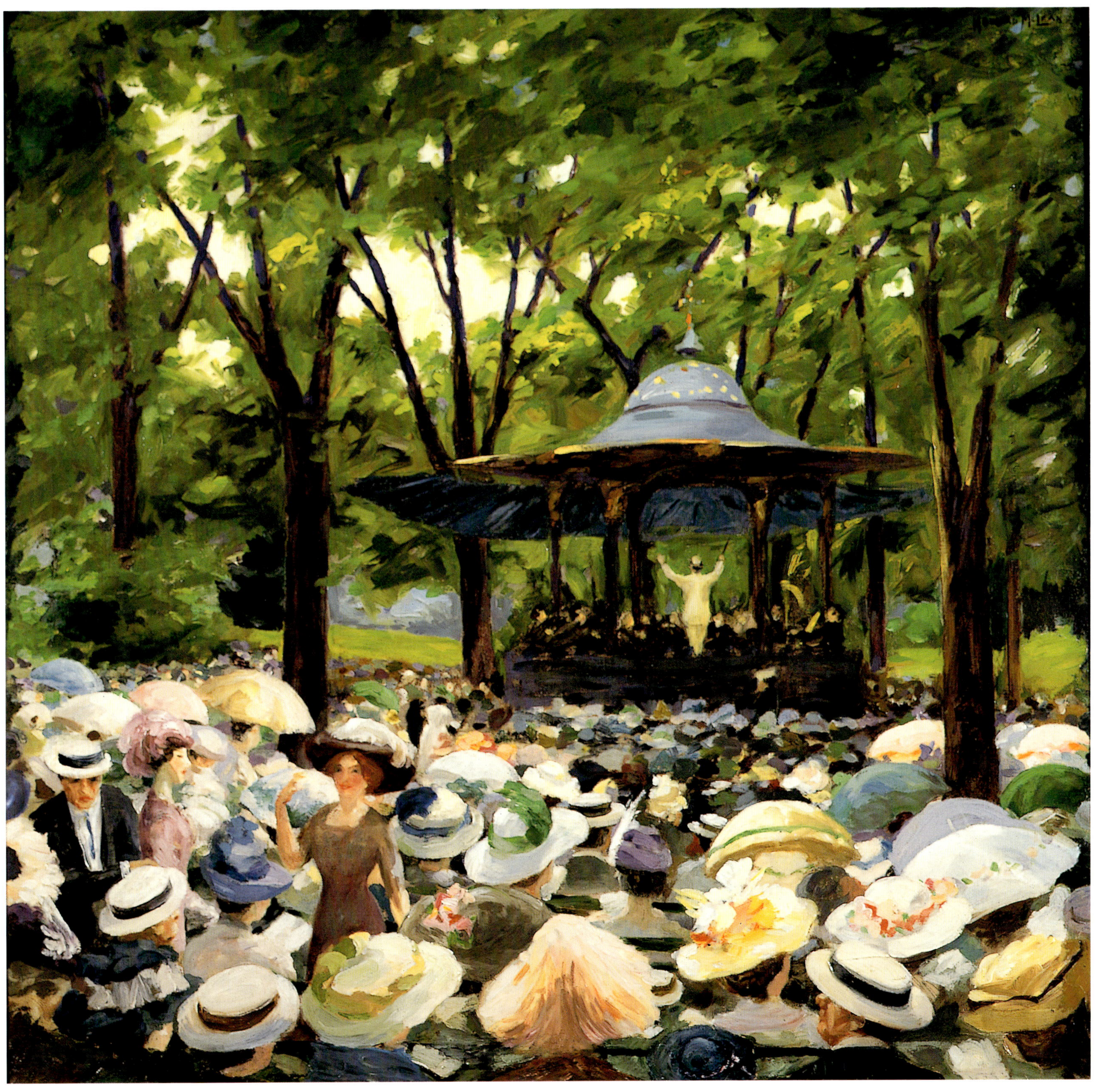

William Glackens 1870–1938

By ten o'clock on summer evenings, Buen Retiro Park in downtown Madrid comes alive. Families stroll and children play as the sweltering heat of the day yields to cool night breezes. In 1906, William Glackens and Edith Dimock, his wife of two years, left for Spain and France on a much-delayed honeymoon. Days studying art in the Prado and evenings relaxing in the cafes and in Buen Retiro Park provided an unending source of material for a painter and illustrator whose work was in demand.

Glackens worked as an artist-reporter for several Philadelphia newspapers after graduating from high school. In 1896, he moved to New York to pursue jobs at the *Herald* and the *World* and to draw illustrations for the *Saturday Evening Post*, *Scribner's*, *Putnam's*, *McClure's*, and other popular magazines. By 1906, when he left for Europe, the demands of this career vied with his desire to paint full time. His work was attracting positive attention from New York critics, and he had won important prizes in museum shows. His paintings and drawings were featured in several exhibitions a year, often with those of his friends Robert Henri, John Sloan, and Everett Shinn, but sales had not yet freed him from illustration work.

His proficiency as a draftsman, though, served him well when he decided to paint the crowds in Retiro Park. Always on the lookout for expressive gestures and body language that conveyed humor or pathos, Glackens discovered a wealth of material in the postures of the adults crowded into the park and in the shenanigans of carefree children. A bonneted baby squirms to get down from her mother's lap; a child crawls on the ground, heedless of her clean white clothes; a little girl flaps her skirt, unaware that her bloomers show; and, at the left, a foppish man in a light-colored hat fans himself.

In the 1890s and early years of the twentieth century, commercial firms produced thousands of stock photographs of cityscapes, beach scenes, and especially streets and parks for magazines, postcards, and guidebooks. Although full of descriptive information, these photographs rarely captured the nuances and visual hierarchies at which Glackens was so adept. According to a widely read critic of the day, Glackens captured "the fluidity of a world in motion," rather than the frozen moments of the photograph.[1] This is especially true of *In the Buen Retiro*, which has preserved the evening's antics for posterity. [VMM]

[1] Joseph Edgar Chamberlin, "Two Significant Exhibitions," *New York Evening Mail*, February 4, 1908, p. 6.

In the Buen Retiro

1906, oil on canvas, 30 × 36 in.
Collection of Ted Slavin

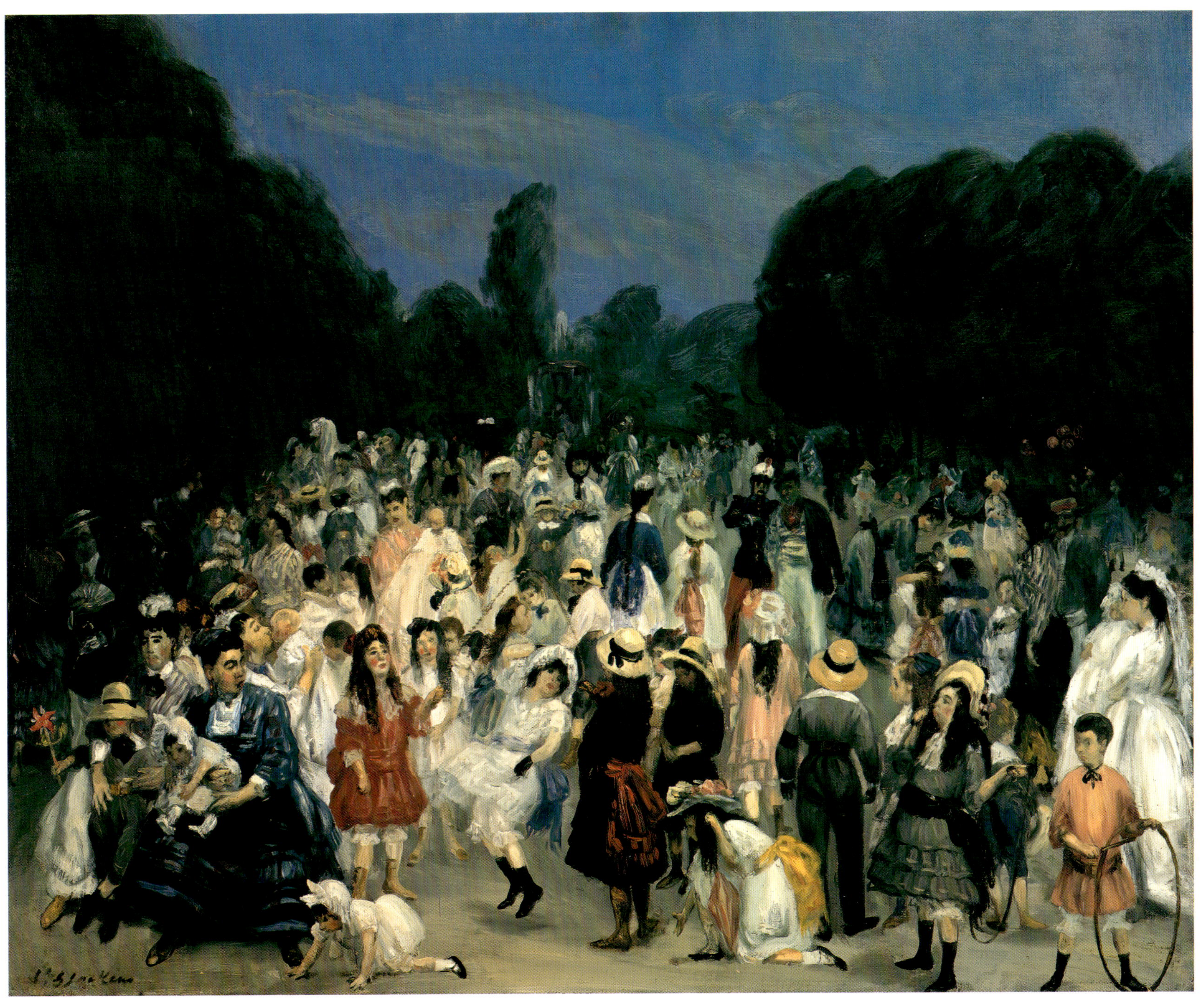

Reginald Marsh 1898–1954

Golf Course Scene is a composite of anecdotes derived from Reginald Marsh's visits to the country clubs around New York City. Elegantly dressed players sip from flasks, bemoan their shanked drives, and send caddies to search for balls lost in the water. Marsh had come to Manhattan in 1920 after graduating from Yale, where he had drawn cartoons for the campus *Record*. He worked as a staff artist for several newspapers, honing his reportorial skills and indulging a lifelong appetite for the hustle of urban life. Marsh came from a privileged background, and his good friend the art historian Lloyd Goodrich recalled that the artist was comfortable in any social setting "from dime-a-dance joints to the Stork Club."[1]

During the 1890s, golf courses sprang up on farmland in New Jersey and Long Island, and by the Roaring Twenties, golf and tennis had become the prestige sports favored by stock-market millionaires. Baggy plus-four trousers and natty shirts started a new fashion sweepstakes. Social posturing on the fairways provided artists with a new theme in American painting, and artists such as Childe Hassam and George Bellows joined Marsh in capturing life on the links.

Golf Course Scene recalls the backdrops and curtains Marsh painted for the Greenwich Village Follies and the Provincetown Theater during these years, and signals his transition from illustration to serious painting in 1923. The artist rarely painted on this scale again until he created his famous murals for the New York Customs House in lower Manhattan. *Golf Course Scene* strikes a balance between sharp observation and gentle humor, a characteristic that would define Marsh's work for the rest of his career. "How good it is to be alive and able to paint," he once said. "What a hole in the life of the painter if the privilege were taken away."[2] [GS]

---

[1] Lloyd Goodrich, "A Tribute to Reginald Marsh," in *Selections from the Felicia Meyer Marsh Bequest* (New York: Whitney Museum of American Art, 1979), n.p.

[2] Reginald Marsh, "Let's Get Back to Painting," *Magazine of Art* 37, no. 8 (December 1944): 293.

Golf Course Scene

1922, oil on canvas on three panels, 72 × 75 in.
The Dicke Collection

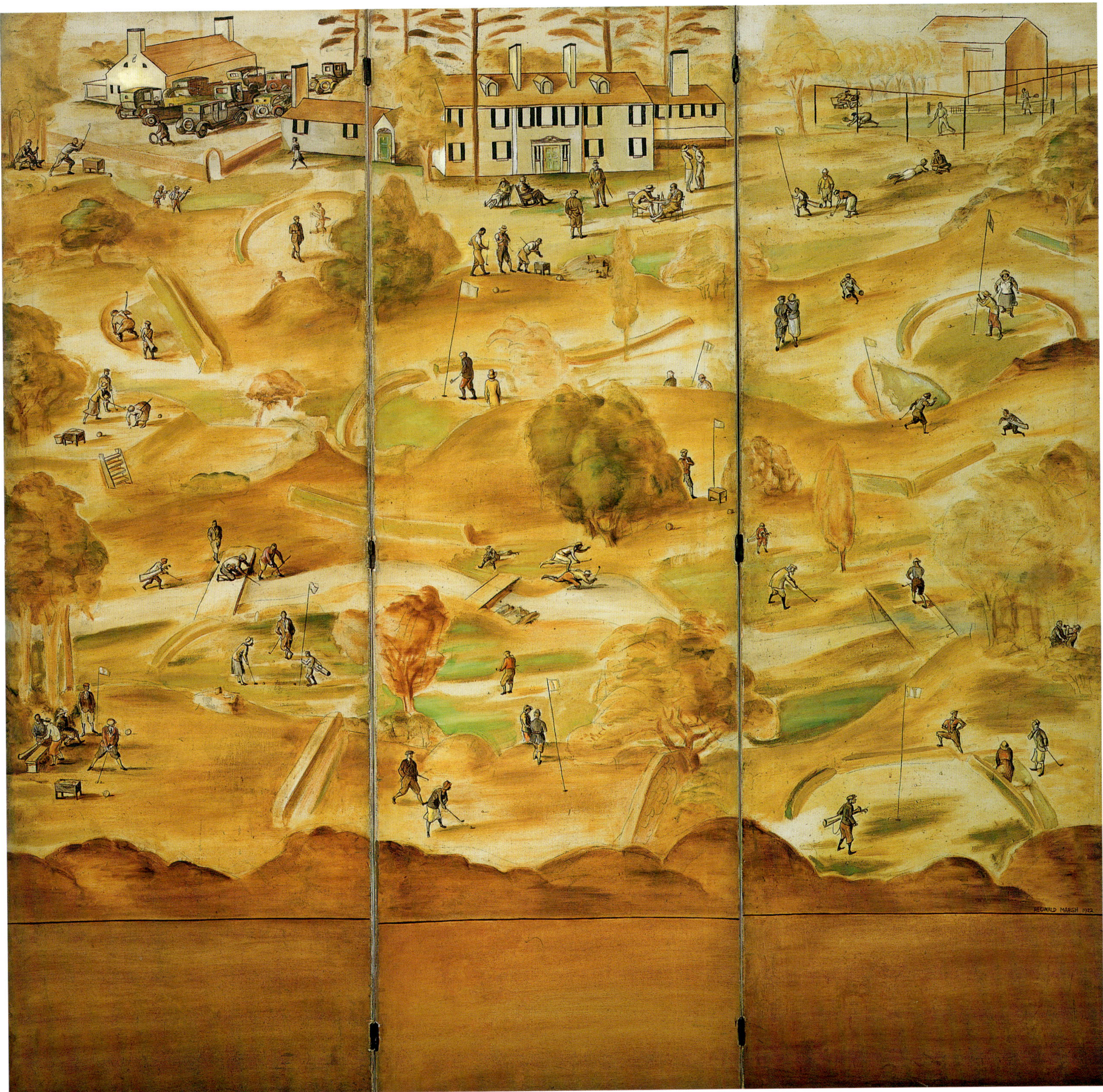
REGINALD MARSH 1922

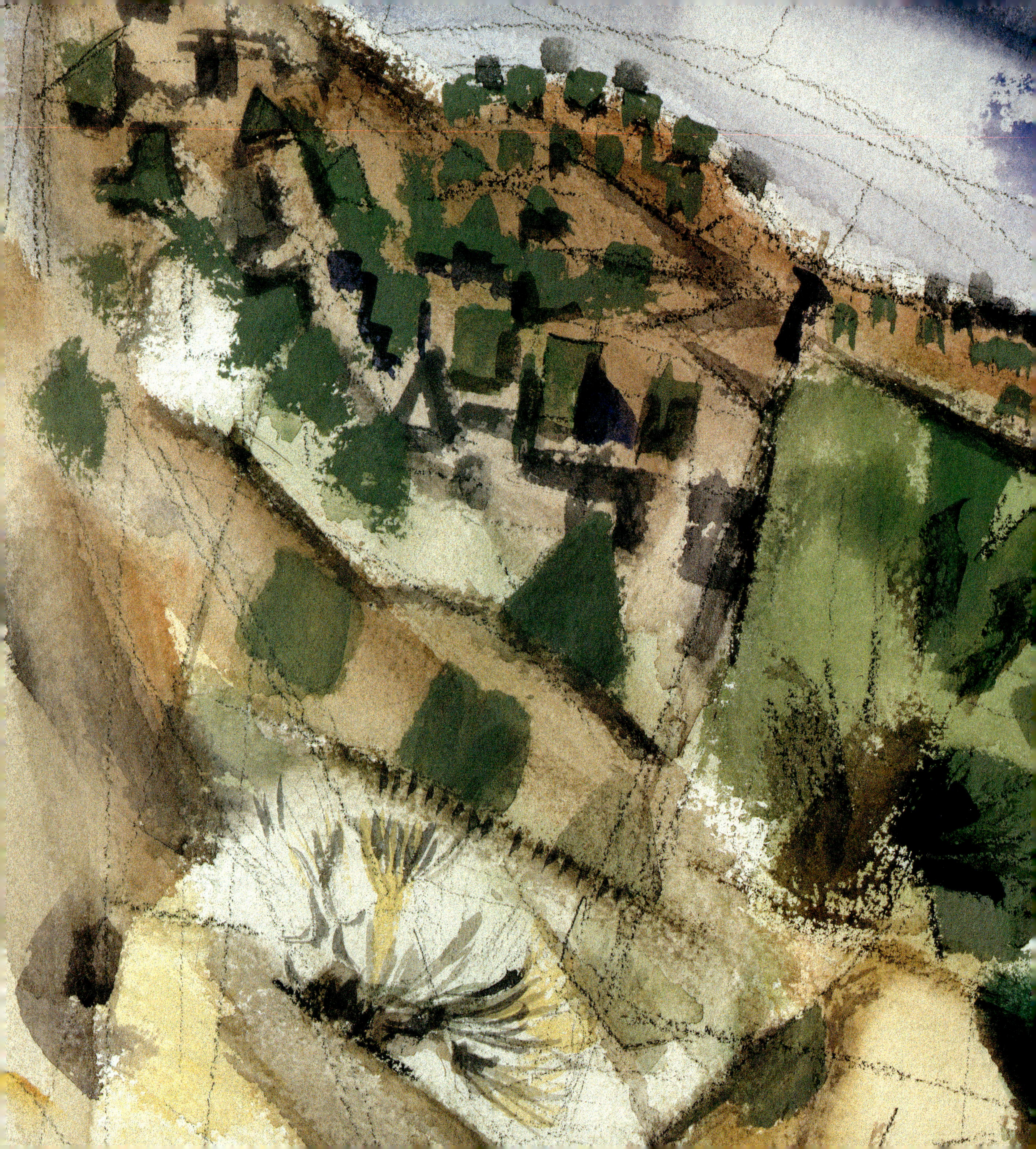

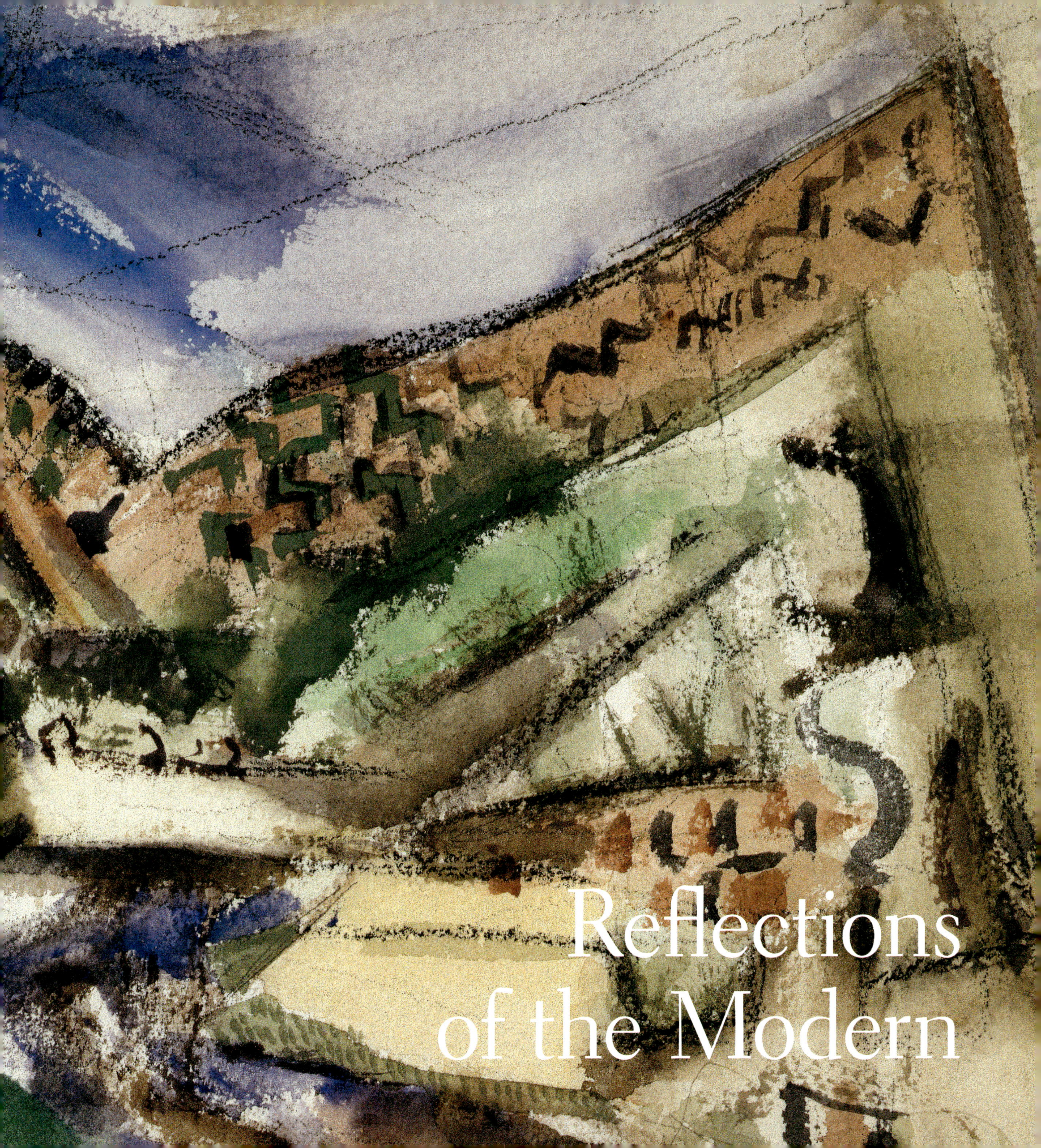
Reflections
of the Modern

Bert Geer Phillips 1868–1956

Bert Geer Phillips settled in Taos in 1898 and helped to establish the Taos Society of Artists, a group of painters who popularized the high country of New Mexico through exhibitions of their work in New York and the Midwest. Phillips had arrived in Taos via a circuitous route. Following a stint at New York's National Academy of Design, Phillips sailed to Paris, where he studied at the Académie Julien. There he met Joseph Henry Sharp, who encouraged Phillips and fellow student Ernest Blumenschein to head west to Taos. Of Taos, Phillips wrote, "… it is the romance of this great pure-aired land that makes the most lasting impression on my mind and heart"; his portraits of Hispanics and Native Americans express an ideal of ancient communities living in harmony with nature.[1]

In *Pueblo Indian Girl with Plum Blossoms*, Phillips clothed his model in a graceful cotton *manta* draped over one shoulder, whitened deerskin boots, a simple bead necklace, and a silver bracelet and ring.[2] A spray of plum blossoms rising out of an earthenware pot and reaching across the green field of her dress underscores the girl's closeness to the natural world.

A strong element of the Taos Society's approach was the affirmation of the Pueblo Indians' innate and complete oneness with nature. In this full-length portrait Phillips adapts a traditional European genre to ennoble his subject, according her the dignity and grace associated with this format. Her enigmatic expression, however, seems to convey the ambivalent relations between Phillips and those who posed for him. In Taos at the turn of the twentieth century, Anglos, Hispanics, and the Pueblo Indians coexisted peacefully but not without tensions. Some aspects of life in the pueblos remained closed to the Taos painters, and Phillips cast these cultural differences in a characteristically positive and poetic light. "Their life is so secretive," he said. "Thousands of years in close communion with nature, a religion and knowledge based upon this, has given them a power we do not possess."[3] In *Pueblo Indian Girl with Plum Blossoms*, Phillips conveys his respect for Pueblo Indian culture with great painterly skill. [GS]

[1] Quoted in Patricia Janis Broder, *Taos: A Painter's Dream* (Boston: New York Graphic Society, 1980), p. 97.

[2] This painting is undated, but was shown at the sixteenth annual exhibition of the Society of Western Artists in Chicago, Des Moines, and St. Louis in the spring of 1912. These elements and an identical hairstyle also appear in the artist's painting *A Daughter of the Water Clan*, shown at the National Academy of Design exhibition in 1911.

[3] Quoted in Julie Schimmel and Robert R. White, *Bert Geer Phillips and the Taos Art Colony* (Albuquerque: University of New Mexico Press, 1994), pp. 177–78.

Pueblo Indian Girl with Plum Blossoms

about 1911, oil on canvas, 66 × 36 in.
Collection of Gerald and Kathleen Peters

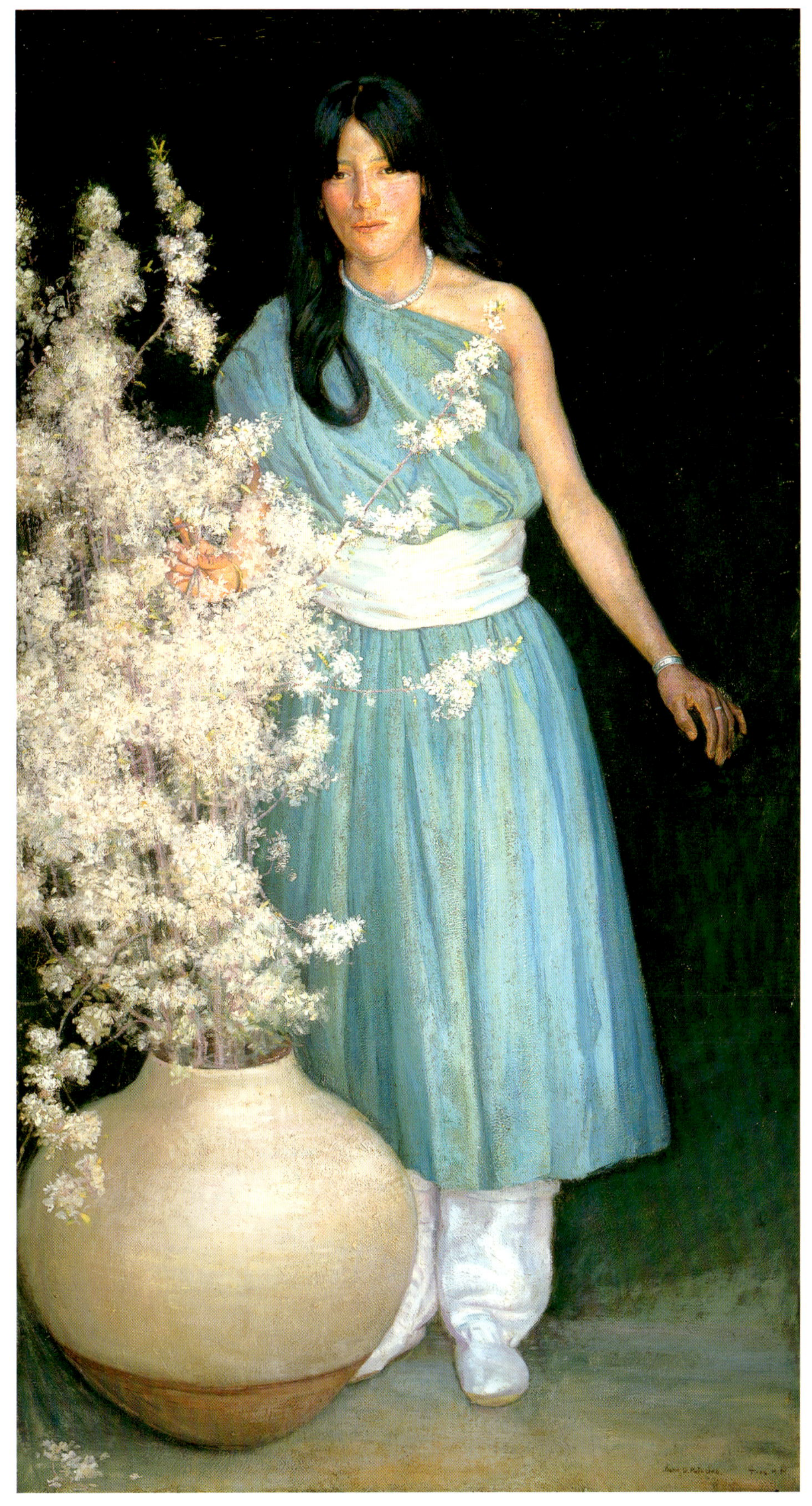

Ernest L. Blumenschein 1874–1960

Ernest Blumenschein recalled his first view of the landscape around Taos and the Sangre de Cristo Mountains in 1898 as "the first great unforgettable inspiration of my life."[1] He made his first trip to the Southwest with fellow artist Bert Geer Phillips at the instigation of Joseph Henry Sharp, who had visited the area five years earlier and spoken glowingly of its beauty and interest. The three artists had become friends at the Académie Julien in Paris and remained close throughout their lives.

Phillips remained in Taos after his first visit, but Blumenschein returned to his studio in New York City and resumed his successful career as an illustrator. Later, dissatisfied with the limitations of illustration, he went back to Paris to continue his studies to become a painter. He was not happy as an expatriate artist and returned to New York. For nine years, beginning in 1910, he spent summers in Taos, sketching and painting. Many other artists had settled there or visited regularly, and they formed the Taos Society of Artists, with which Blumenschein became affiliated.

He moved to Taos in 1919 and continued to draw inspiration from the extraordinary landscape outside the town as well as from the costumes and activities of the native people. In *Untitled (Mountain Wood Gatherers)*, a small group (probably an adult and four children) loads wood onto a donkey. Although they appear in the center foreground in red clothes, their presence is secondary to the splendor of the mountains in the distance and the jagged topography of the valley floor. The figures are smaller than the rocky outcroppings near them and blend with the reddish hue of their surroundings.

Sangre de Cristo is Spanish for "blood of Christ," a name that was probably given to this region because of the brilliant reddish orange glow of the mountains at sunrise and sunset, especially when covered with snow. Here the late afternoon sun emphasizes the deep shadows cast by the rocky surfaces and imparts a cool, lavender light to the distant mountains and clouds. Blumenschein chose an elongated horizontal format to capture the panoramic vista and feel of wide, open space that he relished in New Mexico. There is little sense of human habitation other than the temporary appearance of the figures in the foreground, who take what they need and leave without a trace. Their transience in the landscape contrasts with the eternal and majestic presence of nature. [JM]

[1] Blumenschein, as quoted in William T. Henning Jr., *Ernest L. Blumenschein Retrospective: Colorado Springs Fine Arts Center, March 5–April 16, 1978* (Colorado Springs, CO: The Center, 1978), p. 12.

Untitled (Mountain Wood Gatherers)

1930s, oil on canvas, 23 × 50 in.
Private Collection

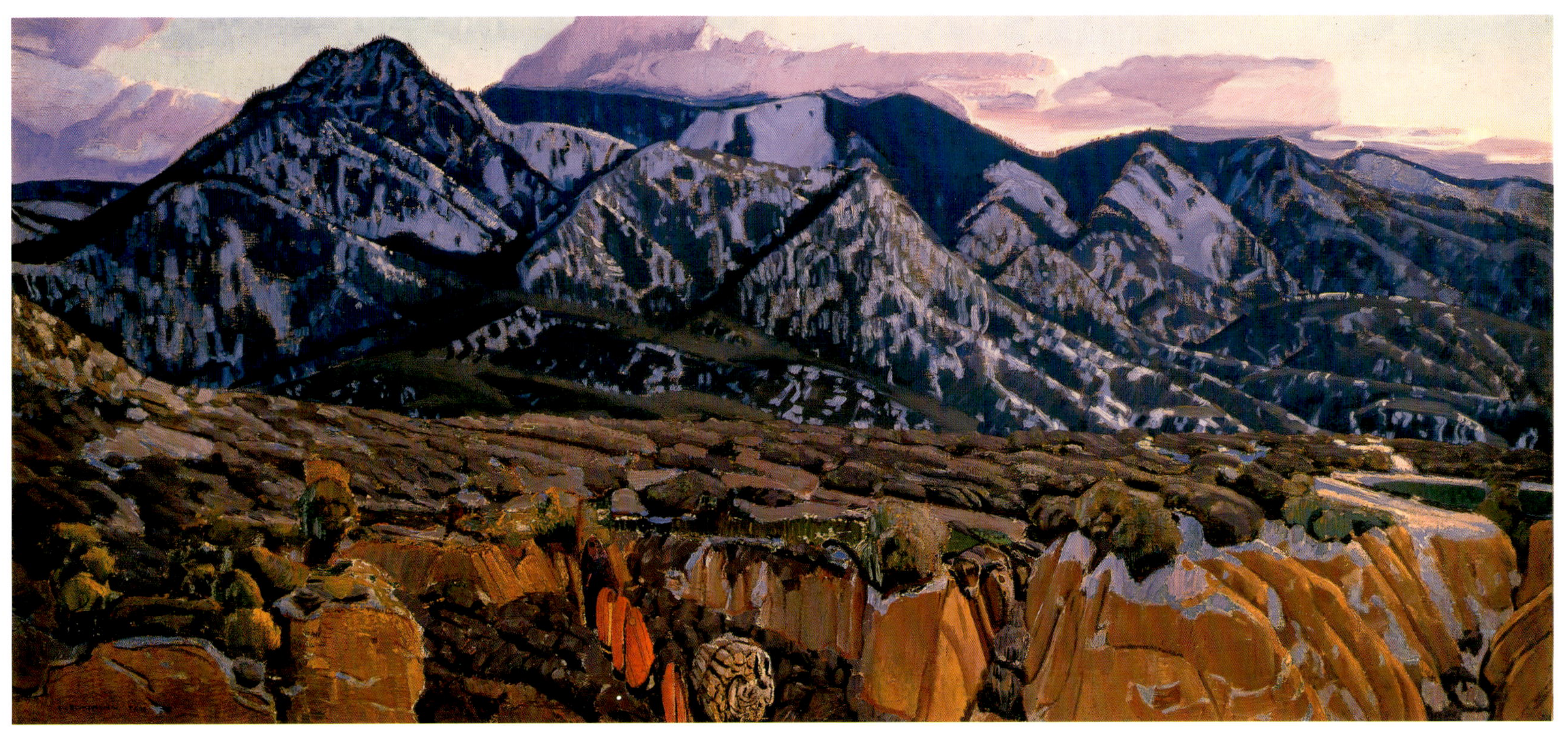

John Marin 1870–1953

Composed entirely of diagonals, sharp angles, curves, and dynamic brushwork, *Taos Canyon* reveals John Marin's exhilaration in his discovery of the New Mexico landscape. Before he traveled to the West, Marin "felt the world was closing in on him. He was tired of 'living in herds,' of swimming in a 'common pool.'"[1] He had spent most of his life in cities: in Paris as a student and in New York as a practicing artist. Friends Georgia O'Keeffe and Rebecca Salsbury James suggested that he join them in New Mexico and arranged an invitation from Mable Dodge Luhan for him to stay at her compound in Taos during the summer of 1929.[2]

Marin was awed by the scale of the sweeping vistas outside Taos and by the intense blue sky, the bright clarity of the light, the unfamiliar combination of arid atmosphere and sudden storms, the jagged Sangre de Cristo range, and the distinctive desert vegetation. Some of his New Mexico landscape watercolors adopted the more traditional progression from foreground to middle ground to distance with recognizable landmarks. Marin created *Taos Canyon*, however, with distorted spatial relationships, fragmented forms, and exaggerated angles, reflecting the vertigo he may have experienced, standing high on the edge of the canyon at the western end of the Rio Hondo looking east. He translated the vegetation—pinyon and juniper, ponderosa pine, and fir and spruce forest—into calligraphic marks and abstract forms. Marin invented details such as the geometric patterns on the rocks in the center foreground that recall motifs found in Indian jewelry, but the scene remains recognizable to anyone familiar with Taos Canyon. [JM]

---

[1] MacKinley Helm, *John Marin* (Boston: Pellegrini and Cudahy and the Institute of Contemporary Art, 1948), p. 64, as quoted in Van Deren Coke, *Marin in New Mexico: 1929 & 1930* (Albuquerque: University Art Museum, University of New Mexico, 1968), p. 5.

[2] At the time, Rebecca Salsbury James was married to photographer Paul Strand. She later divorced Strand and married Bill James. See the entry on Rebecca Salsbury James's *White Hollyhocks (From My Garden)*, p. 140.

Taos Canyon, New Mexico

1929, watercolor on paper, 16 ½ × 22 in.
John and Dolores Beck Collection

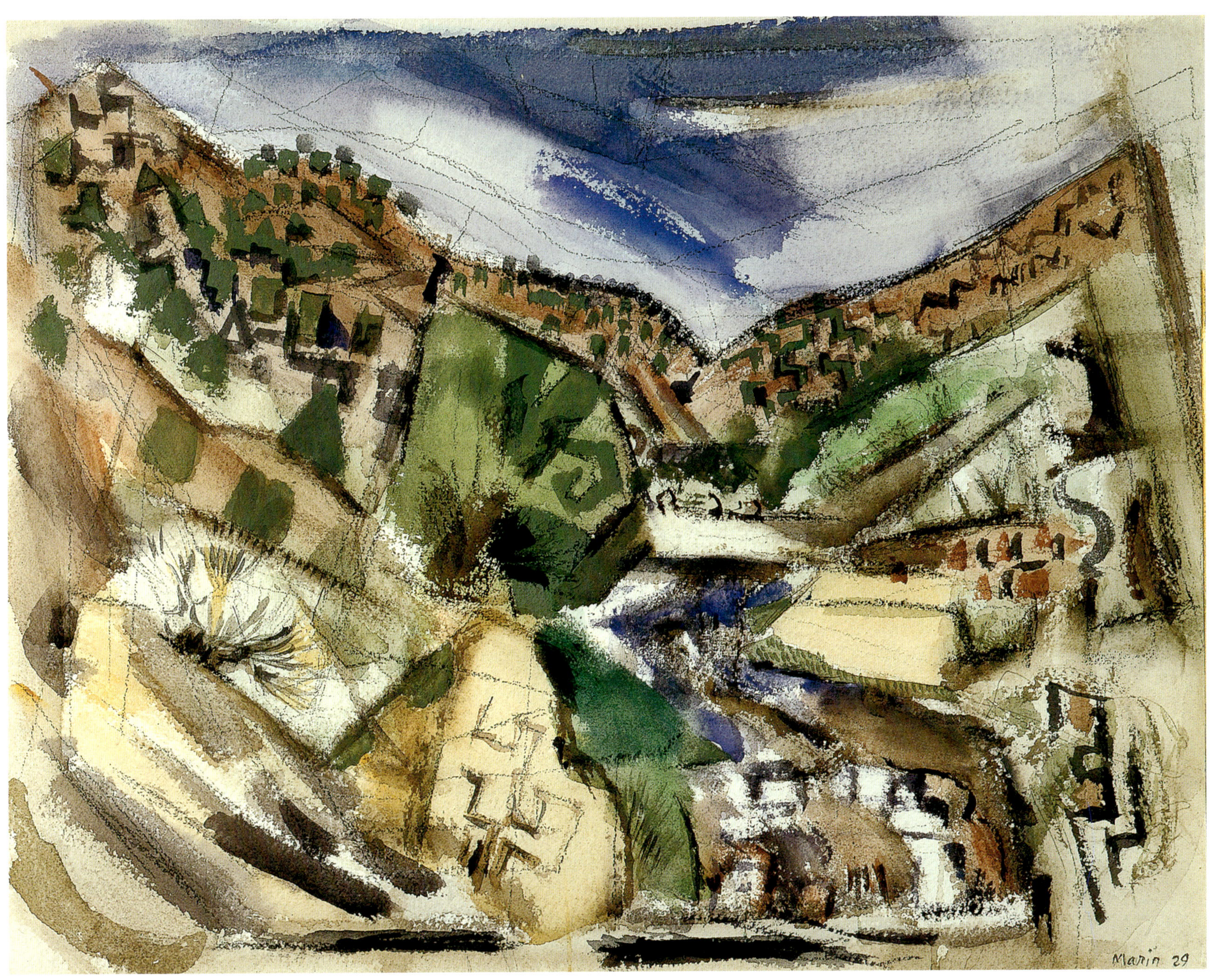
Marin 29

E. Martin Hennings 1886–1956

Sunlit Aspens is one of the rare landscape paintings by E. Martin Hennings that does not include figures. His early academic training stressed drawing and painting from the model, and his commercial work emphasized figures as well. When he moved permanently to Taos from Chicago in 1921, he painted the Spanish and Pueblo Indian peoples of the region, especially the "color and romance of their dress and history."[1]

In New Mexico, Hennings began to paint out-of-doors, and gradually landscape became more important to him than figural work. He spent every autumn painting in the Rio Hondo canyon outside Taos, where golden aspen trees were plentiful. When he used landscape primarily as a setting for people, he favored intimate scenes in which they could fit comfortably, in contrast to the broad, sweeping vistas of other Taos artists. By the 1940s, Hennings had declared: "Landscape plays so important a part of my work.... Nothing thrills me more, when in the fall, the aspen and cottonwoods are in color and with the sunlight playing across them—all the poetry and drama, all the moods and changes of nature are there to inspire one to greater accomplishments from year to year."[2]

The drama of light and shadow in *Sunlit Aspens* was so interesting to Hennings that he did not add figures. He often worked for several weeks, even months, on a single painting, and never signed the work until he was completely satisfied. In a letter to the buyer of this painting, Hennings assured him that it was one of his finest.[3] Painted at the height of his career, *Sunlit Aspens* reveals an artist who has freed himself from the restraints of his academic and commercial beginnings and embraced the Western landscape. [JM]

[1] Hennings as quoted in Robert R. White, "E. Martin Hennings," in Laura M. Bickerstaff, *Pioneer Artists of Taos* (Denver: Old West Publishing, 1983), p. 203.

[2] Ibid.

[3] Hennings to Leighton Wilke, August 31, 1943. The letter is in the possession of the current owners of the painting.

Sunlit Aspens

about 1943, oil on canvas, 30 ⅜ × 36 ¼ in.
Collection of Joffa and Bill Kerr

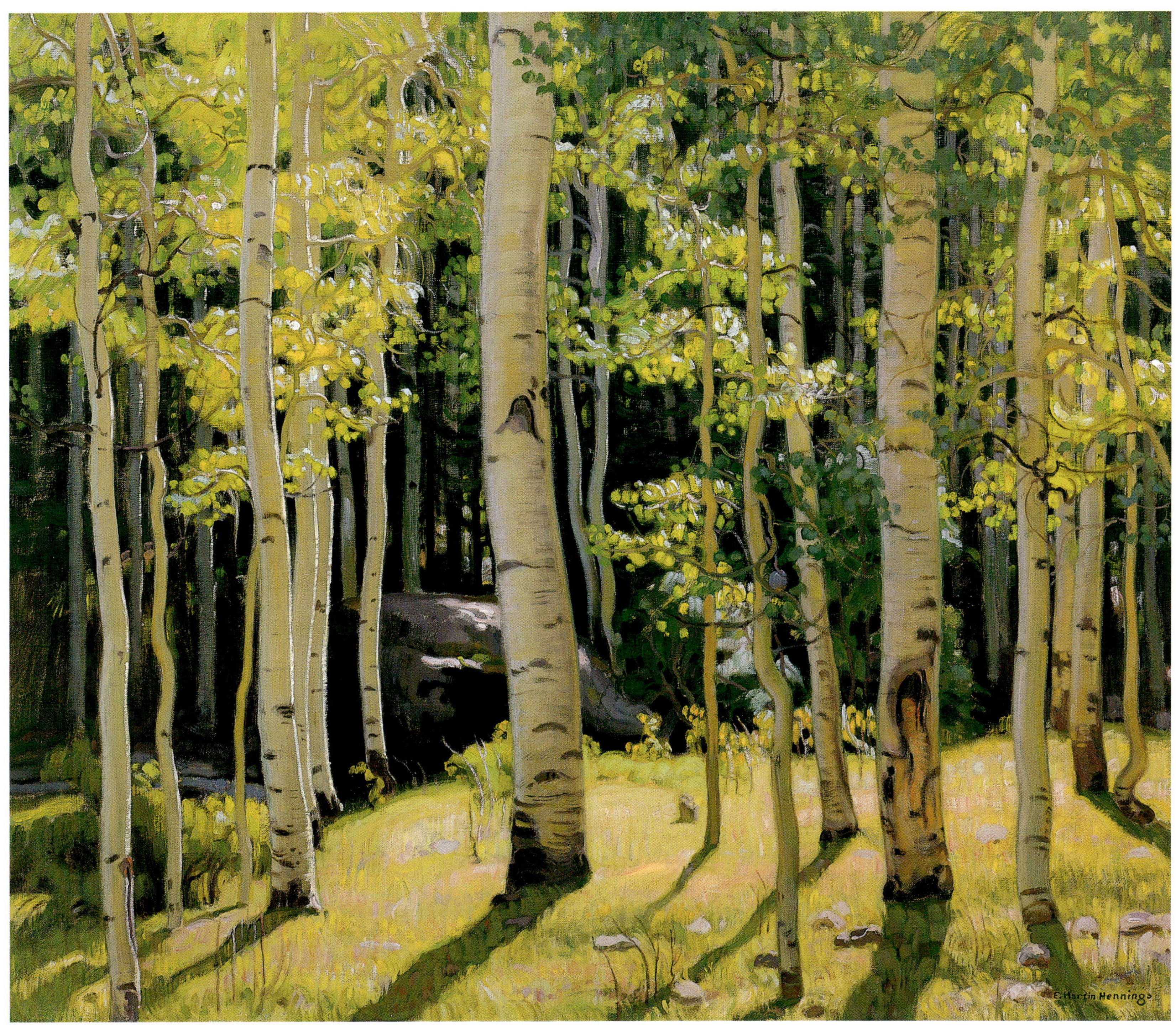
E. Martin Hennings

Rebecca Salsbury James 1891–1968

Rebecca James was born in London, the daughter of Nate Salsbury, who managed Buffalo Bill's Wild West show. She was an outspoken figure in the Alfred Stieglitz circle in New York and a combative but loyal friend to Stieglitz's wife, Georgia O'Keeffe. "Beck" Salsbury was married to photographer Paul Strand when she first came to Taos in 1926. She painted *White Hollyhocks (From My Garden)* after settling there permanently, having divorced Strand and married Bill James, a banker and rancher.

Like many artists in the 1930s, James borrowed from America's folk art traditions to create a truly modern art rooted in the culture rather than in the academies. The technique of reverse oil painting was popular in the nineteenth century among self-taught painters. It involves drawing the details on the back of the glass, then overlaying these with larger areas of color.[1] When the glass is reversed, the forms seemed to float on the background colors, creating a hallucinatory effect that James favored because it expressed an emotional truth rather than a realistic record.

The modulated hues and delicate forms in *White Hollyhocks (From My Garden)* convey little of the outsized personality that led James to insist on the right as a woman to wear trousers among the East Coast's artistic elite. Taos provided James with a social milieu more open to her strong personality. There James's work inevitably drew comparisons with that of the equally strong-minded O'Keeffe, with whom she had shared studio space. The town's most notable arts patron, Mabel Dodge Luhan, compared the "extremely shy and unrevealing" blooms in this painting to O'Keeffe's "large, unembarrassed flower-forms" that demanded the attention of the public.[2] In fact, James's paintings on glass and her efforts to revive a colonial form of embroidery known as *colcha* enabled her to carve her own path among the successful and egotistical artists of Taos. [GS]

---

[1] Dean A. Porter, *Taos Artists and Their Patrons, 1898–1950* (Notre Dame, IN: Snite Museum of Art, University of Notre Dame, 1999), p. 375.

[2] Mabel Dodge Luhan, *Taos and Its Artists* (New York: Duell, Sloan and Pearce, 1947), p. 30.

White Hollyhocks (From My Garden)

before 1947, reverse oil on glass, 24 × 16 1/8 in.
Collection of Lee and Judy Dirks

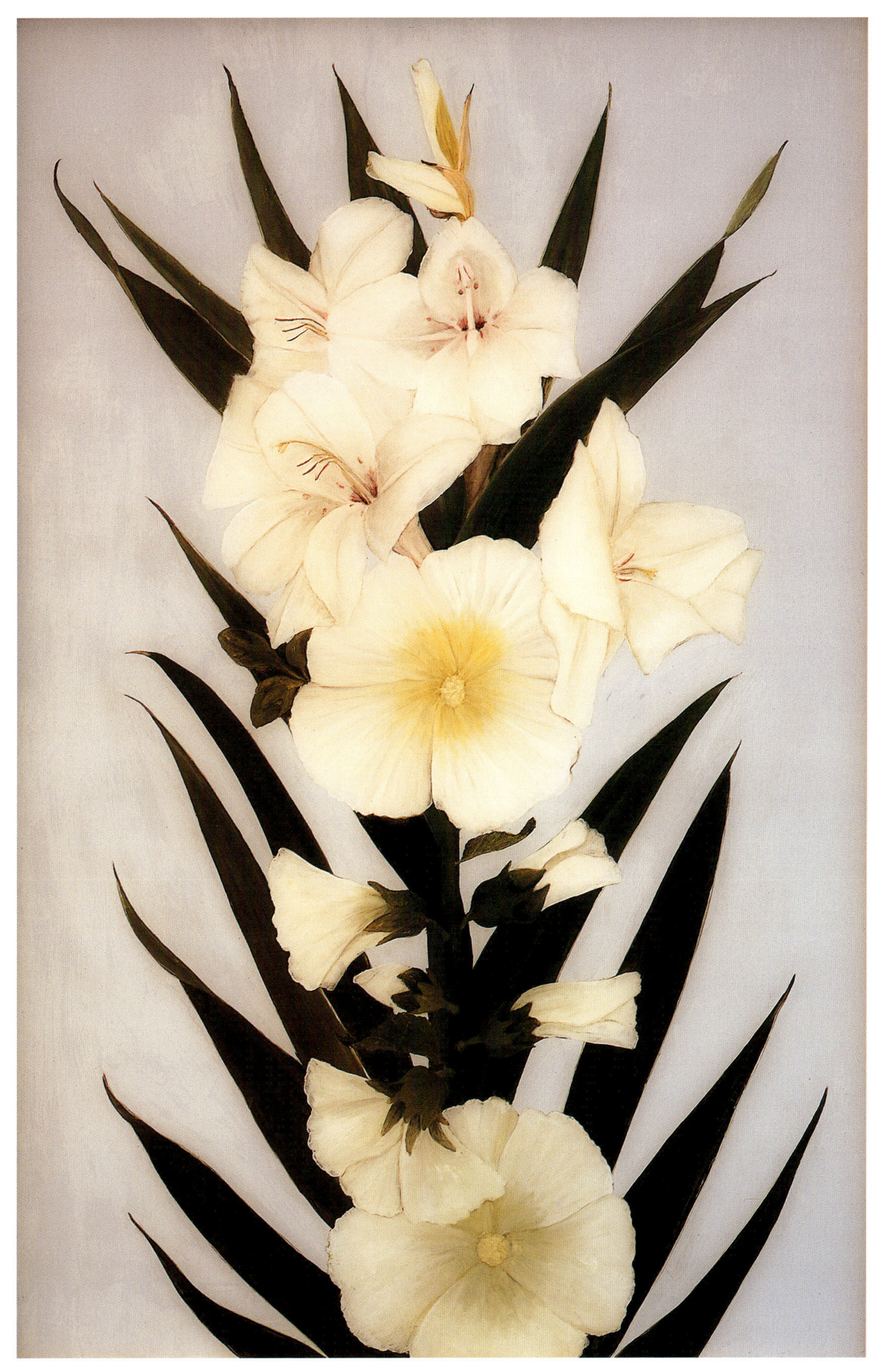

Georgia O'Keeffe 1887–1986

Red Lines is a landmark painting in which Georgia O'Keeffe synthesized modern theories of abstract art with the sensory experience of the physical world around her. O'Keeffe's earlier paintings such as *Blue and Green Music* of 1919 had employed the strong rectangles and rippling streams of pigments seen here, reflecting Arthur Wesley Dow's theory of synesthesia, or the experience of one sense through another. Dow's ideas stirred O'Keeffe's interest in "music [that] could be translated into something for the eye."[1] But *Red Lines* is an abstraction that is nevertheless rooted in the real, a distilled composition of the mountains and skies around Lake George, New York, and transposed from a horizontal format to a vertical one. O'Keeffe was inspired to reorient the image in part by helping Alfred Stieglitz hang the abstract photographs of landscapes and clouds through which he sought to convey an "experience of the spirit."[2] O'Keeffe's painting, however, signals a mature and independent strategy of her own, in which stylized forms and expressive colors would make their way from one series of paintings to another.[3]

Red Lines, in fact, looks forward to the artist's Manhattan paintings of the next few years. Two richly colored verticals at the center reveal a thin seam of light, anticipating the composition and optical tension of light and shadow in such works as *The Shelton with Sunspots* of 1926. The curling, anthropomorphic forms in *Red Lines* will reappear as steam billowing past skyscrapers, and the pale glow at the center will emerge as dazzling globes of light animating the dark towers.[4] The weighty red lines that anchor this canvas contend equally with one another. It is tempting to see in these forms that parallel but do not entirely touch a symbolic echo of Stieglitz and O'Keeffe, who remained uneasily but deeply attached until Stieglitz's death in 1946. The radiant heart of this painting, sheltered by gentle sentinels, evokes the modernist artistic ferment that O'Keeffe and Stieglitz sustained throughout the decade and that provided O'Keeffe with an expressive language that resonated in her work for decades. [GS]

---

[1] O'Keeffe quoted in Judith Zilczer, "'Color Music': Synaesthesia and Nineteenth-Century Sources for Abstract Art," *Artibus et Historiae* 8, no. 16 (1987): 104.

[2] Hunter Drohojowska-Philp, *Full Bloom: The Art and Life of Georgia O'Keeffe* (New York: W. W. Norton, 2004), p. 219; Peter-Cornell Richter, *Georgia O'Keeffe and Alfred Stieglitz* (New York: Prestel, 2001), pp. 63–76.

[3] Peter H. Hassrick, ed., *The Georgia O'Keeffe Museum* (New York: Harry N. Abrams and the Georgia O'Keeffe Museum, 1997), p. 35.

[4] On the optical effects of "halations" and their relation to O'Keeffe's paintings, see Vivian Green Fryd, "Georgia O'Keeffe's *Radiator Building:* Gender, Sexuality, Modernism, and Urban Imagery," *Winterthur Portfolio* 35, no. 4 (Winter 2000): 269–89.

Red Lines

1923, oil on canvas, 25 × 20 in.
Private Collection, Washington, DC

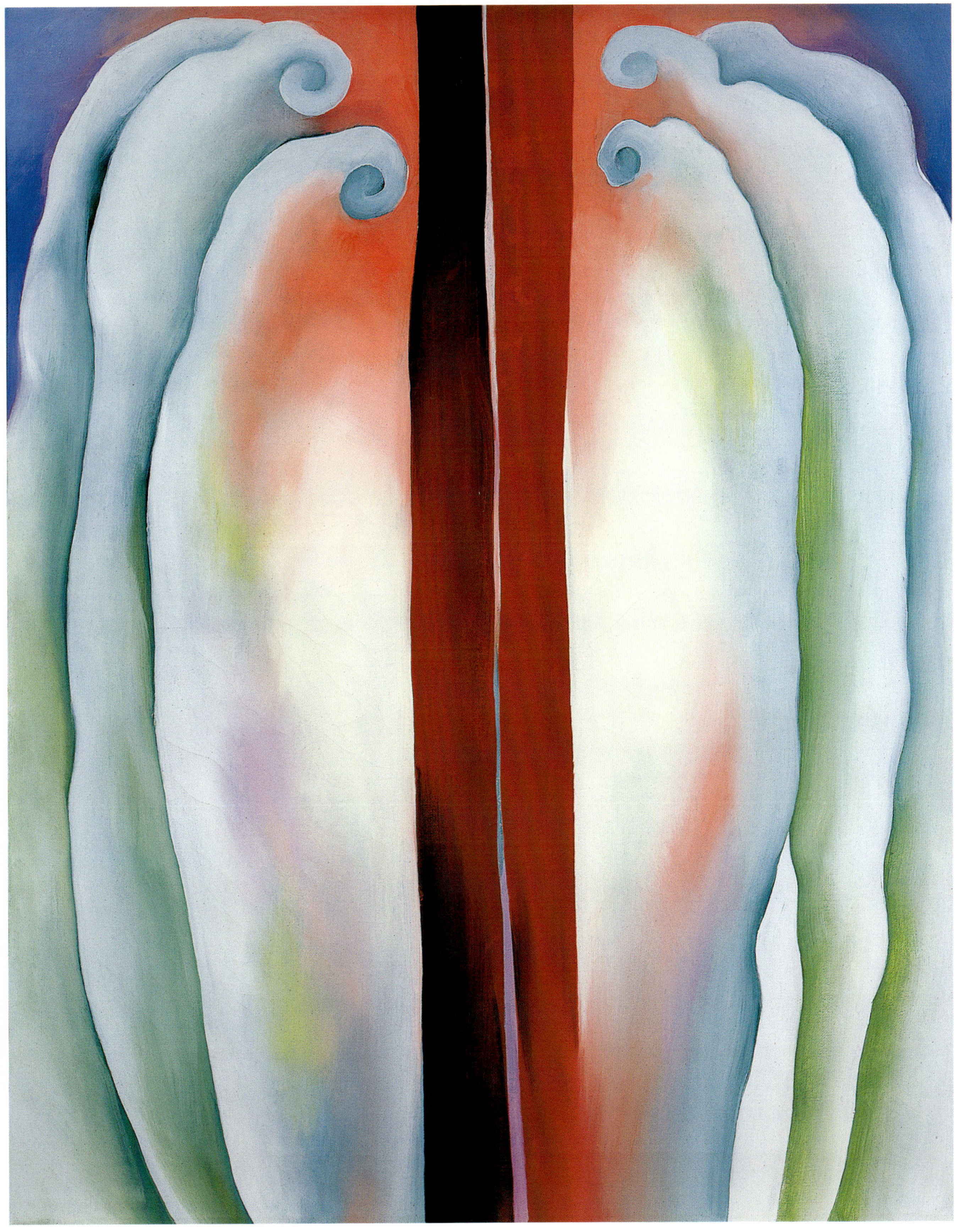

Georgia O'Keeffe 1887–1986

Georgia O'Keeffe spent the summer of 1929 at the Taos estate of Mabel Dodge Luhan. She wrote of her excitement to her sister Catherine, reporting that "I am West again and it is as fine as I remembered it.... There is nothing to say about it except the fact that for me it is the only place."[1] The trip to New Mexico was O'Keeffe's declaration of independence from Alfred Stieglitz's emotional and professional demands. She learned how to drive, making adventurous camping trips into the mountains and out to the pueblos with artist Rebecca Salsbury James, another figure in the Stieglitz circle who had come west with her.[2]

One evening, O'Keeffe and James walked into the hills past a *morada*, one of the small churches built by the Penitentes of northern New Mexico, an ascetic Roman Catholic brotherhood that originated among Europe's Franciscan orders. A great cross of the sort used in the sect's crucifixion rituals loomed between O'Keeffe and the silhouette of Taos Mountain. Decades later, O'Keeffe remembered these crosses, scattered "like a thin dark veil of the Catholic Church spread over the New Mexico landscape."[3] For *Black Cross with Red Sky*, the artist aligned the cross with the mountain, suggesting that the spiritual power of the Penitentes rose out of the old earth itself, as if grafted onto the ancient beliefs of the Indians to whom Taos Mountain was sacred. The sky at end of day glows with a rich red, as though all of nature shared the suffering of the Penitentes who volunteered during Holy Week to be hung from the cross, their hands nailed or bound to the timbers.[4]

O'Keeffe returned to New York in August, exalted by her experience in Taos, physically and emotionally stronger, and resolved to stand her ground with her domineering husband. In February of 1930, *Black Cross with Red Sky* and other works from the summer appeared in Stieglitz's gallery, An American Place. The new paintings announced O'Keeffe as a force to be reckoned with in American modernism. Art critic Henry McBride praised O'Keeffe's vision, realizing—as she clearly had—that "where life manifests itself in greatest ebullience there too is death most formidable."[5] [GS]

---

[1] Quoted in Roxana Robinson, *Georgia O'Keeffe: A Life* (Hanover, NH: University Press of New England, 1999), p. 326.

[2] At the time, Rebecca Salsbury James was married to photographer Paul Strand. She later divorced Strand and married Bill James, a rancher and banker. See the entry on Rebecca Salsbury James's *White Hollyhocks (From My Garden)*, p. 140.

[3] Robinson, *O'Keeffe*, p. 335.

[4] Elizabeth Hutton Turner and Marjorie P. Balge-Crozier, *Georgia O'Keeffe: The Poetry of Things* (New Haven, CT: Yale University Press and the Phillips Collection, 1999), p. 71.

[5] Robinson, *Georgia O'Keeffe*, p. 351.

Black Cross with Red Sky

1929, oil on canvas, 40 × 32 in.
Collection of Gerald and Kathleen Peters

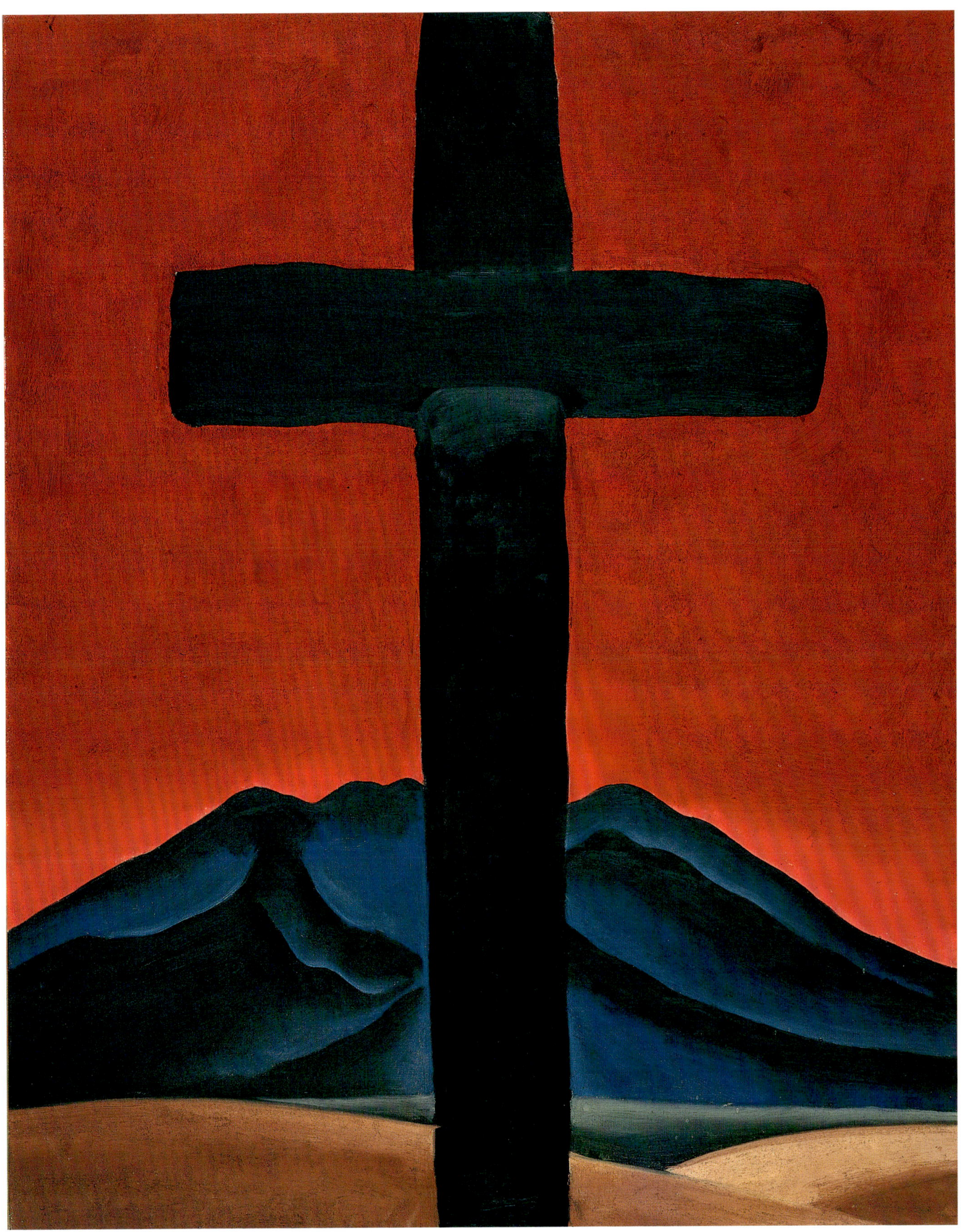

Georgia O'Keeffe 1887–1986

Georgia O'Keeffe created *Birch and Pine Trees—Pink* as a tribute to the black writer and philosopher Jean Toomer, who visited the artist's summer home in Lake George, New York, in 1925. The multiple trunks of a river birch soar upward, their silvery pinks accentuated and embraced by a soft cloud of almost black pines. The image symbolizes a personal bond that O'Keeffe acknowledged in a letter to Toomer written months later. "The feeling that a person gives me that I can not say in words comes in colors and shapes," she wrote. "I never told you—or anyone else—but there is a painting I made from something of you the first time you were here."[1]

The author of the prose poem *Cane*, Toomer was a leading voice in the Harlem Renaissance who believed firmly in the transcendent experiences art and literature could provide. O'Keeffe often kept her distance from the enthusiastic modernists who gathered around her husband, Alfred Stieglitz, choosing, instead, to forge her own path. However, this painting—simultaneously an abstraction, a landscape, and a privately coded portrait of intimate friends—suggests that the artist recognized and embraced Toomer as a kindred spirit.[2]

But if *Birch and Pine Trees—Pink* commemorates a deep friendship, it also captures the claustrophobic environment O'Keeffe struggled against at Lake George. At the upper right, intersecting planes in gray and black suggest the rooftops of the Stieglitz compound, where O'Keeffe felt stifled by the protocols and simmering resentments of her husband's family. Indeed, the full summer pictured in this painting was less appealing to O'Keeffe than autumn, when her relatives moved away and the country opened up with fall colors.[3] In *Birch and Pine Trees—Pink* an exultant orange flare at the upper left suggests such an escape from a dark, oppressive environment. "I wish you could see the place here," she wrote one September to the novelist Sherwood Anderson. "There is something so perfect about the mountains and the lake and the trees... it is really lovely."[4] [GS]

---

[1] Quoted in Hunter Drohowska-Philp, *Full Bloom: The Art and Life of Georgia O'Keeffe* (New York: W. W. Norton, 2004), p. 352.

[2] See Peter H. Hassrick, ed., *The Georgia O'Keeffe Museum* (New York: Harry N. Abrams and the Georgia O'Keeffe Museum, 1997), p. 35: "That O'Keeffe's work could evoke diverse associations is entirely in keeping with her attempt to pare down images to their essential, universal forms."

[3] Roxana Robinson, Part III, "An Ordered Life: Manhattan and Lake George," *Georgia O'Keeffe: A Life* (Hanover, NH: University Press of New England, 1989), pp. 201–312.

[4] Quoted in Charles C. Eldredge, *Georgia O'Keeffe* (New York: Harry N. Abrams and the National Museum of American Art, Smithsonian Institution, 1991), p. 40.

Birch and Pine Trees—Pink

1925, oil on canvas, 36 × 22 in.
Private Collection

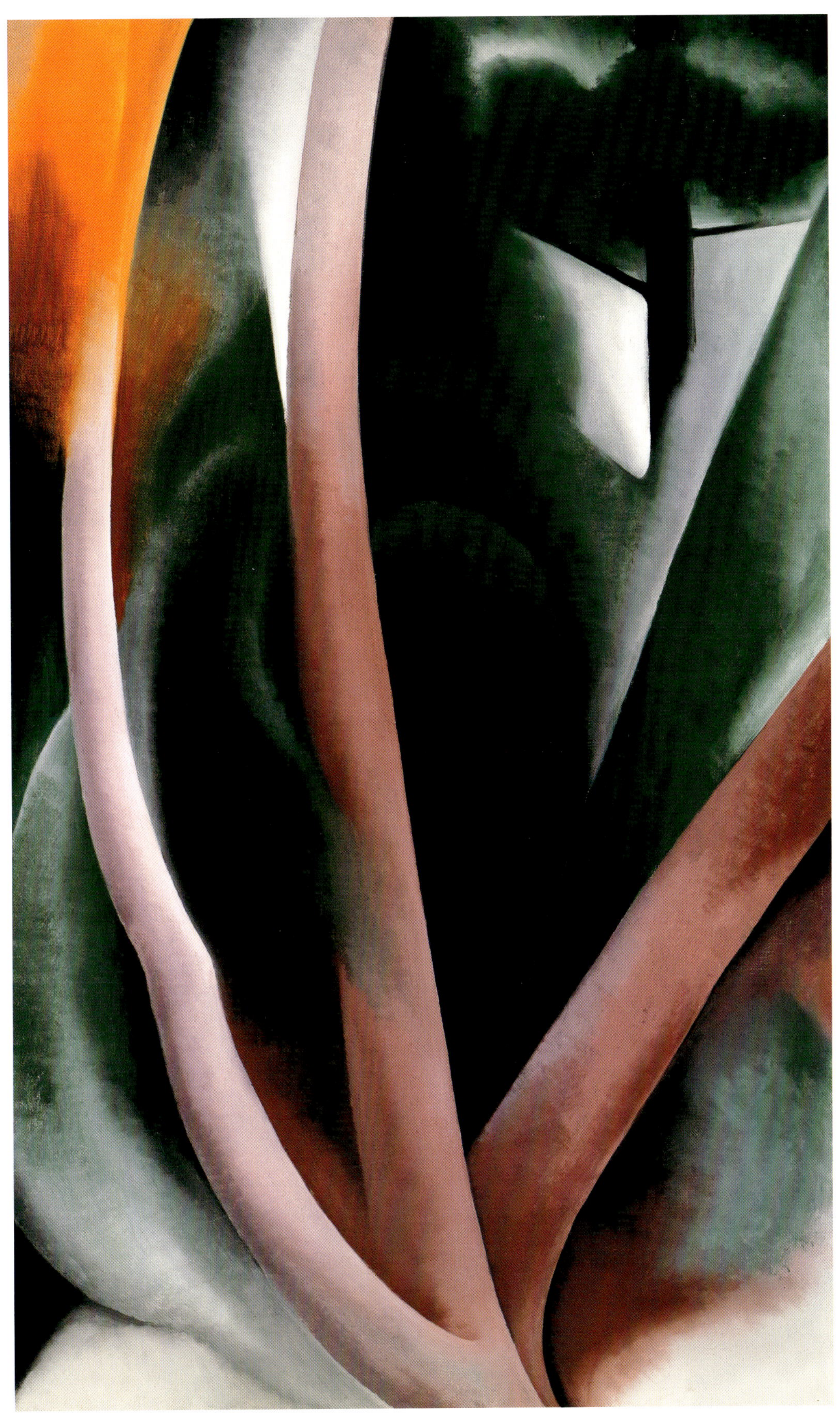

Georgia O'Keeffe 1887–1986

Georgia O'Keeffe returned often throughout the 1930s and 1940s to an area of the Jicarilla Apache Reservation she called the "black place." The artist likened the gray gypsum hills to "a mile of elephants," and steadily abstracted the view until, in *Black Place No. IV*, she expressed not the geography but the feeling of being in the embrace of the land.[1] Contrasting areas of color suggest the scale of the rolling country and the raking light of the desert Southwest. A streak of bright paint at the center of the canvas evokes both a stream enfolded in the hills and a lightning flash in the black maw of a violent storm.

Years before, the artist had begun painting on canvas this size because it was the largest that would fit on the back seat of the Model A Ford she used as a mobile studio. *Black Place No. IV* is a late, highly abstracted work in the Black Place series, and was probably painted in her studio at Ghost Ranch. But the image is rooted in O'Keeffe's physical and emotional memory of the site. "If you ever go to New Mexico," she said, "it will itch you for the rest of your life."[2]

When O'Keeffe created *Black Place No. IV*, she was showing annually at Alfred Stieglitz's An American Place gallery. She had been given a retrospective in 1943 at the Art Institute of Chicago, and was shortly to appear in a second retrospective, at the Museum of Modern Art. Still, she wrote to James Johnson Sweeney at MoMA that, if he should decide not to give her an exhibition, he could rest assured that "it will be alright [*sic*] with me— For myself I feel no need of the showing. As I sit out here in my dry lonely country I feel even less need for all those things that go with the city. And while I am in the city I am always wanting to come back here."[3] [GS]

---

[1] Georgia O'Keeffe, *Georgia O'Keeffe (A Studio Book)* (New York: Viking Press, 1976), n.p.

[2] Quoted in Charles C. Eldredge, *Georgia O'Keeffe* (New York: H. N. Abrams and the National Museum of American Art, Smithsonian Institution, 1991), p. 103.

[3] Quoted in Roxana Robinson, *Georgia O'Keeffe: A Life* (Hanover, NH: University Press of New England, 1999), p. 455.

Black Place No. IV

1944, oil on canvas, 30 × 36 in.
Collection of Lee and Judy Dirks

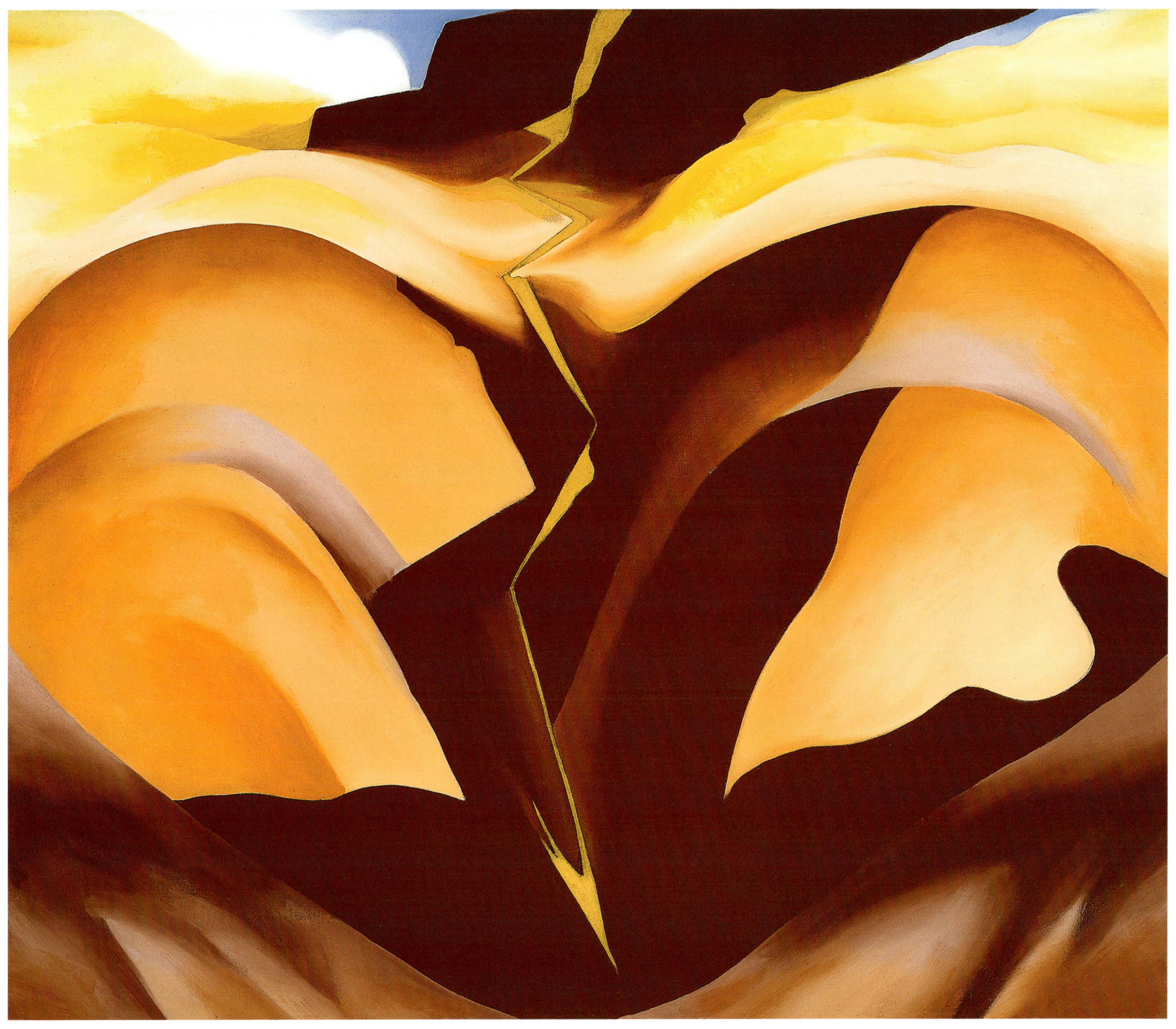

Joseph Stella 1877–1946

Palms is one of the most joyous and sensuous paintings of Joseph Stella's late career. Inspired by the time he spent in Barbados in 1937–38, Stella recalled the soothing warmth, brilliant light, and intense colors of the tropics after he returned to New York. He remembered the exaltation he felt approaching St. Thomas on his way to the island: "The darkness becomes lighter.... The fresh, balmy air and the clarity of the dawn full of young joy, open up the portal of our soul, lighting it up within, chasing away the shadows thickened during the horrible time in ugly America.... The blood rushes through our veins... our artistic powers rise, magically reawakened in the presence of unexpected natural wonders, ready for the highest flights."[1] In *Palms* the colors of the foliage, the house, and the sky, as well as the graceful curves of the tree trunk and palm fronds, create a vision of paradise he remembered in cold, gray New York.

Stella traveled to Barbados with his wife, Mary Geraldine Walter French, who was born in Speightstown. Although they had married before 1916, they lived apart for most of their lives until the mid-1930s. Desperately ill with diabetes, she wished to return to her birthplace to die. Stella was eager to leave inhospitable New York, where his life in a Bronx apartment was constrained, his art was not receiving the recognition it had before the early 1920s, and he was forced to work on a WPA art project. He spent a happy and productive five months in Barbados before going to France and Italy and finally returning to New York. Stella continued to send money and medicine to his wife until her death in 1939, and recalled his pleasurable time in Barbados in some of his most vibrant paintings. In *Palms* the bright red house nestles under a canopy of trees, separated from the road by brilliant red flowers and lush foliage, crowned by a halo of clouds. Man is in harmony with nature in Barbados. Far from the paradisiacal Caribbean island, however, World War II threatened Europe. [JM]

---

[1] Joseph Stella, as quoted in Irma B. Jaffe, *Joseph Stella* (Cambridge: Harvard University Press, 1970), p. 116.

Palms

about 1938–40, oil on canvas, 43 × 24 in.
Private Collection, Washington, DC

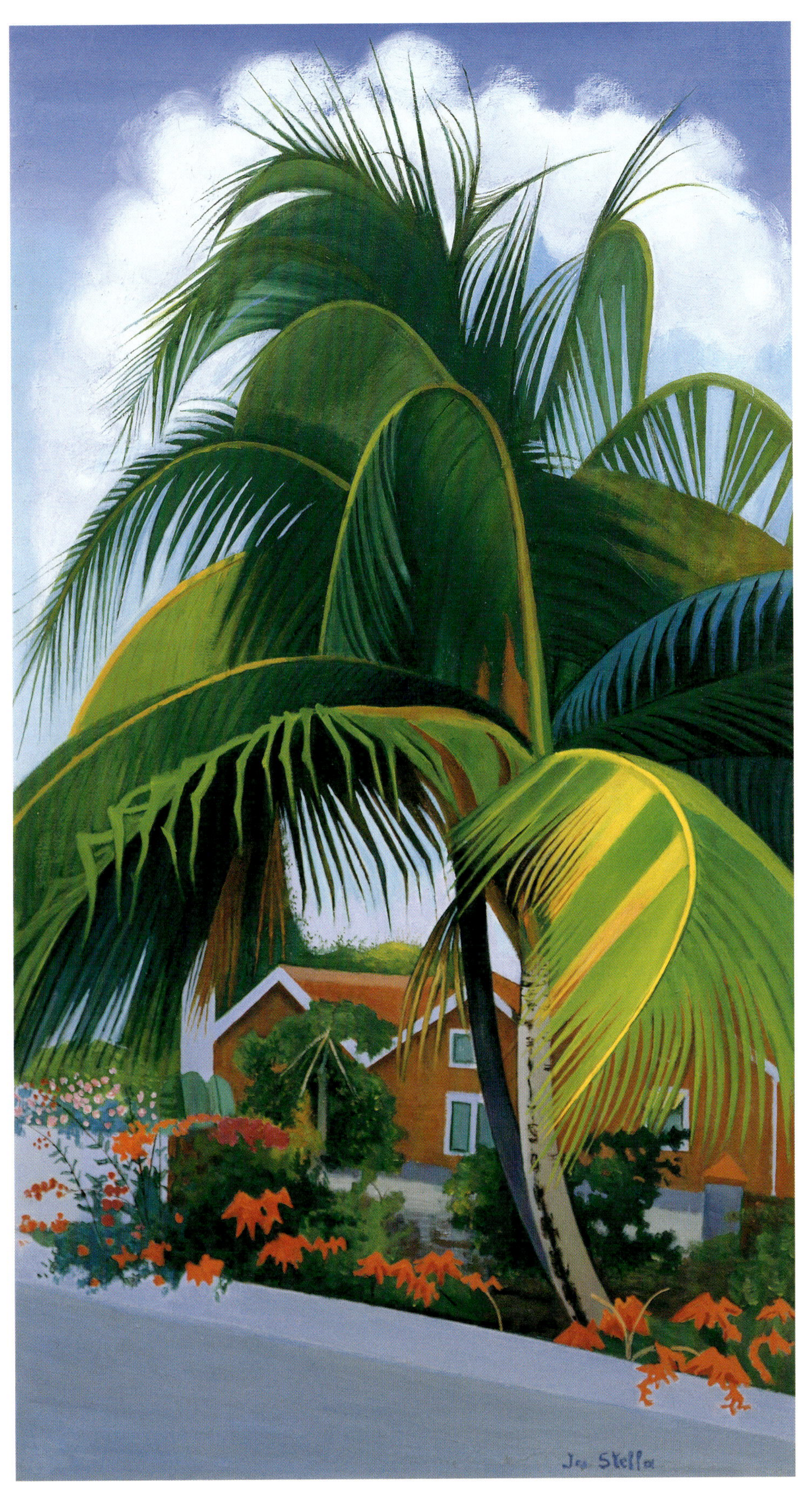
Stella

Rockwell Kent 1882–1971

Rockwell Kent spent two winters in the village of Igdlorssuit on an island above the Arctic Circle, living with a widow named Salamina Fleischer who inspired one of his three books on Greenland. In *Sunday, North Greenland*, the figure at the center gesturing toward the viewer is very likely this woman, who eventually married another Greenlander and died in 1936. The landscape around the rustic church matches this description from *Salamina*, Kent's memoir dedicated to her in 1935: "Standing on the sloping foreland of Igdlorssuit, one looks out as though upon the stage of a great theater. Of that stage, the level plain of the sea is the floor, the great circle of the heavens is the proscenium arch, the two headlands are the wings. Sea, mountains, ice are its one set; sun, moon, and stars the light."[1]

Kent traveled to Greenland as he had to Newfoundland and Tierra del Fuego, searching for exalted landscapes where people struggled at the very limit of survival. *Sunday, North Greenland* and related works such as *Early November: North Greenland* (1932) and *Greenland Winter* (1934–35) depict small communities enduring in the face of all-powerful nature. Greenland's fishing villages represented for the artist a communitarian ideal of mutual effort that meshed with his Communist political sympathies. At the same time, the preindustrial cultures to which Kent periodically fled offered an antidote to the pressures he felt as a husband, father, political figure, and noted artist back in New York City.

Kent was fascinated by the history of the Norse explorers and by the shared heritage of Greenlanders and native peoples across the American continent. Between his trips north, he lectured throughout the United States with the help of films and lantern slides. Like many artists and writers of the Depression years, he looked to the oldest human cultures and the origins of human history for mythic images that helped his audiences transcend their fears of the present. A Los Angeles critic recognized Kent's "quest," placing him among the "restless, uprooted generation [who] ask themselves just what things have lasting value to man."[2] Kent found his answer among the Greenlanders, in whom he saw an enduring culture that was thousands of years old. [GS]

---

[1] Jake Milgram Wien, *Rockwell Kent: The Mythic and the Modern* (New York: Hudson Hills Press and the Portland Museum of Art, 2005), p. 77.

[2] Ibid., p. 72.

Sunday, North Greenland

1933, oil on canvas mounted on board, 28 × 34 in.
John and Dolores Beck Collection

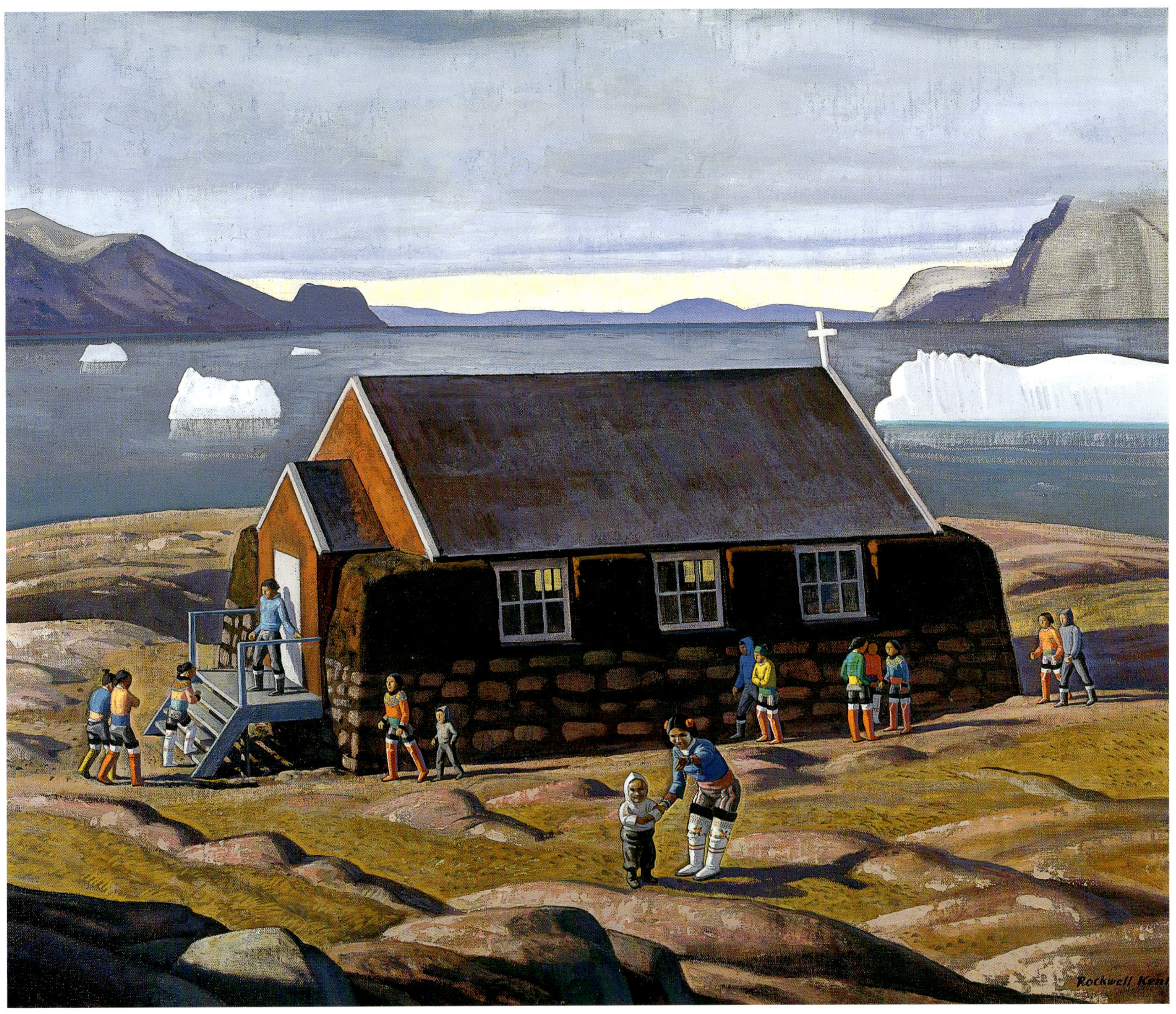
Rockwell Ken

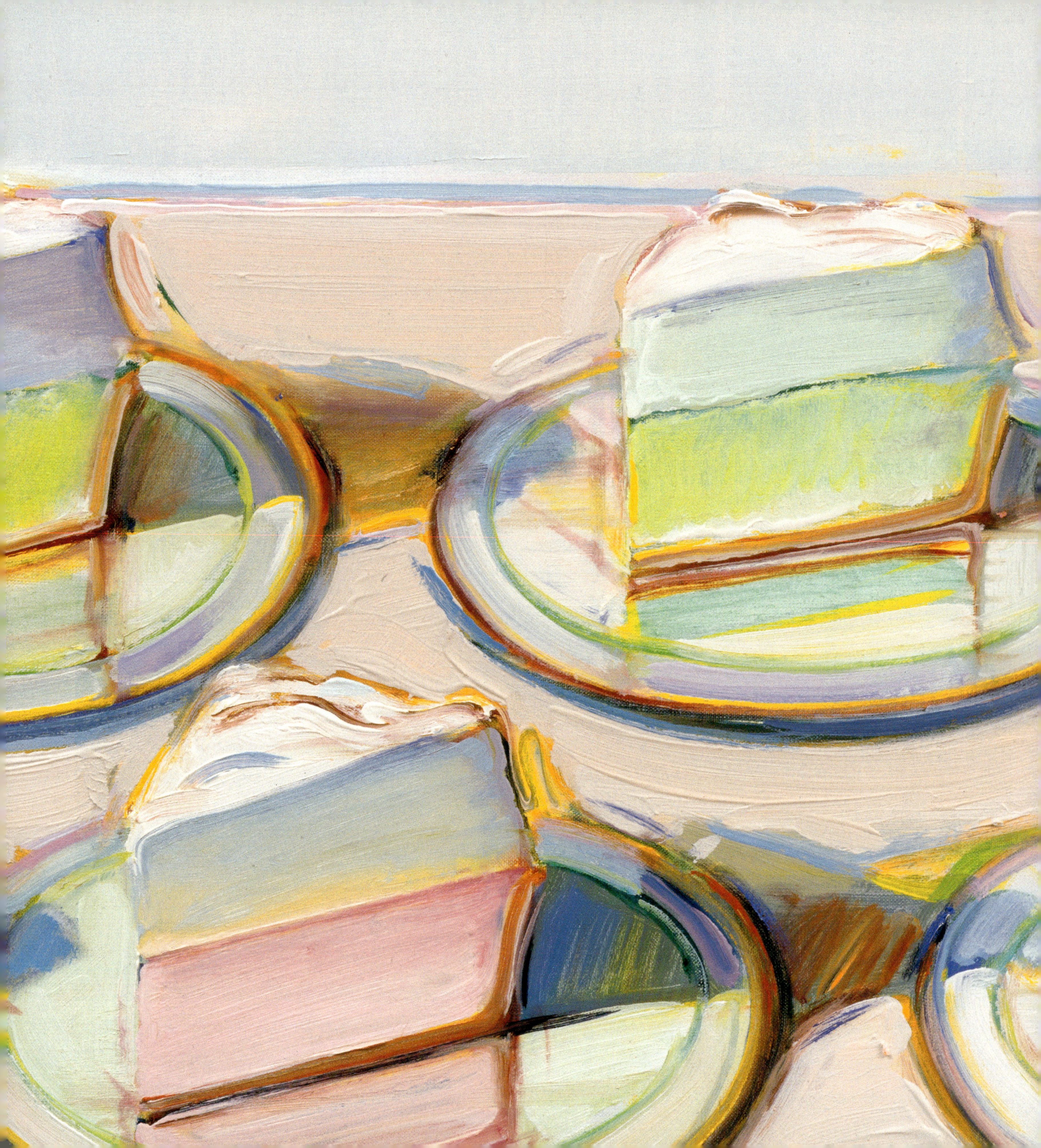

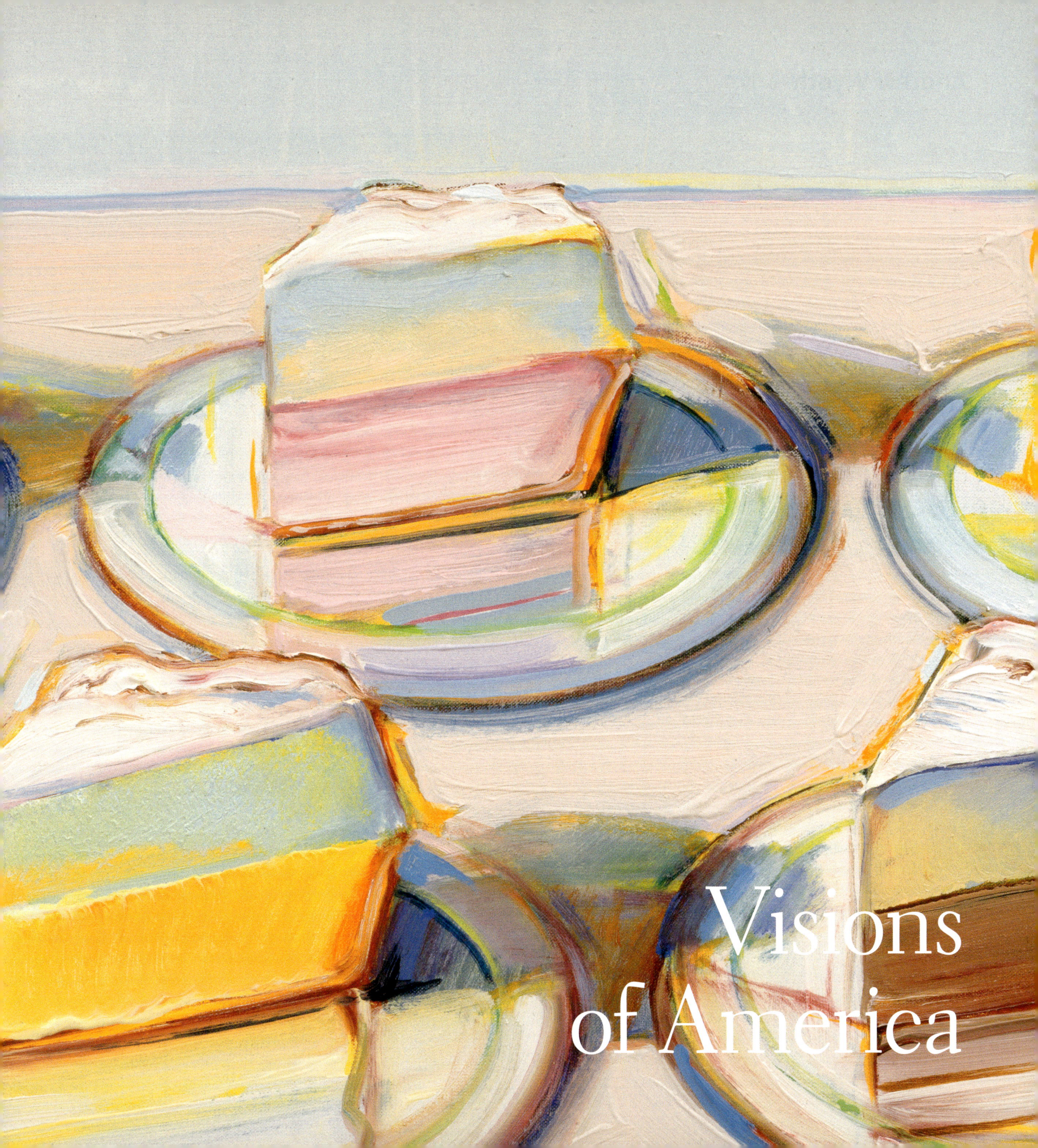
Visions
of America

Andrew Wyeth b. 1917

Thresholds and windows are important motifs for Andrew Wyeth, for whom they signify the degree to which the outside world is allowed to enter his interior realm.[1] In addition to the doors that are the main focus of this work, a strong diagonal of light cuts across the composition from a window, either opened or closed, on another wall of the room.

The watercolor appears to be a meditation on privacy and loss. Wyeth's world revolves around his family, neighbors, and trusted friends. The death of his father and nephew in an automobile accident in 1945 haunted him throughout his life. These themes are strong undercurrents in many of his paintings and watercolors, but he rarely addressed them in a single work as explicitly as in *Open and Closed.*

The doors in the work open into the master bedroom on the first floor of the Broad Cove farmhouse in Cushing, Maine, which belonged to his wife's parents, Mr. and Mrs. Merle D. James.[2] Elizabeth Browning James died in 1959, and Merle James died in November 1963, so the house was probably empty when Wyeth created the watercolor. The white walls show signs of wear, a reference to the lives lived within them. The bedroom is no longer the private space it was when the Jameses were alive, and Wyeth enters it freely now.

Wyeth met his future wife, Betsy James, in Cushing, where both their families had summer homes. He visited his in-laws in this house during his summers in Maine. In 1959, he painted Betsy's mother in a canopy bed in this very room, and in 1970, he again used it as the setting for a painting. By focusing solely on the doors in *Open and Closed* and flattening the space to a single wall with only a narrow view of the space beyond it, the artist minimized its identity as a bedroom. It is less an actual space than an abstract idea. The broad white expanse, defined by both direct and reflected light and shadow, reveals Wyeth's mastery of the subtleties of watercolor. He no longer needed to resort to the dramatic brushwork and more superficial surface effects of some of his earlier works on paper. [JM]

---

[1] Anne Classen Knutson, ed., "Andrew Wyeth's Language of Things," in *Andrew Wyeth: Memory and Magic* (New York: Rizzoli, High Museum of Art, and Philadelphia Museum of Art, 2005), p. 78.

[2] This information was provided by Mary Adam Landa, Wyeth Collection Manager, by email on February 1, 2006.

Open and Closed

1964, watercolor on paper, 21 × 30 in.
Collection of Hacker and Kitty Caldwell

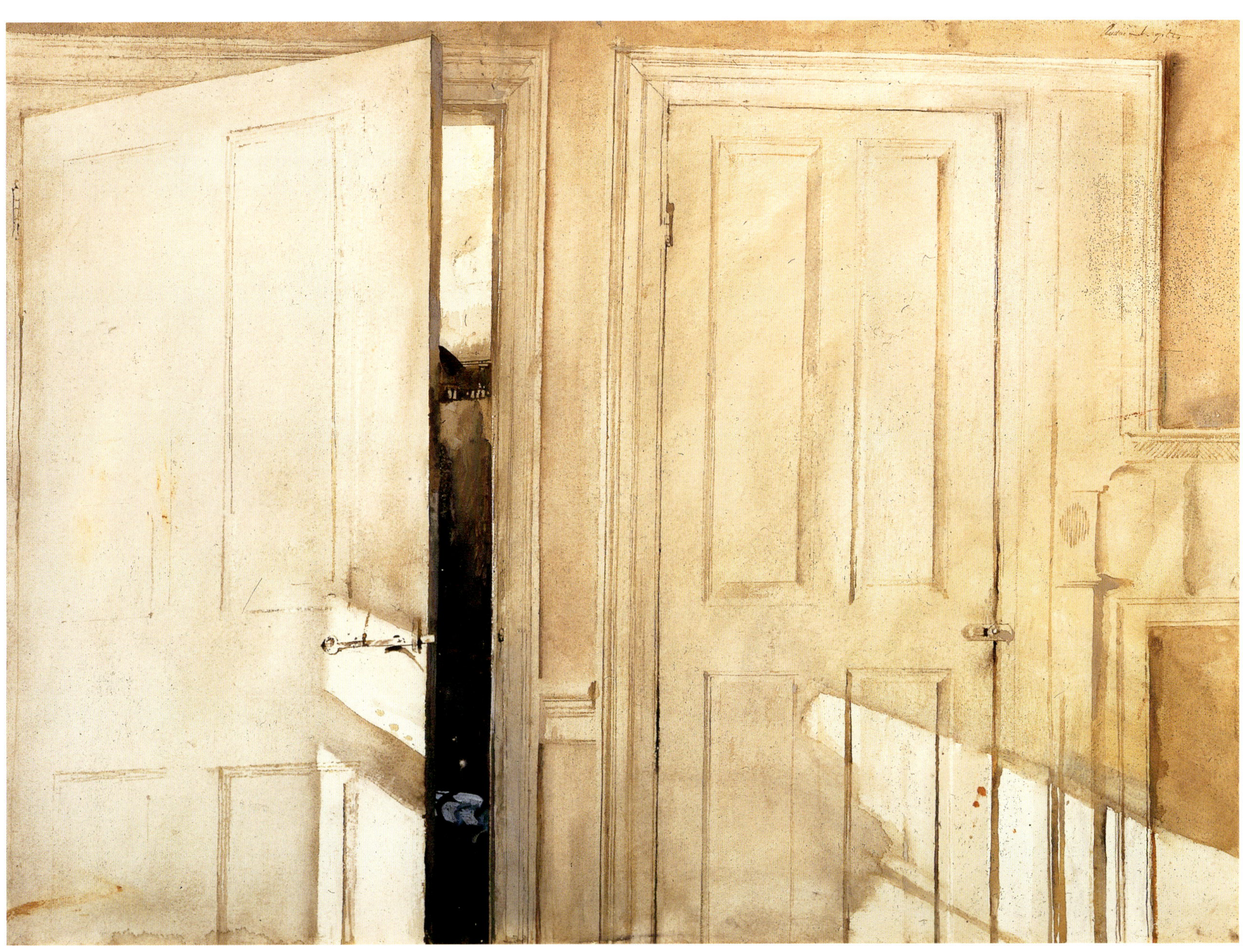

Andrew Wyeth b. 1917

I have such a strong romantic fantasy about things—and that's what I paint.

Andrew Wyeth[1]

Andrew Wyeth carefully chooses the objects he paints and imbues these with mood and meaning. *Logging Scoot* depicts a type of sled used to carry entire logs or loads of firewood from the forest to the mill, pulp yard, or home woodpile. Horses or oxen harnessed to the scoot pull the load over frozen ground or packed trails. The long pole or tongue that rises vertically from the center holds back the load when the scoot is pointed downhill, so that it does not overrun the animals. For Wyeth the logging scoot represents a style of transporting timber more directly in tune with nature than twentieth-century engines and paved roads or rails. It embodies a sense of longing for a simpler time, when people could build their own tools and implements, and animals provide the necessary power.

Wyeth painted *Logging Scoot* in the vicinity of Cushing, Maine, near the farm of his neighbors, Christina Olson and her younger brother, Alvaro. For more than twenty years, the artist enjoyed their friendship and had casual access to their house during the summers he spent in Maine. Christina was one of his favorite models, and he admired the simplicity of their way of life. Alvaro died on Christmas Eve 1967, and Christina died less than a month later. Wyeth made his last paintings of the Olson house and their belongings during the following two summers as the house was gradually emptied of its contents and prepared for sale. It is not known whether this logging scoot belonged to them, but the painting is a tribute to the Olson family, the last of their line. [JM]

---

[1] The quotation is taken from Richard Meryman, "Andrew Wyeth: An Interview"; see Wanda Corn, *The Art of Andrew Wyeth*, with contributions by Brian O'Doherty, Meryman, and E. P. Richardson (Greenwich, CT: New York Graphic Society and Fine Arts Museums of San Francisco, 1973), p. 45.

Logging Scoot

1968, watercolor on paper, 22 × 30 ½ in.
Collection of John and Dolores Beck

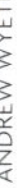

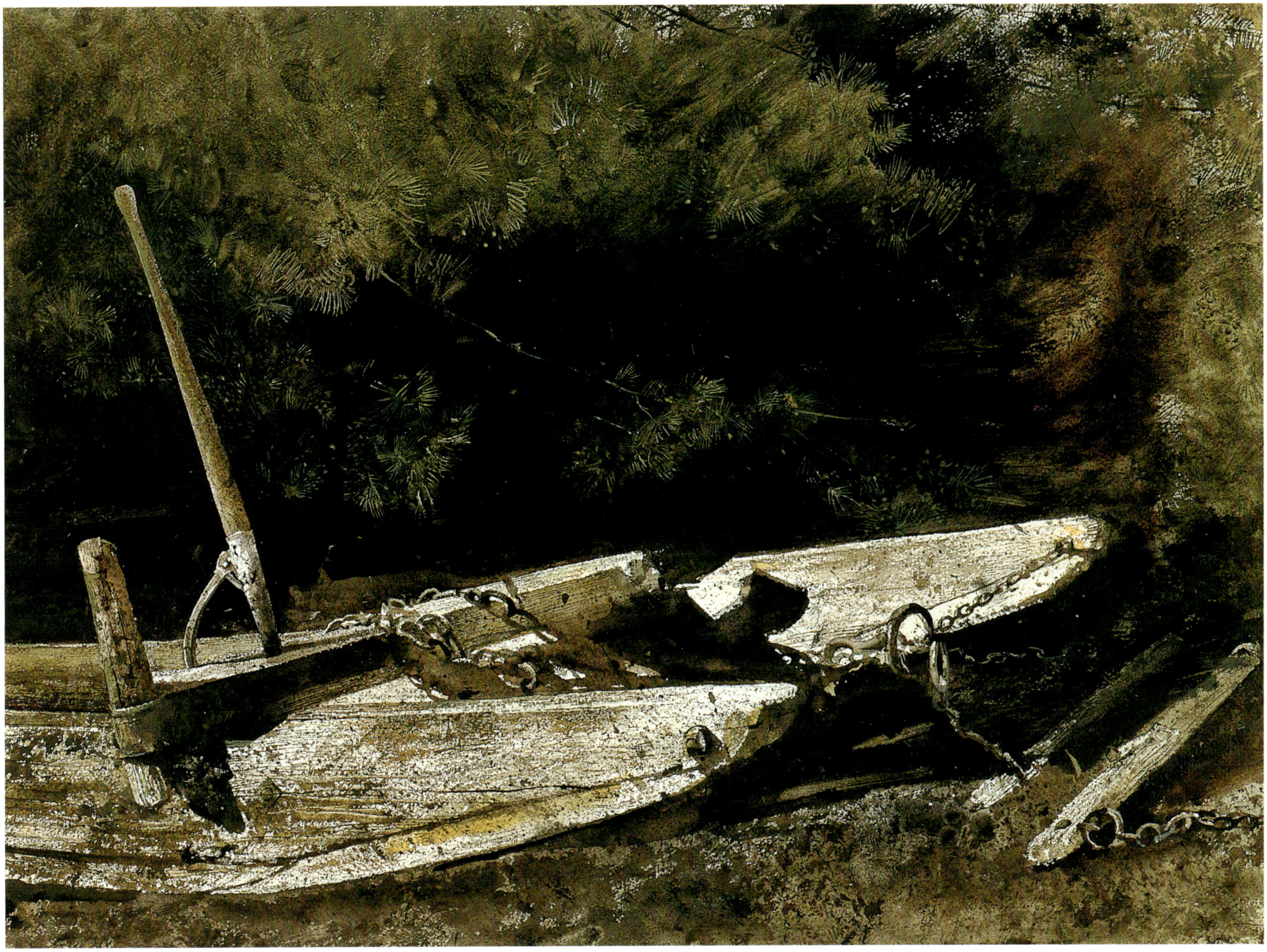

Andrew Wyeth b. 1917

The Quaker is one of Andrew Wyeth's most intriguing symbolic portraits. The two coats hanging from the mantel are from the antique clothing collection of Howard Pyle, the well-known book illustrator who was N. C. Wyeth's teacher. Both Wyeth's father, N. C. Wyeth, and Howard Pyle collected costumes that they used for their illustrations. As a child, Wyeth dressed up in his father's garments to play Robin Hood or the Three Musketeers. He developed a love for vintage clothing and kept an extensive collection himself.

Wyeth often used pieces of clothing to represent the person to whom they belonged. The two coats in this composition evoke Wyeth's only art teacher, his father, as well as his father's teacher. The curator of the 2005 Wyeth exhibition observed that "the coattails seem to move slightly, suggesting a pair of standing figures engaged in conversation."[1] The black Quaker coat in the center represents Wyeth's father, whom he both admired and feared. The more elaborate cream-colored coat represents Pyle, from whom Wyeth learned the importance of historical detail.

Massachusetts-born N. C. Wyeth came to Wilmington, Delaware, to study with Pyle and moved to Chadd's Ford, Pennsylvania, near Wilmington, where Andrew Wyeth continued to live with his wife and family after he married. His father's sudden death in 1945 shocked him and precipitated several important changes in his art. As Wyeth's biographer Richard Meryman has noted, after his father's death "painting after painting would become a posthumous portrait of his father."[2] One of Wyeth's last memories of his father was a visit to the Quaker meeting house to see him in an open casket.

In the painting the window at the left contrasts dramatically with the empty coats. It mediates between the house's dark interior and the sunlight and landscape beyond it. Occupying almost one-third of the picture space, the window is a symbolic self-portrait of Wyeth himself. Both his father and Pyle worked strictly as illustrators, but his father longed to be a fine artist. Wyeth became that artist and paid homage to his artistic heritage in this painting. The two costumes and the dark interior suggest the past, while the landscape and the streaming sunlight evoke the present and Wyeth's break from the tradition of illustration to become a fine artist. [JM]

---

[1] Anne Classen Knutson, ed., "Andrew Wyeth's Language of Things," in *Andrew Wyeth: Memory and Magic* (exhibition catalogue) (New York: Rizzoli, High Museum of Art, Atlanta, and the Philadelphia Museum of Art, 2005), p. 71.

[2] Richard Meryman, as quoted in Knutson, *Andrew Wyeth*, p. 49.

The Quaker

1975, tempera on panel, 36 ¾ × 40 ½ in.
Private Collection

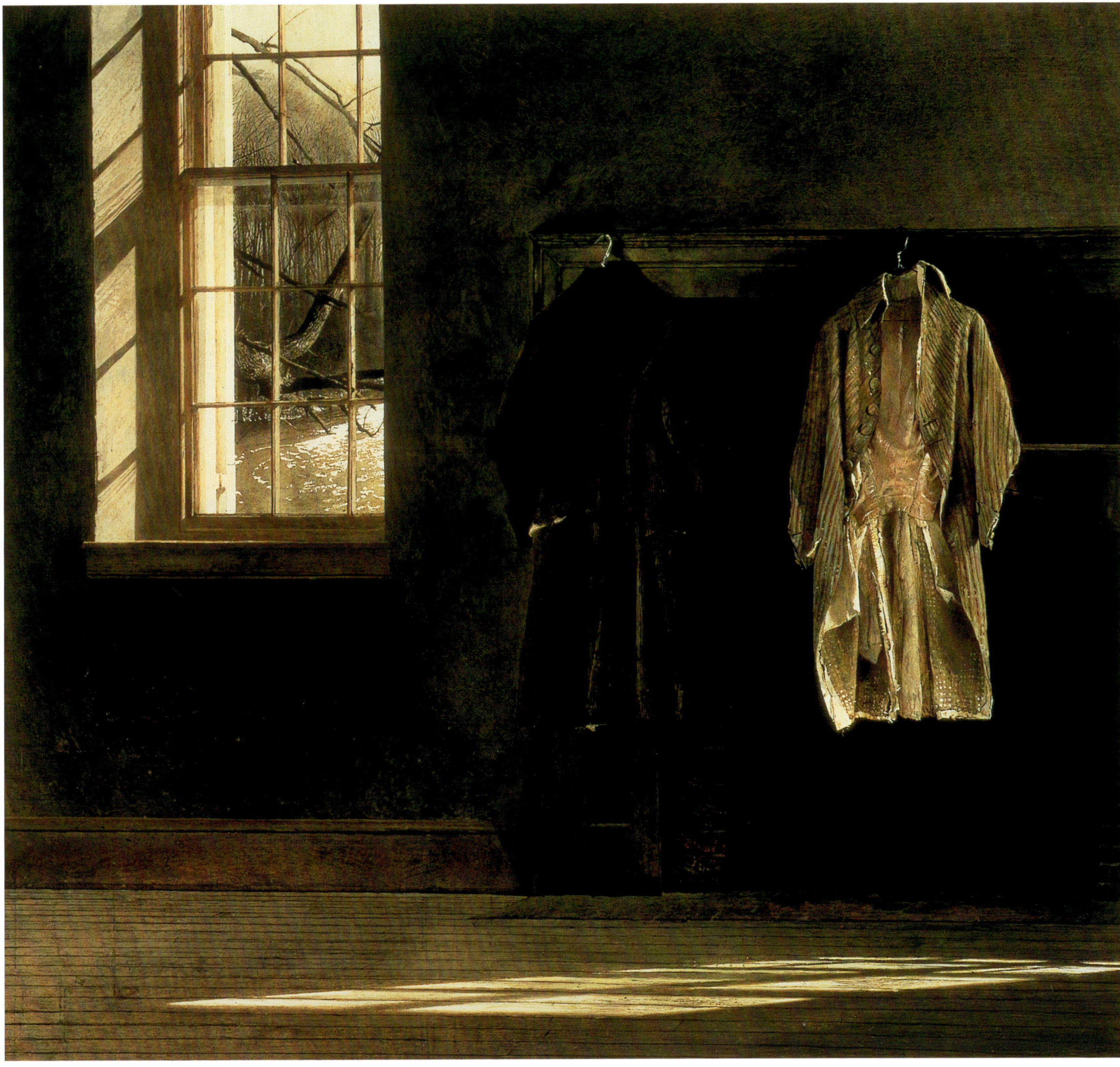

Richard Estes b. 1932

Richard Estes based *Jone's Diner* on a photograph of an eatery on Lafayette Street in lower Manhattan. The ordinary street corner, with parked vehicles, buildings, and signs, is devoid of people except for a silhouette barely visible through the diner's window. The crisp details, uniform light, and sharp shadows seem convincing evidence that Estes has faithfully rendered a photograph he took early one Sunday morning.

Although Estes has been described as a photo realist ever since his work first caught the attention of critics in the early 1970s, neither "photographic" nor "realistic" accurately describes his approach. He starts with photographs, then alters the images as he paints to make the scenes seem more real. Early in his career, Estes worked as a layout and paste-up artist for an ad agency. Manipulating pictures, he soon realized that what the eye sees and the mind understands are not necessarily the same. "The photograph," he once said, "is [not] the last word in reality."[1] Instead, it is the beginning, a kind of filmic sketch that provides the idea for a composition that must be altered to appear real.

Estes selects his subjects based on the photographs, but often returns to a site, sometimes several years later, to take more pictures. Because his subject is the changing urban landscape, the locations may look different: buildings are torn down, stores change hands, new signs replace old ones, so he must choose which elements to include. He then draws freehand, roughing-in basic shapes, emphasizing lines, eliminating details, and moving features around so that the emerging composition no longer matches the original photographs. Occasionally the changes are slight—he may delete a sagging sign or omit a parked car; at other times the alterations are more dramatic. The relative heights of adjacent buildings may change or light poles may be moved, added, or eliminated.

Estes' works, like the "realist" canvases of Edward Hopper, compel speculation. The location in *Jone's Diner*, for example, is a specific New York street corner, yet the painting prompts a sense of déjà vu. Signs and diners like these can be found in cities all across the country. Transcending the specificity of time and place, *Jone's Diner* captures urban life in late twentieth-century America. [VMM]

[1] JoAnn Lewis. "Manhattan Mirror: Previewing a Hirshhorn Exhibit of the Work of Richard Estes," *Washington Post*, January 21, 1979, p. SM16.

Jone's Diner

1979, oil on canvas, 36 × 48 in.
Private Collection, Washington, DC

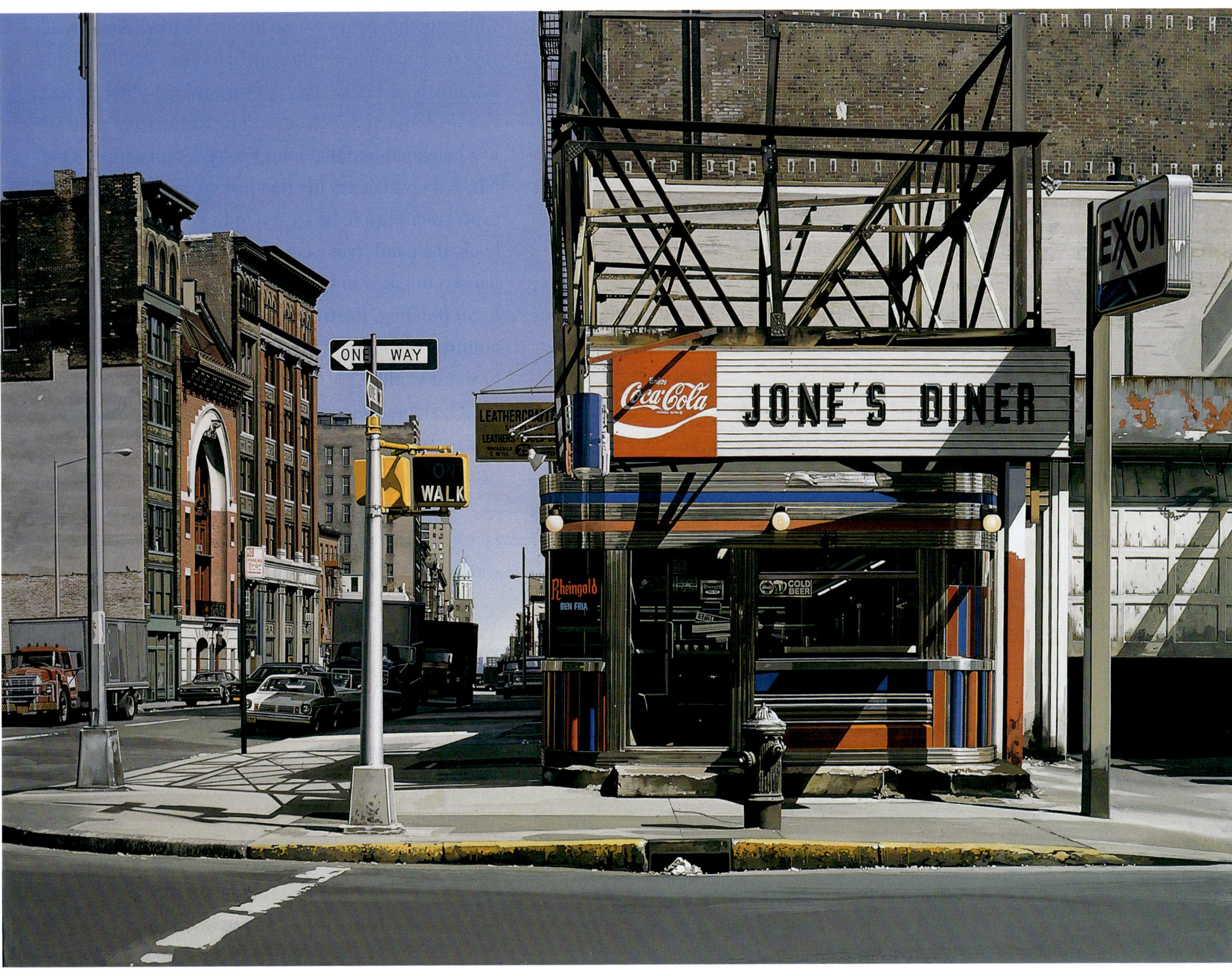
ONE WAY
WALK
Coca-Cola
JONE'S DINER
EXXON
Rheingold
COLD BEER

David Hockney b. 1937

David Hockney was dazzled by the glamour and modernity of Los Angeles when he first arrived from England in 1964. He felt compelled to paint the reality around him and turned away, for a time, from the overt language of desire that had characterized much of his work until then.[1] Nevertheless, *Savings and Loan Building* slyly suggests the creative and sexual freedom that Hockney found in Southern California and that shaped his life thereafter.

The square canvas neatly articulated into subsets of rectangles brings to mind the minimalist painters who, in the 1960s, were offering up the last gasps of high modernist art.[2] Hockney's deeply personal, joyously colored work was not "serious" from the standpoint of these artists or the critics interested only in the properties of paint and surface. In *Savings and Loan Building*, Hockney tweaked the solemnities of the art world, adopting the minimalists' strict calibration of shapes and colors only long enough to disrupt them with a vast cerulean sky and playful palms.

The façade of glass and steel interrupted by small blue rectangles echoes the grid of neighborhoods spangled with swimming pools that Hockney first saw from the air. A phallic radio tower thrusts from the roof of the building, while swaying palms whose fronds are like fountains disrupt the corporate architecture. Hockney employed this imagery once before, in a work from 1964 titled *Building, Pershing Square, Los Angeles*. The earlier painting refers to a neighborhood that John Rechy described in *City of Night*, a novel of gay life that had colored Hockney's expectations before he arrived in Los Angeles.[3] In Rechy's book, the palm trees were silent witnesses to the casual liaisons initiated in Pershing Square. In *Savings and Loan Building*, the trees suggest a subversive counterculture existing under the gaze of the buttoned-down business world.

The basic elements in *Savings and Loan Building* quickly became the dominant motifs in Hockney's paintings. Giant plate-glass windows in suburban homes formed disciplined, middle-class grids against which Hockney contrasted fecund, perenially green gardens and the libidinous energy of young men swimming and sunning beside turquoise pools. [GS]

---

[1] Mark Glazebrook, *David Hockney Paintings, Prints and Drawings 1960–1970* (Boston: Boston Book and Art, 1970), pp. 9–11.

[2] See Paul Melia and Ulrich Luckhardt, *David Hockney: Paintings* (Munich: Prestel-Verlag, 1994), catalogue entry #25.

[3] Paul Melia, ed., *David Hockney* (New York: Manchester University Press, 1995), pp. 53–54.

Savings and Loan Building

1967, acrylic on canvas, 48 × 48 in.
Collection of Nan Tucker McEvoy

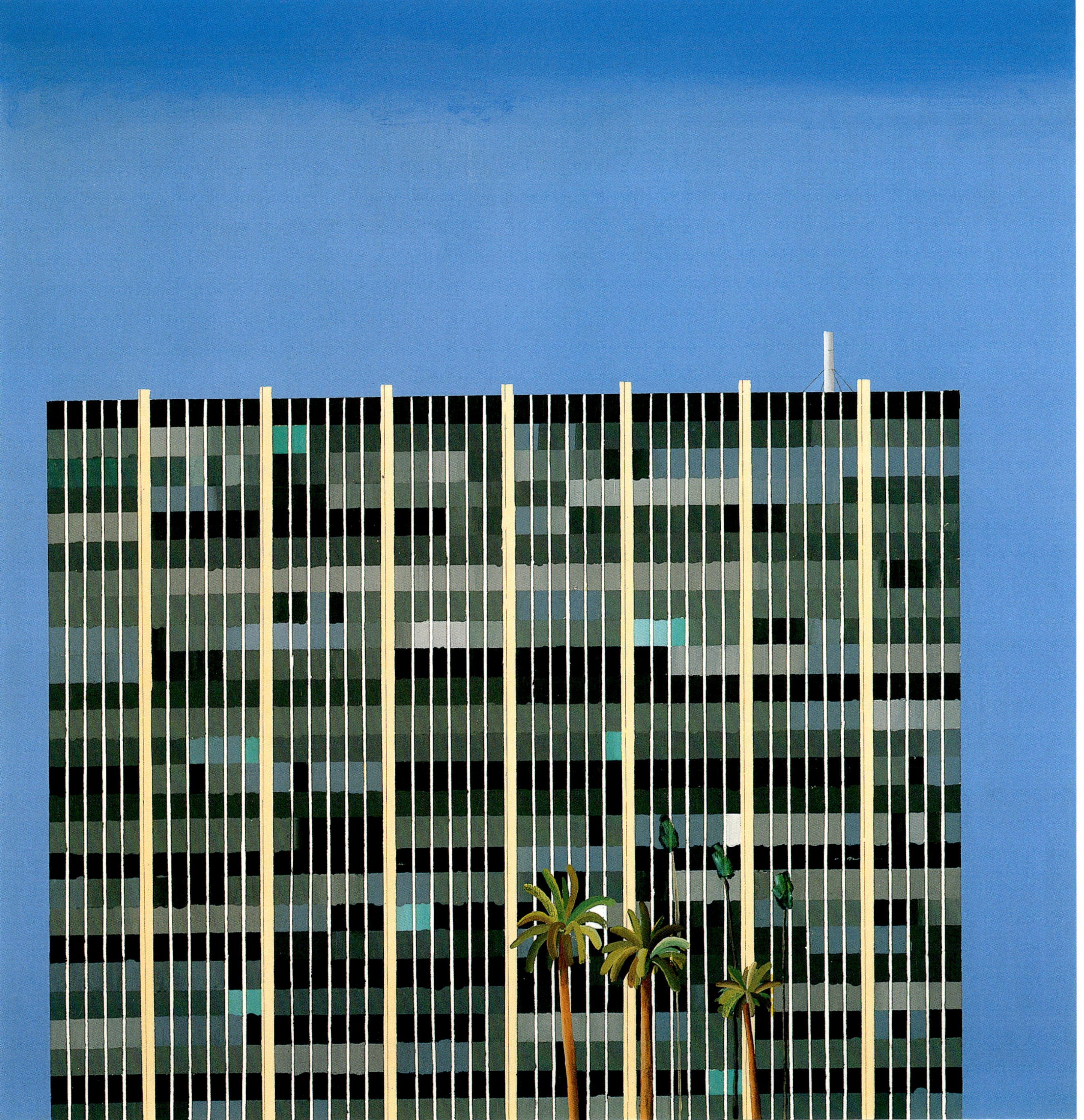

Alice Neel 1900–1984

Alice Neel created portraits when abstract painting ruled the day, and her independent artistic path paralleled a lifelong resistance to society's strictures. Neel was convinced that it was "easy for a woman to be gobbled up" by the expectations of others, and her images of couples, children, and pregnant women resonate with her own losses and hard choices.[1] Her portraits are never idealized, and instead reveal a complex idea of family that Neel wrestled with throughout her career.

The De Vegh twins were daughters of Geza De Vegh, a patron who organized an exhibition on Neel's behalf in 1974 and, years earlier, had restored several paintings that the artist's drug-addicted lover had slashed.[2] In their brilliant red pinafores and white ruffles, the two girls push toward the painting's surface, squeezed by the interior space they occupy. One child slips off the edge of the chair, as though discontented with the chore of posing prettily.

Neel likened herself to a "collector of souls," and this double portrait may be encoded with the memory of her two daughters, one of whom died of diphtheria while the other was taken from the artist while still an infant.[3] Neel often said that she did not make self-portraits because she lived through her subjects as she painted them. In *The De Vegh Twins*, we can look back—perhaps as far as Neel's own childhood—to generations of American girls who, however briefly, did as they were told. [GS]

---

[1] Alice Neel, "Artists and Their Inspiration," *Christian Science Monitor*, October 31, 1977, p. 24.

[2] Linda Chase, *Duos: Alice Neel's Double Portraits* (Naples, FL: Naples Museum of Art, 2001), p. 26.

[3] Patti Goldstein, "Soul on Canvas," *New York*, July 9–16, 1979, p. 76.

The De Vegh Twins

1975, oil on canvas, 48 × 40 in.
Private Collection, Washington, DC

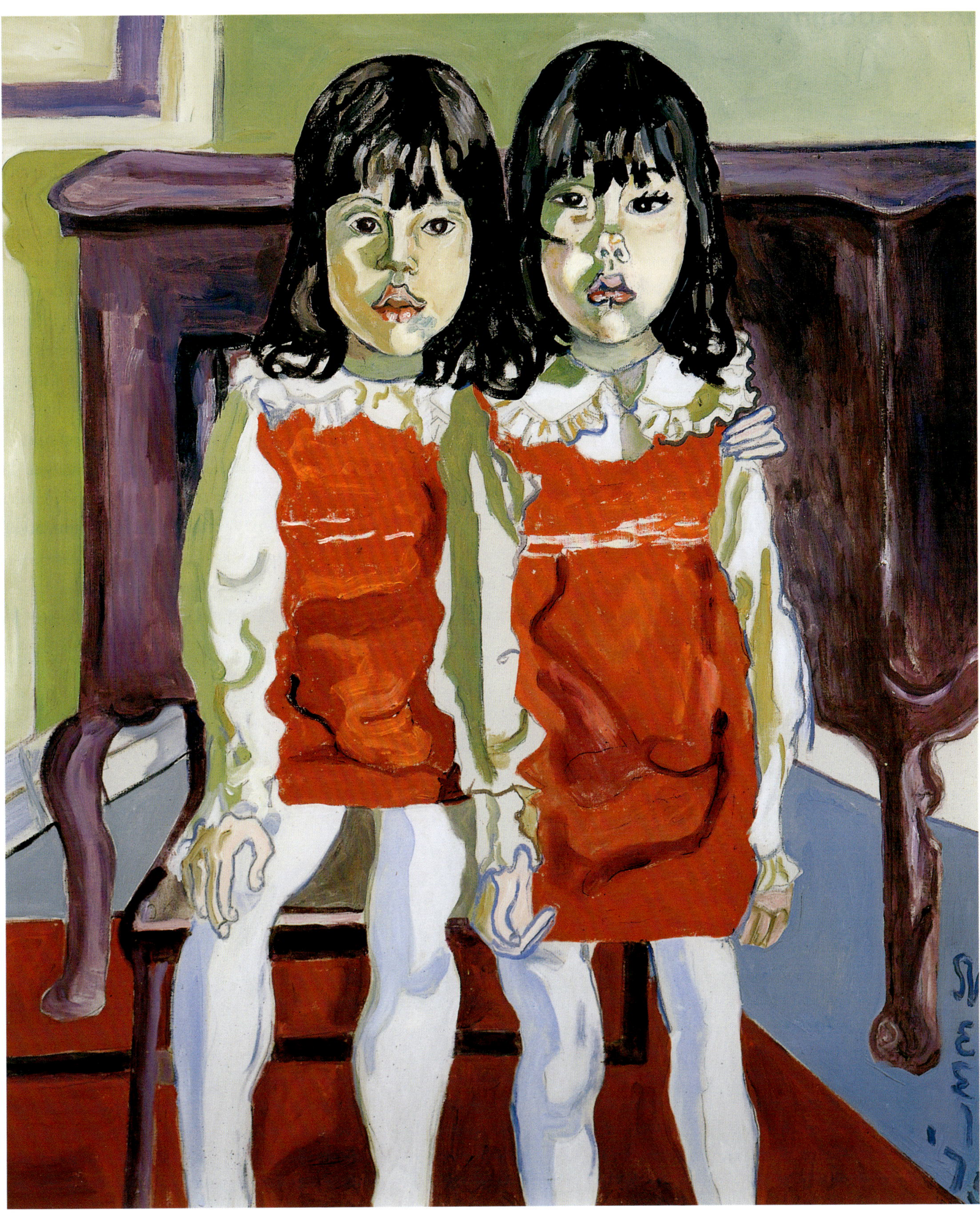

Willem de Kooning 1904–1997

Willem de Kooning painted *Torso* as he was withdrawing from the art scene in New York City and spending more time on the Long Island shore. This painting marks a significant shift in the emotional tone of de Kooning's art and substantiates the painter's opinion in 1959 that "a lot of artists, when they get older they get simpler."[1] De Kooning was painting fewer, larger abstract forms on his canvases, pitting broad swathes of lighter pigment against deeper hues in works that suggested landscapes as well as figures.

As he would throughout his career, de Kooning took a step forward by looking back to earlier successes and reworking them. The central figure in *Torso*, brushed in with thick strokes of pink paint and accented with black, is a gentler daughter of the aggressive goddesses that de Kooning painted throughout the 1950s. The bloated lobster claw that wraps around a barely discernible face and the suggestion of an arm languidly draped over the back of a chair resemble the distorted limbs in *Woman Sitting*, *Pink Lady*, and *Pink Angels*, works from the 1940s that share the pink and green hues of this canvas.

Torso looks forward as well to works de Kooning made after he settled on Long Island in 1963, when he discovered that the women he painted were "very friendly and pastoral, like my landscapes, and not so aggressive."[2] His figures of women would grow more literal and recognizable in the following years before spinning off into thin strands of color at the end of his career. "As for myself," de Kooning asserted in 1964, "Goethe said that when you're sixty you start all over again, and that's what I'm doing."[3] [GS]

---

[1] Willem De Kooning, *Willem de Kooning: Paintings*, essays by David Sylvester, Richard Schiff, and catalogue by Marla Prather (New Haven, CT: Yale University Press and the National Gallery of Art, Washington, DC, 1994), p. 156.

[2] Ibid., p. 177.

[3] Ibid., p. 174.

Torso

late 1950s, oil on canvas, 30 × 20 in.
Collection of Rita J. Pynoos

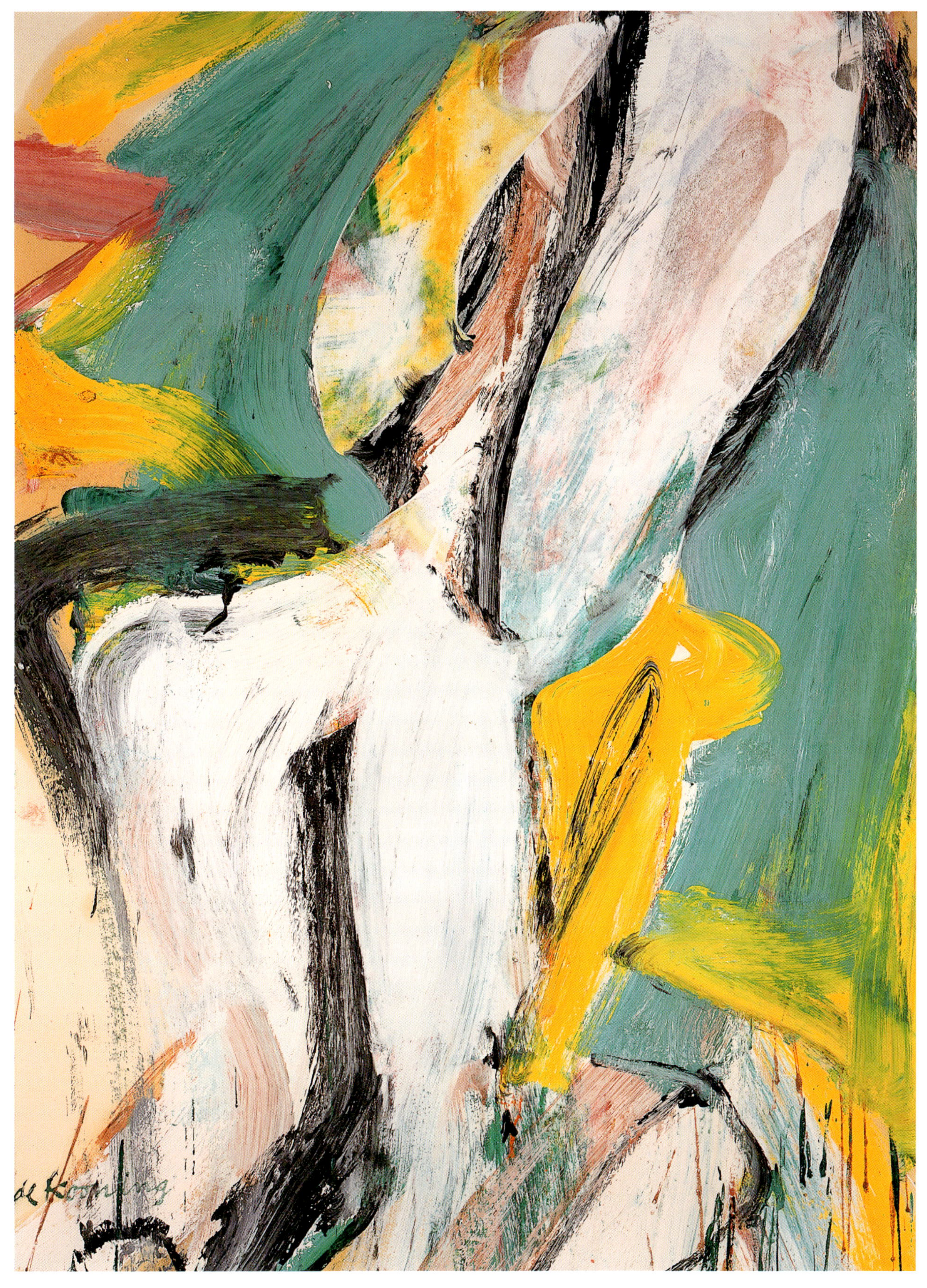
de Kooning

David Smith 1906–1965

VB XXIII grew out of David Smith's visit to Voltri, Italy, in the summer of 1962. Gian Carlo Menotti, director of the Spoleto Festival, had pleaded with Smith to contribute his sculptures, saying, "Italy needs you!" Smith, who felt that his art was more than a match for European tradition, replied, "But what the hell do I need Italy for?"[1] When Smith toured the abandoned factory where he was to work, however, he was thrilled to discover hundreds of tools as well as cut and formed pieces of metal that had been abandoned when the plant closed. Here, among what he called the "found tombs" of an earlier industrial period, Smith created thirty works from the cast-offs he regarded as sculptures in themselves. Smith shipped some of the Voltri remnants to his studio at Bolton's Landing in upstate New York. The works he created there—known as "VBs," "Voltons," or "Voltri-Boltons"—acknowledge his debt to Italy's vanishing artisans, whose skills he sustained in his own art.

When he wrote about his love for industrial materials, the sculptor moved freely between facts and the poetic associations that his "noble junk" inspired. In *VB XXIII*, Smith's stream-of-consciousness translates into a work that shifts between the real and the imagined. *VB XXIII* suggests a figure standing at a table, holding in its hands the basic shapes of circle and square that describe its own form. The piece reflects Smith's process, in which he laid objects out upon a table or on the floor before welding them in upright combinations. Seen this way, the sculpture becomes a self-portrait of the artist at work. Gouges on the perforated standing disc look like finely articulated fingers, delicately pressed together, as if the figure were pondering its next move with the open squares. These resemblances give way momentarily to the "facts," to the weight and texture of the individual components, before the imagination takes over once again. Smith valued both of these experiences. "Sometimes when I start a sculpture," he said, "I begin with only a realized part, the rest is travel [that unfolds] much in the order of a dream."[2] [GS]

---

[1] Quoted in Jay Jacobs, "David Smith Sculpts for Spoleto," *Art News Annual* 29 (1964): 46.

[2] Quoted in Garnett McCoy, ed., *David Smith* (New York: Praeger Publishers, 1973), p. 23.

VB XXIII

1963, welded steel, 69 1/2 × 28 7/8 × 24 in.
Inscribed: *David Smith* and *MaR14–63 V.B XXIII*
Private Collection

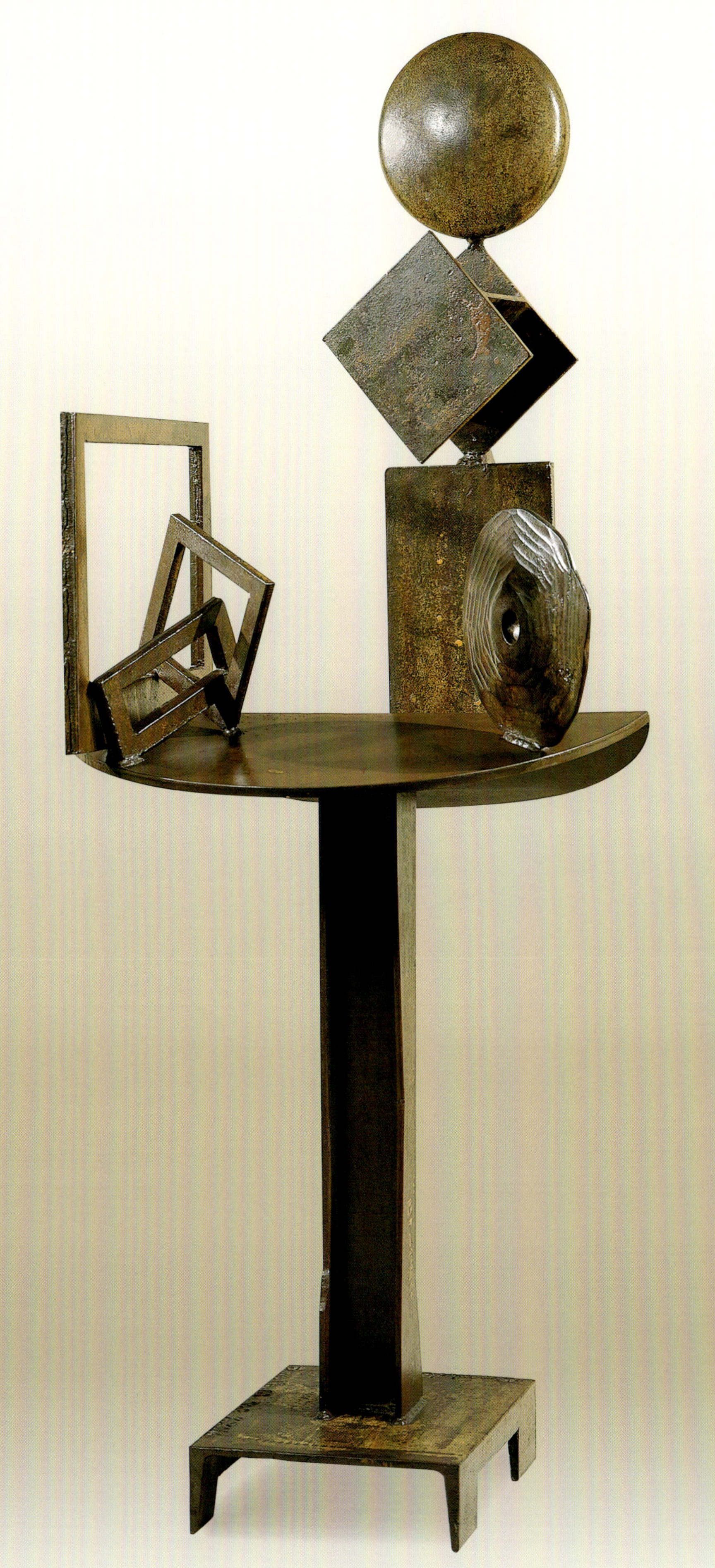

Willem de Kooning 1904–1997

Stowaway distills a range of images that made Willem de Kooning a hero in postwar painting, and reduces line, color, and form—what he called "the three toads in my garden"—to the essentials.[1] The title of this painting suggests that the artist was looking back to the beginning of his career, when he hid in the engine room of a British freighter bound for the United States. Without money or passport, de Kooning came to America dreaming of cowboys, Hollywood goddesses, wealth, and fame. By 1986, he had enjoyed forty years of acclaim as a leading American abstract painter, and *Stowaway* summarizes many episodes in his career.

In his last productive period before illness overtook him, de Kooning drew in charcoal directly on the canvas, then scraped and rubbed successive layers of paint as if he wanted to summon the image as quickly as he could. The more delicate, looping lines evoke his early, biomorphic abstractions, while the push and pull between these hues and the dense white ground recalls such works as *Attic* and *Excavation*, the giant paintings that made de Kooning's reputation in the late 1940s. Suggestions of intertwined arms and legs painted in stronger complementary reds and greens echo the splayed bodies of his notorious Woman series from the 1950s and 1960s.[2]

The lyrical quality of *Stowaway* transforms his once-violent motifs, reflecting the calm and order of de Kooning's late years. In 1978, his estranged wife, Elaine, returned to de Kooning's home on Long Island, where she helped him to stop drinking and carefully maintained his daily routine with the support of studio assistants. Instead of the "melodrama" that de Kooning acknowledged in his earlier images, *Stowaway* reflects the confidence of a man who clearly understood what he had accomplished: "You get old, you get used to yourself. . . . I used to be so nervous I got palpitations. Now I don't have that trouble. I see the canvas, and I begin."[3] [GS]

---

[1] Willem de Kooning, *Willem de Kooning: The Late Paintings, the 1980s*, essays by Gary Garrels and Robert Storr (San Francisco: San Francisco Museum of Modern Art and Walker Art Center, Minneapolis, 1995), p. 16.

[2] Willem de Kooning, *Willem de Kooning: Paintings*, with essays by David Sylvester, Richard Schiff, and catalogue by Marla Prather (New Haven, CT: Yale University Press and the National Gallery of Art, Washington, DC, 1994), pp. 201–02; Robert Rosenblum, "On de Kooning's Late Style," *Art Journal* 48, no. 3 (Fall 1989): 249.

[3] De Kooning, *Willem de Kooning: Paintings*, p. 199.

Stowaway

1986, oil on canvas, 80 × 70 in.
Collection of Rita J. Pynoos

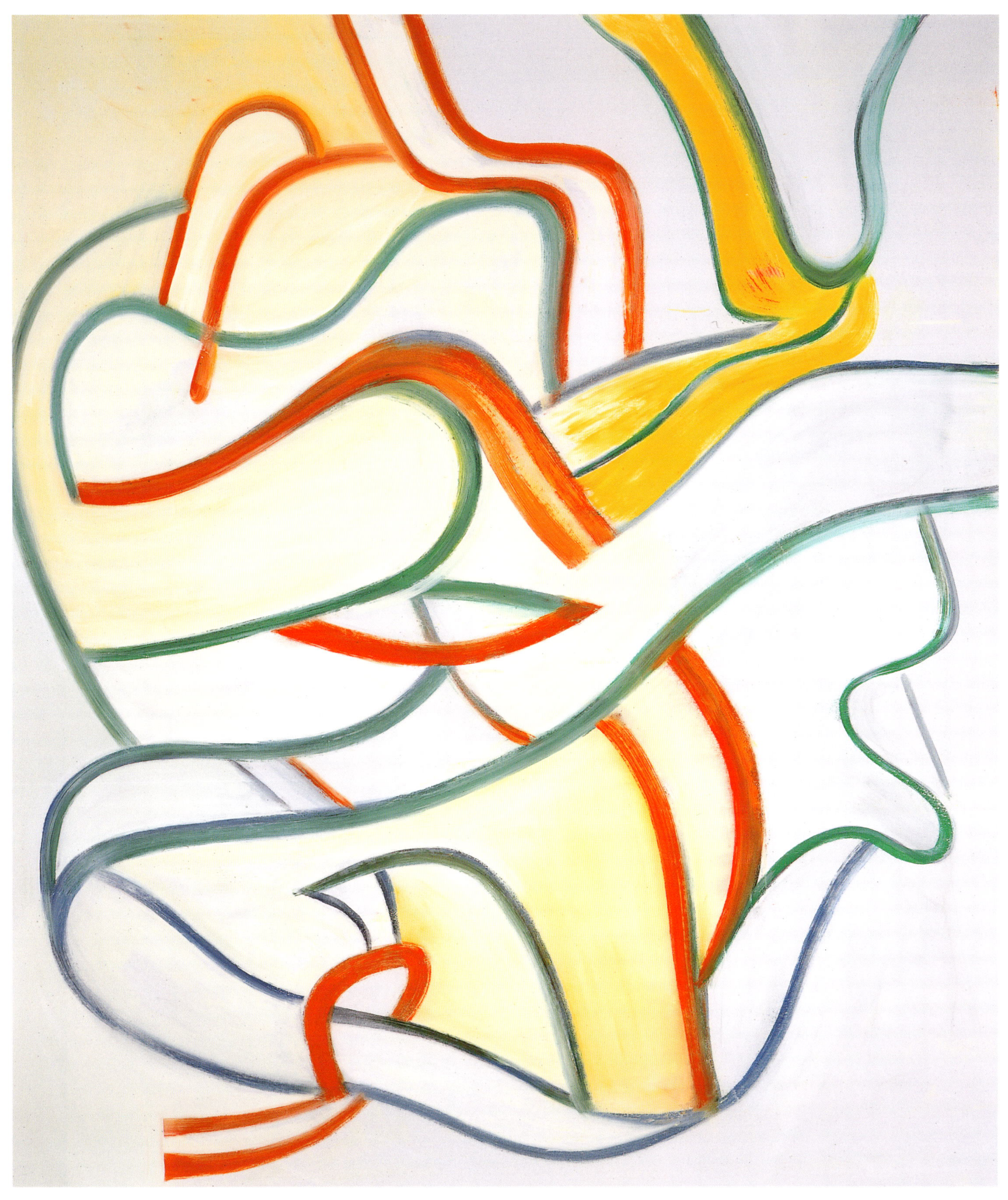

Tom Wesselmann 1931–2004

Great American Nude #94 recalls the collages that made Tom Wesselmann's reputation in the early 1960s. References to flowers and fruit hark back to classical nudes, while the cigarette, teased hair, and leopard skin place this work squarely in the most sensual decade the nation had seen. The "pill" had relaxed the country's sexual mores, the Kennedys were glamorous players, and the women's liberation movement had not yet emerged as a backlash against the shallow promises of the "swinging sixties."

But the graphic nudity and flip references to popular culture in this painting disguise a complex range of ideas and influences. Wesselmann wanted to be a heroic painter like the abstract expressionists, even working for a time with a psychoanalyst as Jackson Pollock and others had done. He reworked the genres of nudes and still lifes with images from his postwar generation, investing his canvases with the frank eroticism he enjoyed in his marriage to a former model, Claire Selley.[1] As he grew more famous, Wesselmann played all the angles in the reaction to his work. He enjoyed the advantages of being labeled a pop artist, but insisted that the cigarettes, Coca Cola bottles, and other ad images were meaningless except as forms and colors competing with one another to produce a "visceral thrill."[2] A particularly conservative critic helped legitimize the work, acknowledging that a Wesselmann nude had pornographic value as an "ideal sexual appliance," but praising the young artist for having assimilated every stream of blue-chip modernist painting, including shaped canvases, minimal art, color field abstraction, and hard-edge painting.[3]

Wesselmann acknowledged the aggressive sexuality of his paintings and claimed that he could "never make [women] as beautiful on canvas as they are in real life."[4] If others wanted to call him a pop artist or a pornographer, he remained convinced that he had done something more. "The female nude was given respectability by the masters—Titian and Manet," he told a journalist. "Then people had to deal with me."[5] [GS]

---

[1] David McCarthy, "Tom Wesselmann and the Americanization of the Nude, 1961–1963," *Smithsonian Studies in American Art* 4, nos. 3–4 (Summer–Fall 1990): 116.

[2] Paul Gardner, "When Is a Painting Finished?" *Artnews* (November 1985): 93; and G. R. Swenson, "What Is Pop Art? Interviews with Eight Painters," *Artnews* (February 1964): 64.

[3] Hilton Kramer, "Form, Fantasy, and the Nude," *New York Times* (February 11, 1968), p. D25.

[4] Lori Simmons Zelenko, "Tom Wesselmann," *American Artist* 46 (June 1982): 103.

[5] Paul Gardner, "Tom Wesselmann," *Artnews* (January 1982): 67.

Great American Nude #94

1967, oil on canvas, 28 ½ × 37 in.
Private Collection, Washington, DC

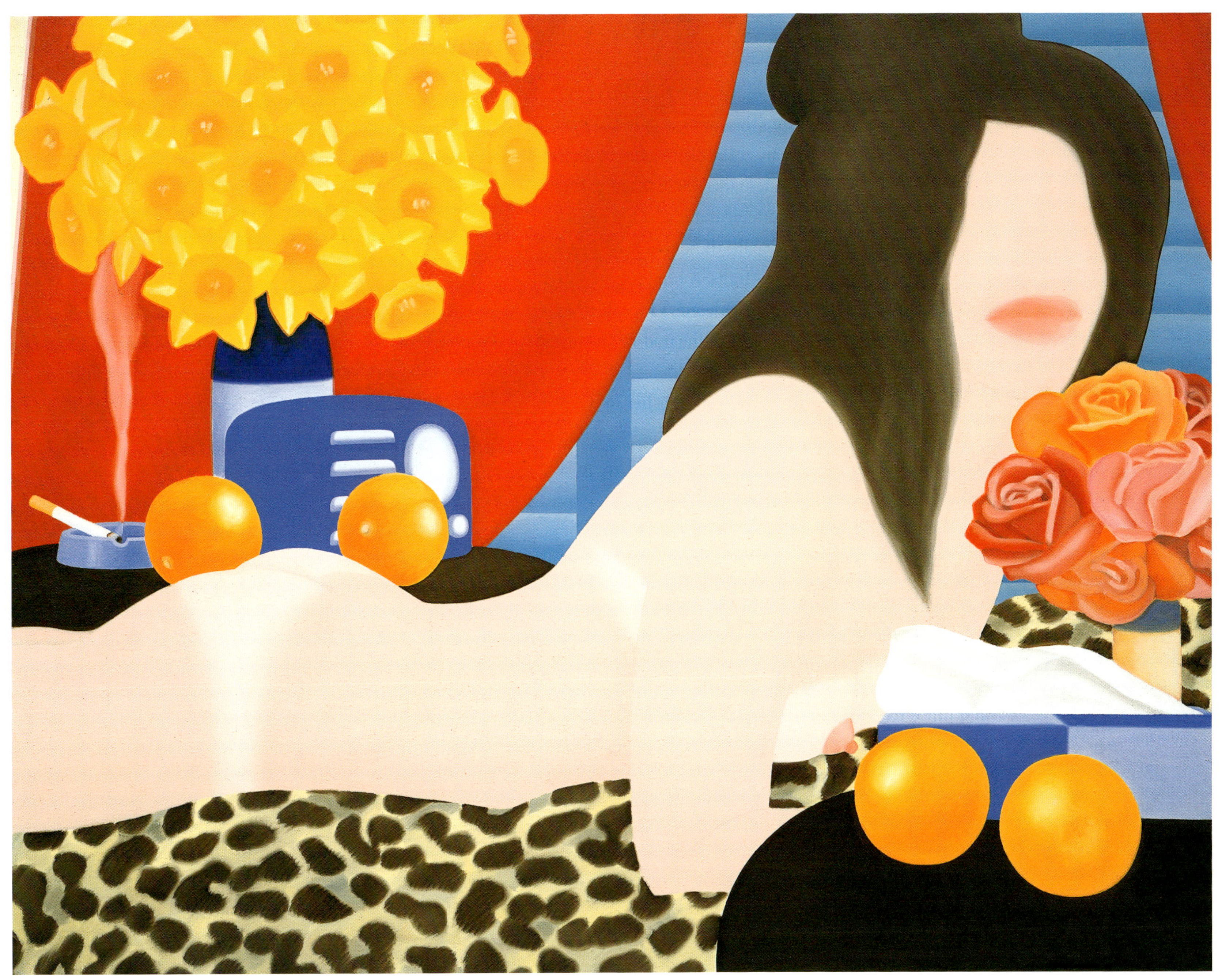

David Hockney b. 1937

Ian Watching Television depicts David Hockney's former lover, Ian Falconer, who, by 1987, had become the painter's assistant. As he did in many of his portraits, Hockney encoded his own image into the likeness of his friend. While Falconer's features are instantly recognizable, he appears with Hockney's trademarks, including the thatch of blond hair, the striped shirt, cigarette, and red sneakers. The large, expressive hand recalls those that hold a pencil or brush in Hockney's self-portraits. A bright flash of light from the television illuminates Falconer's face, further evoking Hockney's self-portraits from the mid-1980s created with laser photocopiers.[1]

The key to this confusion of identities lies in the style of the painting, which links the history of modern painting with Hockney's studio practice. The Picassoesque head and shifting viewpoints pay tribute to the cubists, who Hockney felt taught the world "a different way of looking."[2] Falconer's face is seen both in profile and full view, while legs and feet pointing in different directions suggest his restless movements. *Ian Watching Television* achieves in paint what Hockney captured in his photographic collages, in which multiple images of his companion's hands, face, and limbs record Falconer at work in the studio. The two men were at this time designing sets and costumes in the style of Picasso for Wagner's *Tristan und Isolde*, establishing another symbolic link with the Spanish master, who had designed sets for Wagner's *Parsifal* decades before.

But this image looks forward as well as to the past. Hockney often painted himself and spoke of himself as Picasso's student, and by picturing Falconer as his alter ego, he conveyed to his own pupil the absolute artistic freedom that Picasso had claimed and Hockney celebrated throughout his career.[3] After collaborating with Hockney on two more operas, Falconer embarked on his own career as a theatrical designer and author of children's books. Hockney's *Ian Watching Television* is a self-portrait of the artist as a young man, and a poignant acknowledgment of his role as a mentor to a new generation of painters. [GS]

---

[1] *Self-Portrait, July 1986* employs a laser image of Hockney's striped shirt and a sketch of his face that correspond to these elements in *Ian Watching Television*.

[2] David Hockney and Paul Joyce, *Hockney on "Art": Conversations with Paul Joyce* (London: Little, Brown and Co., 1999), p. 23.

[3] Gert Schiff, "A Moving Focus: Hockney's Dialogue with Picasso," in *David Hockney: A Retrospective* (New York: Harry N. Abrams and the Los Angeles County Museum of Art, 1988), pp. 41–52.

Ian Watching Television

1987, oil on canvas, 40 × 52 in.
Collection of Rita J. Pynoos

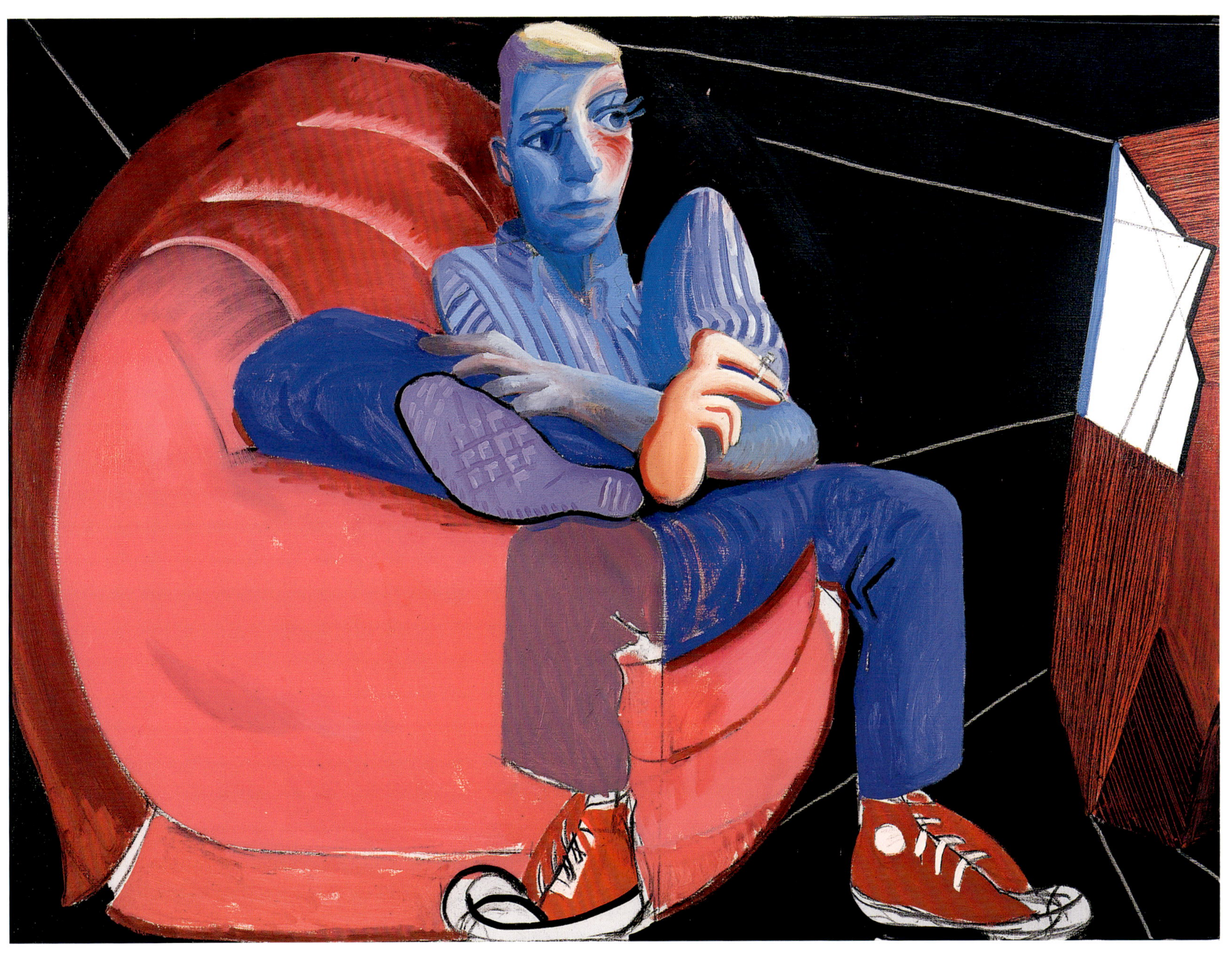

David Bates b. 1952

David Bates's *Sheepsheads and Lemons* carries his thickly painted canvases into three dimensions. The sheepshead fish, a filleting knife, and lemon slices appear to have popped out of the painting, while the frame remains as the support for the sculpture. The artist called attention to his own game by painting a critic's review in one corner with the headline "Sculpture or Painting?" *Sheepsheads and Lemons* demonstrates Bates's debt to folk artists as well as his grasp of art history. His work is undeniably modern and expressive, but it recalls the still-life tradition of trompe l'oeil works by William Harnett and John Frederick Peto in the nineteenth century.

Bates spent most of the 1980s canoeing and fishing in the swampy woodlands of Grassy Lake in western Arkansas. His trips through the wild preserve, accompanied by leathery guides who appear in many of his portraits, generated a body of work that brought the artist glowing reviews and strong sales. Grassy Lake was his "special place," where he felt privileged to participate in the daily dramas of an ancient natural world.[1]

But *Sheepsheads and Lemons* signaled a significant change in his career. As a child, Bates had pleaded for summer vacations on the Texas Gulf Coast, and this work suggests that, although he was still immersed in the imagery of Grassy Lake, he was thinking of another, beloved place. In the lower left corner, Bates painted the travel section of a newspaper, with a headline reading, simply, "The Gulf." He carved and painted sheepsheads, which feed and breed in the gulf shallows rather than inland waters like Grassy Lake. In still other sections of the newspaper, the sports page and a recipe for Cajun catfish suggest the simple pleasures of the coastal cultures that Bates loved all his life. The toothy fish in this work, served up with tasty lemons, offers a wry comment on the food chain that had preoccupied Bates in the Grassy Lake pictures. Shortly after creating *Sheepsheads and Lemons,* Bates shifted the focus of his art, and the symbols in this painted sculpture reappeared throughout the 1990s as emblems of hardworking men in fishing communities along Galveston Island and points east.[2] [GS]

---

[1] Quoted in Marla Price, *David Bates: Forty Paintings* (Fort Worth, TX: Modern Art Museum of Fort Worth, 1988), pp. 10, 27.

[2] See David Bates and Charles Dee Mitchell, *David Bates: The Gulf Coast: Galveston Arts Center, October 4–November 3, 1997* (Galveston, TX: Galveston Arts Center, 1997).

Sheepsheads and Lemons

1986, painted wood and metal, 38 1/2 × 50 1/8 × 4 in.
Collection of Nan Tucker McEvoy

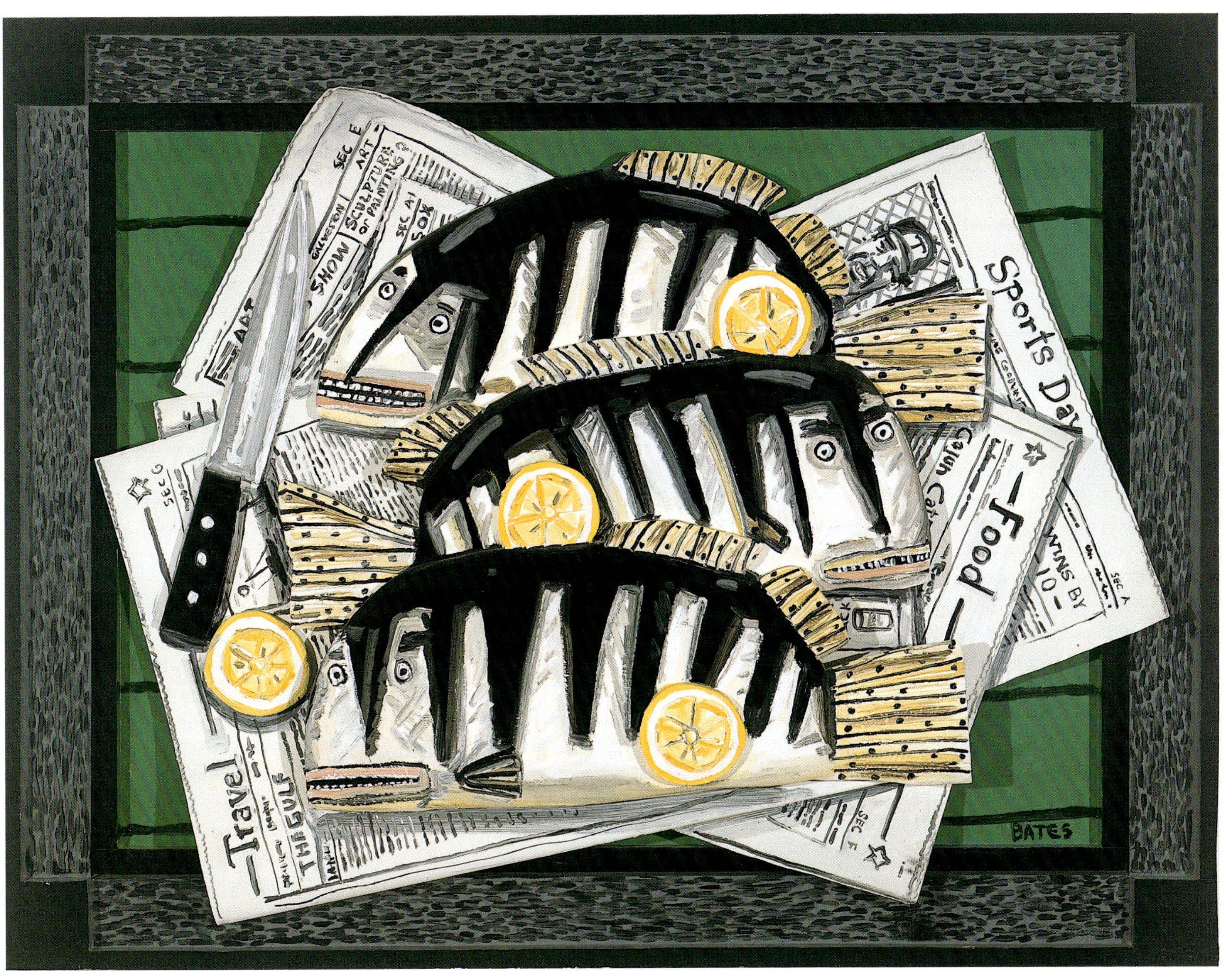
ART
SEC E
SCULPTURE OR PAINTING?
SHOW
Sports Day
Food
Travel
THE GULF
BATES

Wayne Thiebaud b. 1920

Wayne Thiebaud painted cakes, pies, and hot dogs because these familiar things seen in any restaurant across America reminded him of "how gregarious and how close we really are." Whether in Pasadena or on Madison Avenue, he said, "it's the same damn pie," but the little differences of color, light, and shape made him think of how rarely people bother to look for distinctions among themselves.[1] In *Meringues*, each carefully calibrated slice vibrates with "halations," intense shadows in complementary colors that seduce the eye. Rich dollops of paint seem to take on the texture and flavor of the meringues themselves. The countertop looks like pink icing, but then we notice the bluish horizon line at the top, and this no longer seems like a pastry case but a landscape of Pies Across America.

Thiebaud confesses that the exact symbolism of his works continues to elude him, but he admits that, like the customer before the pie counter, he wants to hold on to "just a piece" of that visual experience.[2] When he made his first pie paintings in the early 1960s, Thiebaud could tell that his days as a cartoonist and a poster painter for the movie studios had bubbled to the surface. "Now I have flipped out," he remembers thinking, "that's really crazy, but no one is going to look at these things anyway, so what the heck."[3] On the contrary, Thiebaud's iconic images have reminded critics and admiring friends of Jean-Siméon Chardin's masterful eighteenth-century still lifes, of Claude Monet's impressionist grain stacks, and of the best American pop art. [GS]

---

[1] John Coplans, *Wayne Thiebaud* (Pasadena, CA: Pasadena Art Museum, 1968), p. 26.

[2] Steven A. Nash, "Unbalancing Acts: Wayne Thiebaud Reconsidered," in *Wayne Thiebaud: A Paintings Retrospective* (New York: Thames and Hudson and the Fine Arts Museums of San Francisco, 2000), p. 8.

[3] Ibid., p. 16.

Meringues

1988, oil on canvas, 30 × 30 in.
Private Collection, Washington, DC

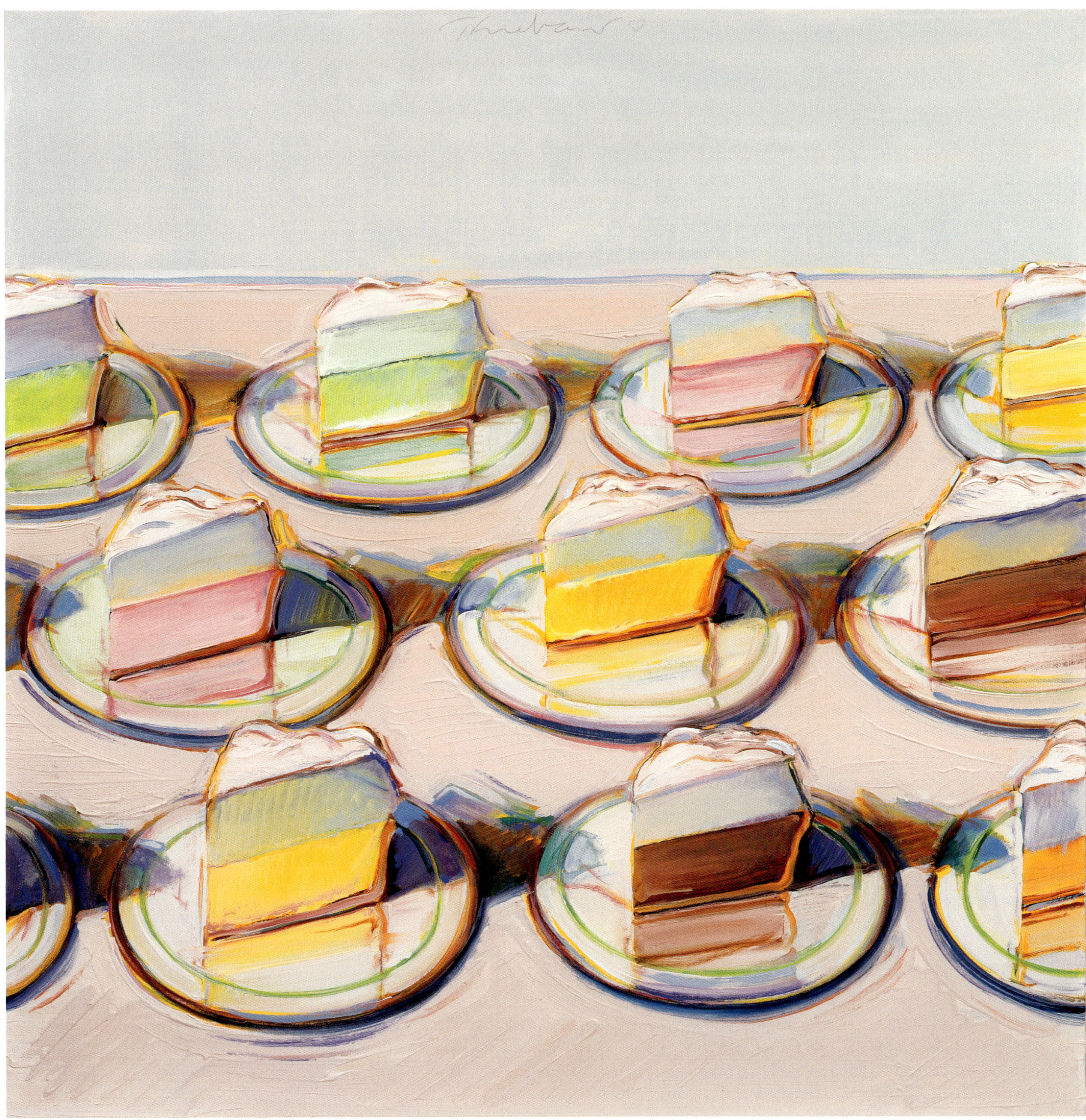

Niki de Saint Phalle 1930–2002

Niki de Saint Phalle maintained that certain tarot cards were dealt to her when she was born—including the moon, symbol of imagination—and that these cards determined her path as an artist.[1] *La Lune* suggests one of the goddess figures who inspired de Saint Phalle to fight all her life against illness, the slights of her family, and the power of men in a sexist society. A version of this work appears in the Garden of Tarot, de Saint Phalle's penultimate project, which she completed not long before her death. The idea came to her in a dream, and in 1979, de Saint Phalle began building sculptures of the most powerful tarot symbols on a rocky plot in Tuscany. The garden was de Saint Phalle's refuge and torment, where, suffering from rheumatoid arthritis and mourning the deaths of friends, she worked for eighteen years, seeking the "garden of paradise" that revealed itself to those who had found inner peace.[2]

The moon's feminine symbolism of childbearing, creation, and ancient taboos calls to mind de Saint Phalle's career, in which she confronted the art world's gender-based prejudices and discomforts. *La Lune* evokes Diana the Huntress, reminiscent of de Saint Phalle's *tirs*, her paintings from the 1960s that she famously shot at with rifles to express her rage at patriarchal Western culture. At the same time, *La Lune* looks forward to the totemlike sculptures of her last years, works that depict mythical creatures and sacred animals of the Pacific Northwest.[3]

The large eye and full lips of this sculpture resemble de Saint Phalle's own features, so that the profile suggests both the goddess and a portrait of the sculptor, her face turned ecstatically to the sky, as if worshipping her patroness. At the base of the sculpture, a blue stream suggests the tides that advance and recede with the moon's phases. Figures of a bear and a dog representing Ursa Major and Canis Minor support a crayfish, a centuries-old tarot symbol that, like the crab, represents Cancer, the constellation associated with the moon. These emblems of darkness and light, of beginnings and endings, point to the cycle of life and the ancient determinations of the stars. As Niki de Saint Phalle said, "We're born without knowing the rules. Yet we must play our hands."[4] [GS]

---

[1] Pontus Hultén, *Niki de Saint Phalle* (Kunst- und Ausstellungshalle der Bundesrepublik Deutschland, 1992), p. 147.

[2] Anna Riera, "Niki de Saint Phalle y el Jardin de los Tarots," *Goya*, no. 270 (May–June 1999): 173–75.

[3] Collette Chattopadhyay, "West Hollywood: Niki de Saint Phalle: Tasende Gallery," *Sculpture* 20, no. 10 (December 2001): 67.

[4] Martha Longenecker, ed., *Niki de Saint Phalle: Insider/Outsider World-Inspired Art* (Mingei International Museum, Japan, 1998), p. 65.

La Lune

1987, mixed media, 118 × 47 ½ × 40 ½ in.
Private Collection, Washington, DC

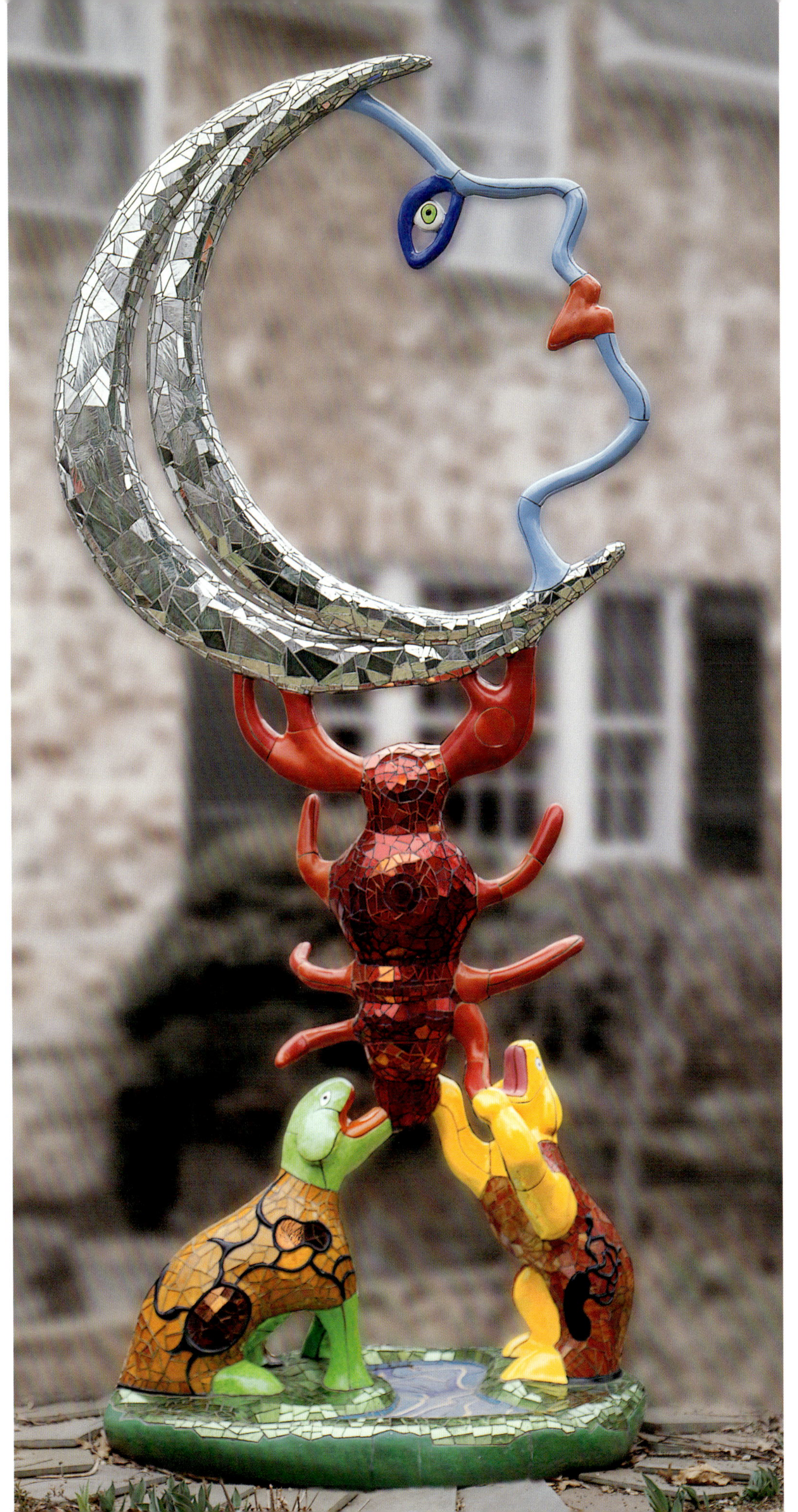

Selected Bibliography

Thomas Anshutz

Archives of American Art, Smithsonian Institution, Washington, DC. Thomas Anshutz to Effie Anshutz, November 11, 1893. Reel 140.

Griffin, Randall. *Thomas Anshutz: Artist and Teacher.* Huntington, NY: Heckscher Museum and the University of Washington Press, Seattle, 1994.

David Bates

Bates, David, and Charles Dee Mitchell. *David Bates: The Gulf Coast: Galveston Arts Center, October 4–November 3, 1997.* Galveston, TX: Galveston Arts Center, 1997.

"David Bates: An Interview." In exhibition catalogue. With preface by Bridget Moore. New York: DC Moore Gallery, 1999.

Price, Marla. *David Bates: Forty Paintings.* Fort Worth, TX: Modern Art Museum of Fort Worth, 1988.

Serwer, Jacquelyn Days. *American Kaleidoscope: Themes and Perspectives in Recent Art.* Contributions by Jonathan P. Binstock, Andrew Connors, Gwendolyn H. Everett, and Lynda Roscoe Hartigan. Washington, DC: National Museum of American Art, Smithsonian Institution, 1996.

George Bellows

Corn, Wanda. "The New New York." *Art in America* 61 (July–August 1973): 59.

Doezema, Marianne. *George Bellows and Urban America.* New Haven, CT: Yale University Press, 1992.

Howells, William Dean. *A Hazard of New Fortunes.* 1890; repr., New York: Signet Classics, 1965.

Quick, Michael, Jane Myers, and Marianne Doezema. *The Paintings of George Bellows. An exhibition catalogue.* New York: H. N. Abrams, 1992.

Zurier, Rebecca, Robert W. Snyder, and Virginia M. Mecklenburg. *Metropolitan Lives: The Ashcan Artists and Their New York.* Washington, DC: National Museum of American Art, Smithsonian Institution and W. W. Norton, 1995.

Robert Blum

Boyle, Richard J. *Robert F. Blum, 1857–1903: A Retrospective Exhibition, April 1 to May 7, 1966.* Cincinnati, OH: Cincinnati Art Museum, 1966.

Lovell, Margaretta. *Venice: The American View, 1860–1920.* San Francisco: Fine Arts Museums of San Francisco, 1984.

Simpson, Marc. "Venice, Whistler, and the American Others." In *After Whistler: The Artist and His Influence on American Painting.* Linda Merill et al. Atlanta: High Museum of Art, 2003.

Weber, Bruce. *Robert Frederick Blum (1857–1903) and His Milieu.* PhD diss. Ann Arbor, MI: University Microfilms International, 1986.

Ernest L. Blumenschein

Eldredge, Charles C., Julie Schimmel, and William H. Truettner. *Art in New Mexico, 1900–1945: Paths to Taos and Santa Fe.* Washington, DC: National Museum of American Art, Smithsonian Institution and Abbeville Press, NY, 1986.

Henning, William T., Jr. *Ernest L. Blumenschein Retrospective: Colorado Springs Fine Arts Center, March 5–April 16, 1978.* Colorado Springs, CO: The Center, 1978.

Dennis Miller Bunker

Archives of American Art, Smithsonian Institution, Washington, DC. Dennis Miller Bunker Papers. Reel 1201.

Hirshler, Erica E. *Dennis Miller Bunker: American Impressionist.* With contributions by David Park Curry, Theodore E. Stebbins, Efrat Adler Porat, and Deanna M. Griffin. Boston: Museum of Fine Arts, 1994.

———. *Dennis Miller Bunker and His Circle.* Boston: Isabella Stewart Gardner Museum, 1995.

Porat, Efrat Adler. "Dennis Miller Bunker: A Tribute to an American Impressionist." *American Art Review* 7, no. 2 (April–May 1995): 113.

White, Nelson C. *Abbott H. Thayer, Painter and Naturalist.* Hartford: Connecticut Printers, 1951.

Mary Cassatt

Barter, Judith A. *Mary Cassatt, Modern Woman.* With contributions by Erica E. Hirshler et al. New York: Harry N. Abrams and the Art Institute of Chicago, 1998.

Carter, S. N. "Exhibition of the Society of American Artists." *Art Journal* 5 (1879): 157.

Mathews, Nancy Mowll, ed. *Cassatt and Her Circle: Selected Letters.* New York: Abbeville Press, 1984.

———. *Mary Cassatt: A Life.* New York: Villard Books, 1994.

Walton, William. "Miss Mary Cassatt." *Scribner's Magazine* 19, no. 3 (March 1896), pp. 358–59.

Frederic Edwin Church

Carr, Gerald. *Frederic Edwin Church: Catalogue Raisonné of Works of Art at Olana State Historic Site,* 2 vols. Cambridge: Cambridge University Press, 1994, vol 1.

Harvey, Eleanor Jones. *The Painted Sketch: American Impressions from Nature, 1830–1880.* New York: Harry N. Abrams and the Dallas Museum of Art, 1998.

Kelly, Franklin, with Stephen Jay Gould, James Anthony Ryan, and Debora Rindge. *Frederic Edwin Church.* Washington, DC: National Gallery of Art, 1989.

Stebbins, Theodore E., Jr. *Close Observation: Selected Oil Sketches by Frederic E. Church: From the Collections of the Cooper-Hewitt Museum.* Washington, DC: Smithsonian Institution Press, 1978.

Treasures from Olana: Landscapes by Frederic Edwin Church. Essay by Kevin J. Avery with introduction by John Wilmerding. Hudson, NY: Olana Partnership, New York State Office of Parks, Recreation and Historic Preservation, and Cornell University Press, 2005.

Cyrus Edwin Dallin

Ahrens, Kent. *Cyrus E. Dallin: His Small Bronzes and Plasters.* Corning, NY: Rockwell Museum, 1995.

Archives of American Art, Smithsonian Institution, Washington, DC. Gorham Manufacturing Company, Bronze Division Records, 5. "Records of Royalties Paid to Sculptors for Casting of Their Works." Reel 3680, frames 96 and 229.

Broder, Patricia Janis. *Bronzes of the American West.* New York: Harry N. Abrams, 1974.

Ewers, John. "Cyrus E. Dallin: Master Sculptor of the Plains Indians." *Montana Magazine of Western History* 18, no. 1 (January 1968), pp. 38–40.

Francis, Rell G. *Cyrus E. Dallin: Let Justice Be Done.* Springville, UT: Springville Museum of Art, 1976.

Museum of Fine Arts, Boston, and Kathryn Greenthal et al. *American Figurative Sculpture in the Museum of Fine Arts Boston.* Boston: Museum of Fine Arts, 1986.

Proske, Beatrice Gilman. *Brookgreen Gardens Sculpture,* 2 vols. Brookgreen Gardens, SC: Trustees of Brookgreen Gardens, 1968–1993.

Willem de Kooning

Garrels, Gary. "Three Toads in the Garden: Line, Color, and Form." In *Willem de Kooning: The Late Paintings, the 1980s.* Essays by Garrels and Robert Storr. San Francisco: San Francisco Museum of Modern Art and Walker Art Center, Minneapolis, 1995.

Sylvester, David, and Richard Schiff. *Willem de Kooning: Paintings.* Catalogue by Marla Prather. New Haven, CT: Yale University Press and the National Gallery of Art, Washington, DC, 1994.

Rosenblum, Robert. "On de Kooning's Late Style." *Art Journal* 48, no. 3 (Fall 1989): 249.

Niki de Saint Phalle

Bourdon, David. "Niki de Saint Phalle: Targets, Nanas, and Tarot." In *Fantastic Vision: Works by Niki de Saint Phalle.* An exhibition catalogue. Roslyn, NY: Nassau County Museum of Fine Art, 1988.

Chattopadhyay, Collette. "West Hollywood: Niki de Saint Phalle: Tasende Gallery." *Sculpture* 20, no.10 (December 2001): 67.

Hultén, Pontus. *Niki de Saint Phalle.* Kunst- und Ausstellungshalle der Bundesrepublik Deutschland, 1992.

Longenecker, Martha, ed. *Niki de Saint Phalle: Insider/Outsider World-Inspired Art.* Japan: Mingei International Museum 1998.

Riera, Anna. "Niki de Saint Phalle y el Jardin de los Tarots." *Goya,* no. 270 (May–June 1999): 173–75.

Arthur Wesley Dow

Dow, Arthur Wesley. *Composition: A Series of Exercises in Art Structure for the Use of Students and Teachers.* 1920; repr., Berkeley, CA: University of California Press, 1997.

Fink, Lois Marie. *American Art at the Nineteenth-Century Paris Salons.* Washington, DC: National Museum of American Art, Smithsonian Institution and Cambridge University Press, 1990.

Green, Nancy E. *Arthur Wesley Dow (1857–1922): His Art and His Influence.* New York: Spanierman Gallery, 1999.

Johnson, Arthur Warren. *Arthur Wesley Dow: Historian, Artist, Teacher.* Ipswich, MA: Ipswich Historical Society, 1934.

Moffatt, Frederick Campbell. "The Breton Years of Arthur Wesley Dow." *Archives of American Art Journal* 15, no. 2 (1975): 2–8.

Sellin, David. *Americans in Brittany and Normandy, 1860–1910.* Phoenix: Phoenix Art Museum, 1982.

George Henry Durrie

Durrie, Mary Clarissa. "George Henry Durrie: Artist." *Antiques* 24, no. 1 (July 1933): 13–15.

Hutson, Martha. *George Henry Durrie, 1820–1863: American Winter Landscapist, Renowned through Currier and Ives.* Santa Barbara, CA: Santa Barbara Museum of Art, 1978.

Simkin, Colin. *George Henry Durrie, Connecticut Artist, 1820–1863.* New Haven, CT: New Haven Colony Historical Society, 1966.

Richard Estes

Arthur, John. "A Conversation with Richard Estes." In *Richard Estes: The Urban Landscape.* Essay by John Canaday. Boston: Museum of Fine Arts and New York Graphic Society, 1978.

Hurwitz, Laurie S. "Richard Estes: Illusion and Reality." *American Artist* 55 (December 1991).

Wilmerding, John. *Richard Estes.* New York: Rizzoli, 2006.

James Earle Fraser

Archives of American Art, Smithsonian Institution, Washington, DC. James Earle Fraser Papers. Reel 2548: 0563–0564.

Craven, Wayne. *Sculpture in America.* New York: Thomas Y. Crowell, 1968.

Kennedy Galleries. *James Earle Fraser, American Sculptor: A Retrospective Exhibition of Bronzes from Works of 1913 to 1953. An exhibition catalogue.* New York: Kennedy Galleries, 1969.

Krakel, Dean Fenton. *End of the Trail: The Odyssey of a Statue.* Norman, OK: University of Oklahoma Press, 1973.

Proske, Beatrice Gilman. *Brookgreen Gardens Sculpture,* 2 vols. Brookgreen Gardens, SC: Trustees of Brookgreen Gardens, 1968–1993.

Tolles, Thayer, ed. *American Sculpture in the Metropolitan Museum of Art. Vol. 2: A Catalogue of Works by Artists Born between 1865 and 1885.* New York: Metropolitan Museum of Art, 2001.

Turner, Frederick Jackson. "The Significance of the Frontier in American History." Address, meeting of the American Historical Association, Chicago, July 12, 1893.

Sanford Robinson Gifford

Harvey, Eleanor Jones. "Tastes in Transition: Gifford's Patrons." In *Hudson River Visions: The Landscapes of Sanford R. Gifford.* Kevin Avery and Franklin Kelly, eds. New Haven, CT: Yale University Press and the Metropolitan Museum of Art, 2003.

Weiss, Ila. *Poetic Landscape: The Art and Life of Sanford Robinson Gifford.* Newark, DE: University of Delaware Press, 1987.

William Glackens

Chamberlin, Joseph Edgar. "Two Significant Exhibitions." *New York Evening Mail*, February 4, 1908, p. 6.

Gerdts, William H. *William Glackens.* Essay by Jorge H. Santis. New York: Abbeville Press, 1996.

Leeds, Valerie Ann. "William Glackens Reappraised." In *William Glackens: American Impressionist.* New York: Gerald Peters Gallery, 2003.

Martin Johnson Heade

Frazier, Nancy. "Mute Gospel: The Salt Marshes of Martin Johnson Heade." *Prospects* 23 (1998): 201.

Stebbins, Theodore E., Jr. *The Life and Work of Martin Johnson Heade: A Critical Analysis and Catalogue Raisonné.* New Haven, CT: Yale University Press, 2000.

———. *Martin Johnson Heade.* With contributions by Janet L. Comey, Karen E. Quinn, and Jim Wright. Boston: Museum of Fine Arts, 1999.

Wilmerding, John, ed. *American Light: The Luminist Movement: 1850–1875.* Washington, DC: National Gallery of Art, 1980.

E. Martin Hennings

Bickerstaff, Laura M. *Pioneer Artists of Taos.* Denver: Old West Publishing, 1983.

Eldredge, Charles C., Julie Schimmel, and William H. Truettner. *Art in New Mexico, 1900–1945: Paths to Taos and Santa Fe.* Washington, DC: National Museum of American Art, Smithsonian Institution and Abbeville Press, NY, 1986.

Rak, Roger. "E. Martin Hennings: Taos Artist." *Color Pattern & Plane: E. Martin Hennings in Taos. An exhibition catalogue.* Essay by Vicki Heltunen. Orange, TX: Stark Museum of Art, 1986.

Robert Henri

Archives of American Art, Smithsonian Institution, Washington, DC. Robert Henri Diary, July 14, 1902, 885:871.

Homer, William Innes. *Robert Henri and His Circle.* Ithaca, NY: Cornell University Press, 1969.

Perlman, Bennard B. *Robert Henri: His Life and Art.* New York: Dover Publications, 1991.

"Pictures by Robert Henri." *New York Times*, April 9, 1902.

Weinberg, H. Barbara, Doreen Bolger, and David Park Curry. *American Impressionism and Realism: The Painting of Modern Life, 1885–1915.* With the assistance of N. Mishoe Brennecke. New York: Metropolitan Museum of Art and Harry N. Abrams, 1994.

David Hockney

Glazebrook, Mark. *David Hockney Paintings, Prints and Drawings 1960–1970.* Boston: Boston Book and Art, 1970.

Hockney, David, and Paul Joyce. *Hockney on "Art": Conversations with Paul Joyce.* London: Little, Brown and Co., 1999.

Hockney, David. *That's the Way I See It.* Nikos Strangos, ed. London: Thames & Hudson, 1993.

Melia, Paul, and Ulrich Luckhardt. *David Hockney: Paintings.* Munich: Prestel-Verlag, 1994, catalogue entry no.25.

Melia, Paul, ed. *David Hockney.* New York: Manchester University Press, 1995.

Schiff, Gert. "A Moving Focus: Hockney's Dialogue with Picasso." In *David Hockney: A Retrospective.* New York: Harry N. Abrams and the Los Angeles County Museum of Art, 1988.

Winslow Homer

Cikovsky, Nicolai, Jr., and Franklin Kelly. *Winslow Homer.* New Haven, CT: Yale University Press and the National Gallery of Art, Washington, DC, 1995.

Cooper, Helen A. *Winslow Homer Watercolors.* New Haven, CT: Yale University Press and the National Gallery of Art, Washington, DC, 1986.

Junker, Patricia A., with Sarah Burns et al. *Winslow Homer: Artist and Angler.* Dallas, TX: Amon Carter Museum and the Fine Arts Museums of San Francisco, 2002.

Taylor, Sue, ed. *Winslow Homer in Gloucester.* Chicago: Terra Museum of American Art, 1990.

Wilmerding, John. *Winslow Homer.* New York: Praeger Publishers, 1972.

Edward Hopper

Levin, Gail. *Edward Hopper: A Catalogue Raisonné.* 4 vols. New York: Whitney Museum of Art and W. W. Norton, 1995.

Levin, Gail. *Edward Hopper: An Intimate Biography.* New York: Knopf, 1995.

Mecklenburg, Virginia M. *Edward Hopper: The Watercolors.* Washington, DC: National Museum of American Art, Smithsonian Institution and W. W. Norton, 1999.

Wagstaff, Sheena, ed. *Edward Hopper.* With contributions by David Anfam et al. London: Tate Publishing, 2004.

Henry Inman

Bolton, Theodore. "Henry Inman: An Account of His Life and Work." *Art Quarterly* 3 (Autumn 1940).

Cosentino, Andrew J. *The Paintings of Charles Bird King (1785–1862).* Washington, DC: Smithsonian Institution Press and the National Collection of Fine Arts, 1977.

Gerdts, William H. *The Art of Henry Inman.* Washington, DC: National Portrait Gallery, 1987.

"Henry Inman." *Bulletin of the American Art-Union*, no. 5 (August 1850): 69–73.

McKenney, Thomas L., and James Hall. *History of the Indian Tribes of North America with Biographical Sketches and Anecdotes of the Principal Chiefs*, 3 vols. Frederick Webb Hodge, ed. 1836–44; repr., Totowa, NJ: Rowman and Littlefield, 1972.

Parke-Bernet Galleries. Sale Number 3056, May 21, 1970, Lot 10, p. 24.

Viola, Herman J. *The Indian Legacy of Charles Bird King*. Washington, DC: Smithsonian Institution Press, 1976.

Rebecca Salsbury James

Luhan, Mabel Dodge. *Taos and Its Artists*. New York: Duell, Sloan and Pearce, 1947.

McCausland, Elizabeth. "Rebecca Salsbury James." In *Paintings of Glass, Third New York Exhibition*. New York: Martha Jackson Gallery, 1954.

Porter, Dean A. *Taos Artists and Their Patrons, 1898–1950*. Notre Dame, IN: Snite Museum of Art, University of Notre Dame, 1999.

David Johnson

Baur, John I. H. "'. . . the exact brushwork of Mr. David Johnson,' An American Landscape Painter, 1827–1908." *American Art Journal* 12, no. 4 (Autumn 1980): 34, 57–62.

Johnson, David. *Catalogue of Paintings in Oil*. New York: Fifth Avenue Art Galleries and Ortgies, 1890.

Owens, Gwendolyn. *Nature Transcribed: The Landscapes and Still Lifes of David Johnson (1827–1908): An Exhibition*. Ithaca, NY: Herbert F. Johnson Museum of Art, Cornell University, 1988.

Eastman Johnson

Allen, Brian T. *Sugaring Off: The Maple Sugar Paintings of Eastman Johnson*. Williamstown, MA: Sterling and Francine Clark Art Institute, 2004.

Archives of American Art, Smithsonian Institution, Washington, DC. *The Works of the Late Eastman Johnson*, N. A. Roll N51, frame 1015.

Carbone, Teresa A., and Patricia Hills. *Eastman Johnson: Painting America*. New York: Brooklyn Museum of Art and Rizzoli, 1999.

Rockwell Kent

Archives of American Art Journal 12, no. 1 (January 1972): 13.

Kelly, Gemey. *Rockwell Kent: The Newfoundland Work*. Halifax, NS: Dalhousie Art Gallery, 1987.

West, Richard V. *"An Enkindled Eye": The Paintings of Rockwell Kent, a Retrospective Exhibition*. Contributions by Fridolf Johnson and Dan Burne Jones. Santa Barbara, CA: Santa Barbara Museum of Art, 1985.

Wien, Jake Milgram. *Rockwell Kent: The Mythic and the Modern*. New York: Hudson Hills Press and the Portland Museum of Art, 2005.

Zurier, Rebecca, Robert W. Snyder, and Virginia M. Mecklenburg. *The Ashcan Artists and Their New York*. Washington, DC: National Museum of American Art, Smithsonian Institution and W. W. Norton, 1995.

John La Farge

Adams, Henry. "The Mind of John La Farge." In *John La Farge: Essays*. New York: Abbeville Press, Carnegie Museum of Art, and National Museum of American Art, Smithsonian Institution, 1987.

———. "William James, Henry James, John La Farge and the Foundations of Radical Empiricism." *American Art Journal* 17, no. 1 (Winter 1985): 63.

Foster, Kathleen A. "The Still-Life Painting of John La Farge." *American Art Journal* 11, no. 3 (July/Summer 1979).

Gerdts, William H., and Russell Burke. *American Still-Life Painting*. New York: Praeger, 1971.

Pyne, Kathleen A. *Art and the Higher Life: Painting and Evolutionary Thought in Late Nineteenth-Century America*. Austin, TX: University of Texas Press, 1996.

Stein, Roger. *John Ruskin and Aesthetic Thought in America, 1840–1900*. Cambridge, MA: Harvard University Press, 1967.

Tuckerman, Henry T. *Book of the Artists: American Artist Life: Comprising Biographical and Critical Sketches of American Artists*. 1867; repr., New York: James F. Carr, 1966.

Yarnall, James L. *Nature Vivante: The Still Lifes of John La Farge*. New York: Jordan-Volpe Gallery, 1995.

Fitz Henry Lane

Wilmerding, John, ed. *American Light: The Luminist Movement: 1850–1875*. With contributions by Lisa Fellow Andrus. Washington, DC: National Gallery of Art, 1980.

Wilmerding, John. *Fitz Henry Lane*. 1971; repr., Danvers, MA: Bradford & Bigelow and the Cape Ann Historical Museum, 2005.

———. *Paintings by Fitz Hugh Lane*. Washington, DC: National Gallery of Art, 1988.

John Marin

Fine, Ruth E. *John Marin*. Washington, DC: National Gallery of Art and Abbeville Press, New York, 1990.

Reich, Sheldon. *John Marin: A Stylistic Analysis and Catalogue Raisonné*. Tucson: University of Arizona Press, 1970.

Sanstrom, Robert Louis. *John Marin's Paintings of the Maine Seacoast: An Investigation of the Use and Appearance of the Natural Elements in the Marine Paintings of John Marin and Their Importance to the Artist*. Ann Arbor, MI: University Microfilms International, 1984.

Reginald Marsh

Cohen, Marilyn. *Reginald Marsh's New York: Paintings, Drawings, Prints and Photographs*. New York: Whitney Museum of Art and Dover Publications, 1983.

Goodrich, Lloyd. "A Tribute to Reginald Marsh." In *Selections from the Felicia Meyer Marsh Bequest*. New York: Whitney Museum of American Art, 1979.

Marsh, Reginald. "Let's Get Back to Painting." *Magazine of Art* 37, no. 8 (December 1944): 293.

Howard White McLean

Zurier, Rebecca, Robert W. Snyder, and Virginia M. Mecklenburg. *Metropolitan Lives: The Ashcan Artists and Their New York.* Washington, DC: National Museum of American Art, Smithsonian Institution and W. W. Norton, 1995.

Thomas Moran

Anderson, Nancy K. *Thomas Moran.* With contributions by Thomas P. Bruhn, Joni L. Kinsey, and Anne Morand. Washington, DC: National Gallery of Art and Yale University Press, 1997.

Clark, Carol. *Thomas Moran, Watercolors of the American West: Text and Catalogue Raisonné.* Austin, TX: University of Texas Press and the Amon Carter Museum of Western Art, Forth Worth, 1980.

Drake, Alexander? "Thomas Moran's Water-Color Drawings." *Scribner's Monthly* 5, no. 3 (January 1873), p. 394.

Harvey, Eleanor Jones. *Thomas Moran and the Spirit of Place.* Dallas: Dallas Museum of Art, 2001.

Moran, Thomas. "Notebook." Unpublished mss., 1874–1882. Thomas Gilcrease Institute of American History and Art, Tulsa, Oklahoma.

Raymond, R. W. "The Heart of the Continent: The Hot Springs and Geysers of the Yellow Stone Region." *Harper's Weekly*, April 5, 1873.

Alice Neel

Carr, Carolyn Kinder. *Alice Neel's Women.* New York: Rizzoli, 2002.

Chase, Linda. *Duos: Alice Neel's Double Portraits.* Naples, FL: Naples Museum of Art, 2001.

Goldstein, Patti. "Soul on Canvas." *New York Magazine*, July 9–16, 1979, p. 76.

Neel, Alice. "Artists and Their Inspiration." *Christian Science Monitor*, October 31, 1977, p. 24.

Georgia O'Keeffe

Drohojowska-Philp, Hunter. *Full Bloom: The Art and Life of Georgia O'Keeffe.* New York: W. W. Norton, 2004.

Eldredge, Charles C. *Georgia O'Keeffe.* New York: Harry N. Abrams and the National Museum of American Art, Smithsonian Institution, 1991.

Fryd, Vivian Green. "Georgia O'Keeffe's Radiator Building: Gender, Sexuality, Modernism, and Urban Imagery." *Winterthur Portfolio* 35, no. 4 (Winter 2000): 269–89.

Hassrick, Peter H., ed. *The Georgia O'Keeffe Museum.* New York: Harry N. Abrams and the Georgia O'Keeffe Museum, 1997.

Lynes, Barbara Buhler, *O'Keeffe, Stieglitz, and the Critics, 1916–1929.* Chicago: University of Chicago Press, 1991.

———. *Georgia O'Keeffe: Catalogue Raisonné.* 2 vols. Washington, DC: National Gallery of Art, 1999.

O'Keeffe, Georgia. *Georgia O'Keeffe (A Studio Book).* New York: Viking Press, 1976.

Richter, Peter-Cornell. *Georgia O'Keeffe and Alfred Stieglitz.* New York: Prestel, 2001.

Robinson, Roxana. *Georgia O'Keeffe: A Life.* Hanover, NH: University Press of New England, 1999.

Turner, Elizabeth Hutton, and Marjorie P. Balge-Crozier. *Georgia O'Keeffe: The Poetry of Things.* New Haven, CT: Yale University Press and the Phillips Collection, 1999.

Zilczer, Judith. "'Color Music': Synaesthesia and Nineteenth-Century Sources for Abstract Art." *Artibus et Historiae* 8, no. 16 (1987):104.

William McGregor Paxton

Chabourne, Janice H. *The Boston Art Club, Exhibition Record 1873–1909.* Karl Gabosh, and Charles O. Vogel, eds. Madison, CT: Sound View Press, 1991.

Fairbrother, Trevor J., Erica Hirshler, Theodore Stebbins, and William Vance. *The Bostonians: Painters of an Elegant Age, 1870–1930.* Boston: Museum of Fine Arts, 1986.

Lee, Ellen. *William McGregor Paxton, 1869–1941.* Indianapolis: Indianapolis Museum of Art, 1978.

St. Botolph Club. *Paintings by Mr. William M. Paxton.* Boston: 1904.

Sarah Miriam Peale

Griffith, Priscilla Stump. Diary entry for January 28th, 1841. Unpublished mss., private collection.

Hirshorn, Anne Sue. "Sarah Miriam Peale." In *American Women Artists: 1819–1947: The Neville-Strass Collection.* Hagerstown, MD: Washington County Museum of Fine Arts, 2003.

Lloyd, Phoebe. *Death and American Painting: Charles Willson Peale to Albert Pinkham Ryder.* PhD diss., City University of New York, 1980.

———."Posthumous Mourning Portraiture." In *A Time to Mourn: Expressions of Grief in Nineteenth-Century America.* Martha V. Pike and Janice Gray Armstrong, eds. New York: Museums at Stony Brook, 1980.

Perry, Claire. *Young America: Childhood in Nineteenth-Century Art and Culture.* New Haven, CT: Yale University Press and the Iris & B. Gerald Cantor Center for Visual Arts, Stanford University, 2006.

Guy Pène du Bois

Fahlman, Betsy. *Guy Pène du Bois: Artist about Town.* Washington, DC: Corcoran Gallery of Art, 1980.

———. *Guy Pène du Bois, Painter of Modern Life.* New York: James Graham and Sons, 2004.

Levine, Louis. "The Philosophy of Henry Bergson and Syndicalism." *New York Times*, January 16, 1913, p. SM4.

Pène du Bois, Guy. *"The Art Critic." Artists Say the Silliest Things.* New York: American Artist Group, 1940.

John Frederick Peto

Frankenstein, Alfred. *John F. Peto.* Brooklyn: Brooklyn Institute of Arts and Sciences, 1950.

Gerdts, William H., and Russell Burke. *American Still-Life Painting.* New York: Praeger, 1971.

Lubin, David. "Masculinity, Nostalgia, and the Trompe l'Oeil Still-Life Paintings of William Harnett." In *Picturing a Nation: Art and Social Change in Nineteenth-Century America.* New Haven, CT: Yale University Press, 1994.

Nemerov, Alexander. *The Body of Raphaelle Peale: Still Life and Selfhood, 1812–1824.* Berkeley, CA: University of California Press, 2001.

Wilmerding, John. *Important Information Inside: The Art of John F. Peto and the Idea of Still-Life Painting in Nineteenth-Century America.* Washington, DC: National Gallery of Art, 1983.

Bert Geer Phillips

Broder, Patricia Janis. *Taos: A Painter's Dream.* Boston: New York Graphic Society, 1980.

Eldredge, Charles C., Julie Schimmel, and William H. Truettner. *Art in New Mexico, 1900–1945: Paths to Taos and Santa Fe.* Washington, DC: National Museum of American Art, Smithsonian Institution and Abbeville Press, NY, 1986.

Schimmel, Julie, and Robert R. White. *Bert Geer Phillips and the Taos Art Colony.* Albuquerque: University of New Mexico Press, 1994.

Maurice Prendergast

Ivinski, Pamela A. *Maurice Prendergast: Paintings of America.* An exhibition catalogue. New York: Adelson Galleries, 2003.

Matthews, Nancy Mowll. *The Art of Leisure: Maurice Prendergast in the Williams College Museum of Art.* Williamstown, MA: Williams College Museum of Art, 1999.

Wattenmaker, Richard J. *Maurice Prendergast.* New York: Harry N. Abrams and the National Museum of American Art, Smithsonian Institution, 1994.

Theodore Robinson

Baur, John I. H. *Theodore Robinson, 1852–1896.* New York: Brooklyn Museum of Art, 1946.

Brinton, Christian. "American Painting at the Panama-Pacific Exposition." *International Studio* (August 1915): 30.

Frick Art Reference Library, New York. Theodore Robinson Diaries: 1892–1896. Unpublished mss.

Larkin, Susan. *The Cos Cob Art Colony: Impressionists on the Connecticut Shore.* New Haven, CT: Yale University Press, 2001.

———. "Light, Time, and Tide: Theodore Robinson at Cos Cob." *American Art Journal* 23, no. 2 (1991): 85.

John Singer Sargent

Kilmurray, Elaine, and Richard Ormond, eds. *John Singer Sargent.* Washington, DC: National Gallery of Art, 1999.

Ormond, Richard, and Elaine Kilmurray. *John Singer Sargent: Complete Paintings,* vol. 1. New Haven, CT: Yale University Press and the Paul Mellon Centre for Studies in British Art, 1998.

Simpson, Marc. "Reconstructing the Golden Age: American Artists in Broadway, Worcestershire, 1885 to 1889." PhD diss., Yale University, 1993.

Simpson, Marc, with Richard Ormond and H. Barbara Weinberg. *Uncanny Spectacle: The Public Career of the Young John Singer Sargent.* New Haven, CT: Yale University Press and the Sterling and Francine Clark Institute, Williamstown, MA, 1997.

Everett Shinn

DeShazo, Edith. *Everett Shinn, 1876–1953: A Figure in His Time.* New York: Clarkson N. Potter, 1974.

Weber, Bruce. *Homage to the Square: Picturing Washington Square, 1890–1965.* New York: Berry-Hill Galleries, 2001.

"What Is the Most Beautiful Spot in New York?" *New York Times,* June 18, 1911, p. SM4.

Wong, Janay. *Everett Shinn: The Spectacle of Life.* New York: Berry-Hill Galleries, 2000.

Francis A. Silva

Baur, John I. H. "Francis A. Silva: Beyond Luminism." *Magazine Antiques* 118 (November 1980): 1021.

Mitchell, Mark D. *Francis A. Silva (1835–1886): In His Own Light.* New York: Berry-Hill Galleries, 2002.

Silva, Francis A. "American vs. Foreign-American Art." *Art Union* 1, nos. 6–7 (June–July 1884): 131.

John Sloan

Elzea, Rowland. *John Sloan's Oil Paintings: A Catalogue Raisonné,* vol. 1. Newark, DE: University of Delaware Press, 1991.

St. John, Bruce, ed. *John Sloan's New York Scene: From Diaries, Notes and Correspondence, 1906–1913.* New York: Harper & Row, 1965.

David Smith

Giménez, Carmen, Rosalind E. Krauss, David Anfam et al. *David Smith: A Centennial.* New York: Guggenheim Museum, 2006.

Jacobs, Jay. "David Smith Sculpts for Spoleto." *Art News Annual* 29 (1964): 46.

Krauss, Rosalind E. *Terminal Iron Works: The Sculpture of David Smith.* Cambridge: MIT Press, 1971.

McCoy, Garnett, ed. *David Smith.* New York: Praeger Publishers, 1973.

Wilkin, Karen. *David Smith.* New York: Abbeville Press, 1984.

Joseph Stella

Baur, John I. H. *Joseph Stella.* New York: Praeger, 1971.

Haskell, Barbara. *Joseph Stella.* New York: Whitney Museum of American Art, 1994.

Jaffe, Irma B. *Joseph Stella.* Cambridge: Harvard University Press, 1970.

Edmund C. Tarbell

Baldwin, Maurice. "The Whistler Memorial Exhibition." *New England Magazine* (May 1904): 292.

Cox, Kenyon. "The Recent Work of Edmund C. Tarbell." *Art in America* 14, no. 70 (January 15, 1909): 254–60.

Fairbrother, Trevor. "Edmund C. Tarbell's Paintings of Interiors." *Antiques* (January 1987): 232–34.

Fairbrother, Trevor J., Erica Hirshler, Theodore Stebbins, and William Vance. *The Bostonians: Painters of an Elegant Age, 1870–1930.* Boston: Museum of Fine Arts, 1986.

Wayne Thiebaud

Coplans, John. *Wayne Thiebaud.* Pasadena, CA: Pasadena Art Museum, 1968.

Nash, Steven A. and Adam Gopnik. *Wayne Thiebaud: A Paintings Retrospective.* New York: Thames and Hudson and the Fine Arts Museums of San Francisco, 2000.

Louis Comfort Tiffany

Jaffe, Harold. *The Age of Tiffany: Glass, Paintings, Bronzes, Furniture: February 6–March 15, 1981.* Greenvale, NY: C. W. Post Art Gallery, 1981.

McKean, Hugh F. *The "Lost" Treasures of Louis Comfort Tiffany.* New York: Doubleday, 1980.

"Some Examples of American Glass Work at Paris." *Art Interchange* (June 1900): 131.

Stover, Donald L. *The Art of Louis Comfort Tiffany: An Exhibition Organized by the Fine Arts Museums of San Francisco from the Collection of the Charles Hosmer Morse Foundation, M. H. de Young Memorial Museum, 25 April through 8 August, 1981.* San Francisco: Fine Arts Museums of San Francisco, 1981.

Tiffany, Louis Comfort. "American Art Supreme in Colored Glass." *Forum* 15 (1893): 624.

Wearn, Cecilia. "The Industrial Arts in America." *International Studio* 11, no. 2 (September 1897): 158.

Adolph Alexander Weinman

Broder, Patricia Janis. *Bronzes of the American West.* New York: Harry N. Abrams, 1974.

Gurney, George. *Sculpture and the Federal Triangle.* Washington, DC: Smithsonian Institution Press, 1985.

Proske, Beatrice Gilman. *Brookgreen Gardens Sculpture*, 2 vols. Brookgreen Gardens, SC: Trustees of Brookgreen Gardens, 1968–1993.

Tolles, Thayer, ed. *American Sculpture in the Metropolitan Museum of Art. Vol. 2: A Catalogue of Works by Artists Born between 1865 and 1885.* New York: Metropolitan Museum of Art, 2001.

Tom Wesselmann

Gardner, Paul. "Tom Wesselmann." *Artnews* (January 1982): 67.

———. "When Is a Painting Finished?" *Artnews* (November 1985): 93.

Hunter, Sam. *Tom Wesselmann.* New York: Rizzoli, 1994.

Kramer, Hilton. "Form, Fantasy, and the Nude." *New York Times*, February 11, 1968, p. D25.

McCarthy, David. "Tom Wesselmann and the Americanization of the Nude, 1961–1963." *Smithsonian Studies in American Art* 4, nos. 3–4 (Summer–Fall 1990): 116.

Swenson, G. R. "What Is Pop Art? Interviews with Eight Painters." *Artnews* (February 1964): 64.

Zelenko, Lori Simmons. "Tom Wesselmann." *American Artist* 46 (June 1982): 103.

James McNeill Whistler

Broun, Elizabeth. "Thoughts That Began with the Gods: The Content of Whistler's Art." *Arts Magazine* 62, no. 2 (October 1987): 40.

Dorment, Richard, and Margaret F. MacDonald. *James McNeill Whistler.* With contributions by Nicolai Cikovsky Jr., Ruth E. Fine, and Geneviève Lacambre. London: Tate Gallery Publications, 1994.

Sutton, Denys. *James McNeill Whistler: Paintings, Etchings, Pastels and Watercolours.* London: Phaidon Press, 1966.

Young, Andrew MacLaren, Margaret MacDonald, and Robin Spencer. *The Paintings of James McNeill Whistler.* New Haven, CT: Yale University Press and the Paul Mellon Centre for Studies in British Art, 1980.

Andrew Wyeth

Corn, Wanda. *The Art of Andrew Wyeth.* Greenwich, CT: New York Graphic Society and Fine Arts Museums of San Francisco, 1973.

Hoving, Thomas. *Andrew Wyeth: An Autobiography.* New York: Bulfinch Press, 1998.

Knutson, Anne Classen, ed., Kathleen Foster, Michael Taylor, and Christopher Crosman. *Andrew Wyeth: Memory and Magic.* New York: Rizzoli, High Museum of Art, and Philadelphia Museum of Art, 2005.

Wyeth, Andrew, and Betsy James Wyeth. *Andrew Wyeth: Close Friends.* Jackson, MS: Mississippi Museum of Art and University of Washington Press, 2001.

Image Credits

The Flowering of Liberty

Sarah Miriam Peale, *Mary Leypold Griffith (1838–1841)*, photo by Harriet Wise, Frederick, Md.; Henry Inman, *Mistippee*, photo by Mike Jensen, Atlanta, Ga.; Fitz Henry Lane, *View of Norwich*, David Stansbury Photography, Springfield, Mass.; Francis A. Silva, *Evening in Gloucester Harbor*, photo by Eduardo Calderón; David Johnson, *The Torne at Ramapo*, David Stansbury Photography, Springfield, Mass.; Eastman Johnson, *Cardplaying at Fryeburg, Maine*, photo by Gene Young, SAAM; Martin Johnson Heade, *Newburyport Meadows I*, photo by Gene Young, SAAM; Martin Johnson Heade, *Cattleya Orchid with Two Brazilian Hummingbirds*, photo by Gene Young, SAAM; Winslow Homer, *Girl in the Hammock*, photo by Jay York, Portland, Maine; John F. Peto, *Beer Mug, Book, and Pipe*, photo courtesy of Berry-Hill Galleries, New York, N.Y.; James McNeill Whistler, *Harmony in Grey: Chelsea in Ice*, photo by John Bellenis.

Destiny and Desire

John Singer Sargent, *François Flameng and Paul Helleu*, photo by Steve Oliver, Altadena, Calif.; John Singer Sargent, *Garden Study with Lucia and Kate Millett*, photo courtesy of the National Gallery of Art, Washington, DC; John La Farge, *Hollyhocks*, photo by Steve Oliver, Altadena, Calif.; John La Farge, *Bowl of Flowers*, photo by Steve Oliver, Altadena, Calif.; Mary Cassatt, *Reading "Le Figaro,"* photo by Mark Gulezian, Takoma Park, Md.; Adolph Weinman, *Chief Blackbird—Ogalalla Sioux*, photo by Josh Nessky; James Earle Fraser, *End of the Trail*, photo by Josh Nessky.

From Innocence to Experience

Theodore Robinson, *The Anchorage, Cos Cob*, photo by Bibb Gault, San Antonio, Tex.; Winslow Homer, *Watching Ships, Gloucester*, photo by Ira Shank, San Francisco, Ca.; Thomas Anshutz, *Sand Burr*, photo courtesy of Graham Gallery, New York, N.Y.; Edmund Tarbell, *Girl Cutting Patterns*, photo by Bibb Gault, San Antonio, Tex.

The Work of the World

Rockwell Kent, *Tugboat on the Hudson*, by permission of the Plattsburgh State Art Museum, Plattsburgh College Foundation, Rockwell Kent Gallery and Collection; photo by Jay York, Portland, Maine; George Bellows, *Noon*, photo by Gene Young, SAAM; John Sloan, *Easter Eve*, photo by Gene Young, SAAM; William Glackens, *The Purple Dress*, photo by Gene Young, SAAM; Robert Henri, *Far Rockaway*, photo courtesy of Jordan-Volpe Gallery, New York, N.Y.; Reginald Marsh, *Golf Course Scene*, © 2006 Estate of Reginald Marsh/Art Students League, New York/Artists Rights Society (ARS), New York.

Reflections of the Modern

Bert Geer Phillips, *Pueblo Indian Girl with Plum Blossoms*, photo by Josh Nessky; Ernest Blumenschein, *Untitled (Mountain Wood Gatherers)*, photo by Josh Nessky; John Marin, *Taos Canyon, New Mexico*, © 2006 Estate of John Marin/Artists Rights Society (ARS), New York; E. Martin Hennings, *Sunlit Aspens*, photo by Garth Dowling Photography, Jackson, Wyo.; Georgia O'Keeffe, *Red Lines*, © 2006 The Georgia O'Keeffe Museum/Artists Rights Society (ARS), New York; photo by Gene Young, SAAM; Georgia O'Keeffe, *Black Cross with Red Sky*, © 2006 The Georgia O'Keeffe Museum/Artists Rights Society (ARS), New York; photo by Josh Nessky; Georgia O'Keeffe, *Birch and Pine Trees—Pink*, © 2006 The Georgia O'Keeffe Museum/Artists Rights Society (ARS), New York; Georgia O'Keeffe, *Black Place No. IV*, © 2006 The Georgia O'Keeffe Museum/Artists Rights Society (ARS), New York; Joseph Stella, *Palms*, photo by Gene Young, SAAM; Rockwell Kent, *Sunday, North Greenland*, by permission of the Plattsburgh State Art Museum, Plattsburgh College Foundation, Rockwell Kent Gallery and Collection; photo by Jay York, Portland, Maine.

Visions of America

Andrew Wyeth, *Open and Closed*, photo courtesy of the Wyeth Foundation, Chadds Ford, Pa.; Andrew Wyeth, *Logging Scoot*, photo courtesy of the Wyeth Foundation, Chadds Ford, Pa.; Andrew Wyeth, *The Quaker*, photo courtesy of the Wyeth Foundation, Chadds Ford, Pa.; Richard Estes, *Jone's Diner*, photo by Gene Young, SAAM; David Hockney, *Savings and Loan Building*, © David Hockney; photo by Ira Shank, San Francisco, Calif.; Alice Neel, *The De Vegh Twins*, © Estate of Alice Neel; photo by Gene Young, SAAM; Willem De Kooning, *Torso*, © 2006 The Willem de Kooning Foundation/Artists Rights Society (ARS), New York; photo by Steve Oliver, Altadena, Calif.; Willem de Kooning, *Stowaway*, © 2006 The Willem de Kooning Foundation/Artists Rights Society (ARS), New York; photo by Steve Oliver, Altadena, Calif.; David Hockney, *Ian Watching Television*, © David Hockney; photo by Steve Oliver, Altadena, Calif.; David Bates, *Sheepsheads and Lemons*, courtesy of the artist; photo by Ira Shank, San Francisco; Wayne Thiebaud, *Meringues*, photo by Mark Gulezian, Takoma Park, Maryland; Niki de Saint Phalle, *La Lune*, © 2006 Artists Rights Society (ARS), New York/ADAGP, Paris; photo by Gene Young, SAAM.